T0357579

"*Oral Roberts and the Rise of the Prosperity Gosp* fully researched addition to the Eerdmans serie offers an account that combines the insight of biography with the breadth of scholarly research, furthering the conversation about the origins of prosperity gospel influences that have come to conquer Pentecostal and other charismatic forms of Christianity. Root's work gives the reader a deep understanding of Oral Roberts the person, and then follows the growth of that fragile human into a figure whose success, according to his own lights, must be the work of God. But what about his failures? Jonathan Root helps us understand how Roberts, and American Christianity, persist in prosperity teaching and seeking the seed faith that always promises a better tomorrow. A much-needed work about a surprisingly overlooked figure in American religion."

—AMY ARTMAN, Missouri State University

"Fascinating. Timely. This lively book resurrects Oral Roberts as the preacher of modern capitalism we can no longer ignore."

—KATE BOWLER, Duke Divinity School

"No monochromatic portrait can ever capture Oral Roberts, America's premiere televangelist. Roberts was, to his detractors, a cynical pitchman; to his acolytes, an unabashedly sincere evangelist in whose presence miracles were not unknown. In this important and deeply contextualized biography, Jonathan Root meticulously portrays the Oral who defined the crossroads of modern American faith, combining deep sincerity and personal guile, yearning search and steely eyed shrewdness, salvific promise and practical help. Root meticulously portrays this religious pioneer as a fascinating, frustrating man who mirrors back the calico qualities of ourselves as seekers."

—MITCH HOROWITZ,
PEN Award–winning author of *Occult America* and *Uncertain Places*

"Few Americans could captivate an audience or sell them on the gospel like Oral Roberts. Jonathan Root's smart, engaging, and original biography demonstrates how Roberts, whose life was equal parts hope and tragedy, engaged with the major issues of his era and reshaped the Christian faith to reach a consumer culture during the television age."

—MATTHEW AVERY SUTTON, author of
*Double Crossed: The Missionaries Who Spied
for the United States during the Second World War*

LIBRARY OF RELIGIOUS BIOGRAPHY

Mark A. Noll, Kathryn Gin Lum, and Heath W. Carter, series editors

Long overlooked by historians, religion has emerged in recent years as a key factor in understanding the past. From politics to popular culture, from social struggles to the rhythms of family life, religion shapes every story. Religious biographies open a window to the sometimes surprising influence of religion on the lives of influential people and the worlds they inhabited.

The Library of Religious Biography is a series that brings to life important figures in United States history and beyond. Grounded in careful research, these volumes link the lives of their subjects to the broader cultural contexts and religious issues that surrounded them. The authors are respected historians and recognized authorities in the historical period in which their subject lived and worked.

Marked by careful scholarship yet free of academic jargon, the books in this series are well-written narratives meant to be read and enjoyed as well as studied.

Titles include:

*The Religious Journey of **Dwight D. Eisenhower**:*
Duty, God, and Country
by Jack M. Holl

*One Soul at a Time: The Story of **Billy Graham***
by Grant Wacker

*The Miracle Lady: **Katherine Kuhlman***
and the Transformation of Charismatic Christianity
by Amy Collier Artman

Mother of Modern Evangelicalism:
*The Life and Legacy of **Henrietta Mears***
by Arlin Migliazzo

*Strength for the Fight: The Life and Faith of **Jackie Robinson***
by Gary Scott Smith

For a complete list of published volumes, see the back of this volume.

Oral Roberts
and the **Rise**
of the **Prosperity Gospel**

Jonathan Root

WILLIAM B. EERDMANS PUBLISHING COMPANY
GRAND RAPIDS, MICHIGAN

Wm. B. Eerdmans Publishing Co.
4035 Park East Court SE, Grand Rapids, Michigan 49546
www.eerdmans.com

Published 2023

Book design by Leah Luyk

Printed in the United States of America

29 28 27 26 25 24 23   1 2 3 4 5 6 7

ISBN 978-0-8028-7727-7

Library of Congress Cataloging-in-Publication Data

A catalog record for this book is available from the Library of Congress.

This book is dedicated to the memory of
Robert "Crocodile Bob" Linder.

CONTENTS

CONTENTS

FOREWORD

"WHAT'S AN ORAL ROBERTS?" This is a question that followed Oral Roberts during the 1970s, as he and his eponymous university began receiving national attention. Although this question initially reflected confusion about the meaning of the name that Oral Roberts University and its successful basketball team carried, it serves today as a point of departure for reflecting on Roberts's career, influence, and legacy. Because Roberts fulfilled an array of ministerial roles and built numerous institutions during his lifetime, potential answers to this question eventually became abundant. But as Jonathan Root argues in this illuminating and engaging religious biography, one answer stands above all others. Oral Roberts was, Root tells us, a "microcosm of the state of evangelical Christianity at the end of the twentieth century." At least three significant features of that state come into view through the story Root offers, helping us understand Roberts's religious worlds and their legacy today.

First, Roberts preached an evangelical gospel of prosperity that measured itself in numerical success, and the numbers that counted most were dollars, attendance figures, forecasted revenue, and ratings. In some ways, this preoccupation with money and attention built on centuries of evangelical tradition. Throughout the nineteenth and earlier twentieth centuries, numerous renowned revivalists and ministers used advertising, marketing, commercial publishing, and other business methods to amplify their audiences. Expanding audiences and donation revenue not only enabled additional outreach but also served as supposed evidence of spiritual effectiveness and divine favor.

Just as other evangelicals developed techniques and traditions that reflected their own cultural and economic contexts, Roberts knit together an array of ideas and practices that defined his own life and times. At the heart of his particular synthesis lay a Pentecostal belief in the material reality of God's power, a confidence in popular theologies of positive-thinking prosperity, and a devotion to the promises of postwar capitalism despite its potential perils. All of these influences were apparent in Roberts's recurrent call for Christians to practice "seed faith," the conviction that God will grant spiritual and material prosperity to people who plant proverbial "seeds" through sacrificial giving. A teaching that Roberts justified with reference to biblical passages such as 3 John 1:2, seed faith did not define money as the only object that God recognized as potential seeds. But even though Roberts discussed healing and other blessings that people could receive on account of their varied sacrifices, discussions of seed faith most typically focused on the material success or wealth that grew from faithful monetary gifts to Christian causes.

Situating Christians in a transactional relationship with a God who asks followers to give in exchange for divine favor, seed faith is easy to condemn as manipulative or misleading. It can sound like a scam. And Root's narrative offers countless details that justify serious condemnation. As Root and other scholars of evangelical theologies of prosperity have pointed out, those theologies tend to promise individual prosperity without challenging structural sources of inequity, suffering, and oppression that lead people to desire or need a dose of prosperity. As a result, Roberts's teachings were most accessible and appealing to white Christians, who experienced far less harm from structures of inequity than Christians of color. Roberts almost always joined many other white evangelical leaders in insisting that everyone had equal access to the "Blessing Pact" and its means of pleasing a colorblind God. Yet by teaching Christians to seek God's favor within their social structures rather than critiquing or rebuilding them, Roberts and other evangelicals essentially sanctified those structures and their harms—including the inequities and violence of racism and capitalism.

In addition to inviting readers to consider how Roberts and other evangelicals have affirmed what Root describes as "capitalism's core values of power and accumulation," Root empathetically and attentively reveals how those apparent theological compromises and their complementary practices could take shape within evangelical culture despite the seemingly good and pious intentions of leaders and laypeople. Root explains, for example, that Roberts amplified his emphasis on seed faith in a time of national economic uncertainty. With inflation, unemployment, deindustrialization, and rising energy costs all causing economic unease during the 1970s, Roberts presented seed faith as a straightforward consumer transaction with God because that framework inspired confidence and security.

If Roberts ultimately capitalized on his followers' economic desperation, he also sought to give them hope.

This empathetic yet critical approach to the story of Roberts's career guides how Root presents a second feature of Roberts's microcosm: Roberts's pioneering approach to televangelism and institution building. For many critics of religion in general and evangelical Christianity in particular, the most prominent televangelists of the 1980s distill several of the most pernicious practices and priorities associated with contemporary religions—including the financial enrichment of leaders, the emphasis of those same leaders on the need for congregations to make financial contributions, and an apparent priority of stylish performance over theological substance. But Root emphasizes how Roberts continually treated television as a vehicle of spiritual enrichment, and he attempted to elevate the entertainment appeal of his television specials in order to enhance their reach and spiritual impact. When he founded Oral Roberts University in the early 1960s, he did so in the hope that it would serve as a training ground for evangelism and an engine of Christian culture.

The avowed objectives of Roberts's initiatives do not erase their flaws, but they do provide insight into the process through which he and other evangelicals often have wrapped their flaws in cocoons of evangelical theology and tradition. Because the expanse of evangelical Christianity encompasses a variety of religious cultures and lacks any central ecclesiastical institutions, particular leaders and institutions—from parachurch organizations to commercial corporations such as publishing houses—always have wielded extraordinary religious authority. Within that framework, authorized evangelicals have been able to orient how lay evangelicals interpret their world and understand their obligations within it.

Today, both insiders and outsiders often view evangelical Christianity as theologically conservative; but it more typically is a site of creativity, with evangelicals continually transforming innovative interpretations of the Bible and new cultural practices into new religious orthodoxies. So it was that Roberts pursued many peculiar and pernicious practices. At Oral Roberts University, for example, weight loss became a requirement of employment for overweight people, due to Roberts's view that God's promise of salvation involved the mind, spirit, and body. Roberts's expectant faith in God's blessing led him to invest millions of dollars in expanding his university and health complex despite abundant evidence that it would fail. Even though he supported racial integration more than some of his fellow white evangelical leaders, he only occasionally viewed racial segregation as a practice that required deliberate prophetic correction. And this list could go on—including realms of activity such as seed faith, televangelism, and the accumulation of wealth.

The perpetual creativity of evangelical Christianity brings a third feature of Roberts's microcosm into view: the difficulty of change. Through Root's detailed and chronological narrative of Roberts's life, we are able to see many moments where Roberts might have gone a different way. Root concludes that Roberts became "corrupted by power," but Roberts could have put his power toward other ends. Yet the same theological and cultural inertia that elevated him also undermined his willingness to pursue paths that contradicted his theological teachings or his traditions of authority. Root provides a particularly clear window into this process through his analysis of Roberts's prolonged effort to build a $100 million medical complex during a time of financial hardship for his university.

What does Oral Roberts ultimately reveal about the state of evangelicalism in the twentieth century—and today? Root concludes that Roberts reveals how difficult it is for Christians to engage with and speak to the societies and cultures they live in "without completely rejecting or accepting the dominant culture." But if dominant cultures provide the milieu within which forms of Christianity take shape, rejection and acceptance are impossible objectives. What, then, can we do in the space between? We can try to pay attention to the priorities that we embrace, the justifications we invent for our practices, and our willingness to accept failure or pursue change. Through his successes and failures in each of these areas, Oral Roberts lived a life that we all can learn from—whether we are Christian or have other commitments. What is an Oral Roberts? It is a you, and a me.

Daniel Vaca

ACKNOWLEDGMENTS

This project would have never been completed without the help of people who are far more intelligent and capable than me. I am grateful to a long list of people who read drafts, listened patiently as the project developed, and, most importantly, offered friendship. Hunter Hampton, Darin Tuck, Cassandra Yacovazzi, Brandon Flint, Scott Anderson, Joshua Nudell, and Victor McFarland all participated at some stage in the process. I am forever in their debt. I'm especially thankful for John Wigger, my PhD advisor at the University of Missouri. John read every chapter and offered invaluable feedback and advice. Toward the end of the project, when I was discouraged about ever finishing it, John was there to give encouragement. I truly could not have finished the book without his words of wisdom.

Every writer agrees that we could never complete our work without the help of librarians and archivists. Mark Roberts, Daniel Isgrigg, and Roger Rydin at Oral Roberts University pointed me toward sources, answered endless questions about Oral Roberts, and made me feel welcome. I am especially thankful for Daniel, who scanned documents when my job(s) and the COVID-19 pandemic made travel impossible. Writers also could never complete our work without capable editors. Thank you to David Bratt, now of BBH Literary, and Heath Carter for believing in the project from the beginning and for welcoming me to the Library of Religious Biography. Thank you also to Laurel Draper. Their enthusiasm for the book was a guiding light.

Every historian is heavily indebted to remarkable history teachers. I have been blessed with some of the best: Mr. Charles Applehanz and Professors Mark Jantzen, Penelope Moon, Bob Linder, Al Hamscher, John Wigger, Chip Callahan, Steven Watts, and Catherine Rymph.

And, of course, there is my family. My siblings and their spouses, Matthew and Emily Piper Root, Hannah Joy and Kay Peterson Root, and Elizabeth

ACKNOWLEDGMENTS

Root, have been a constant source of enjoyment and support throughout the project. Finally, my parents, Darren and Ann Root. They have been my most vocal cheerleaders, have offered a place to sleep and food to eat when I needed it, and have bought more than their fair share of groceries. I love you all.

Introduction

ORAL ROBERTS RECEIVED NEARLY SIX MILLION LETTERS a year in the early 1970s. Most of these letters were prayer requests regarding illnesses or personal and family problems. Other letters asked for information on Oral Roberts University (ORU). Many letters contained money, or what Oral called a "seed," both an investment in Roberts's growing ministry and a promise of future personal wealth or fulfillment. Roberts sometimes publicly read letters—always omitting names so he wouldn't betray a person's privacy—but some names had to be shared. At an ORU chapel service on January 26, 1973, he told the students that John Lennon had recently sent him a handwritten letter. The ex-Beatle was candid about his history with drug abuse—"I am, I hate to say," he wrote, "under the influence of pills now, I can't stop"—his feelings of childhood abandonment—"maybe if I'd had a father like you, I would have been a better person"—his failed first marriage and its effects on his son Julian, his arrests for drug possession and check forgery, his regret for saying that the Beatles were more popular than Jesus, and his role in the breakup of the Beatles, admitting that he asked the rest of the Fab Four for a "divorce." He also asked Oral about Christianity, wanting to know what it could do for him, if it was phony, and if God loved him, and said that he liked watching Oral's TV show, especially Richard and the World Action Singers. Oral said he immediately wrote back and sent a copy of the *Miracle of Seed Faith* to Lennon, in which he laid out the gospel to the musician and his wife, Yoko Ono, and told them he and the entire ORU student body were praying for their salvation and happiness.[1]

Years later, Jason Aycock, a student at the time, remembered the effect the letter had on the ORU community. "The majority of students at that time were converted hippies. We called ourselves Jesus Freaks," he recalled. "When John Lennon writes to Oral Roberts, you can believe it had a huge impact. There was hardly a dry eye in the place." Oral asked Aycock and the rest of the students to sign their names and write a note on a roll of butcher paper to send to Lennon. Aycock said, "I know personally, my

1

heart went out to him, and I thought of him often after that and wondered if he was happier later in life. It certainly seemed he was happier in the few years leading up to his death."[2]

Even though Oral was a skilled communicator, his daughter-in-law at the time, Patti Roberts, remembered that he couldn't sell a punchline. He always messed up, "but the show he put on was much funnier than the joke could have ever been."[3] The same year he corresponded with Lennon, Oral took his comedic chops to a national audience when he appeared on the popular counterculture sketch comedy *Rowan & Martin's Laugh-In*. When asked his opinion of the popular rock opera *Jesus Christ Superstar*, he said, "I enjoyed it very much, but I like the book a whole lot better." The next joke: "You know, there's a phrase that's sort of religious that comes to mind when I hear *Laugh-In*'s been on for six years: holy mackerel."[4] That same year, Oral did a scene in Archie Campbell's barbershop for the television show *Hee Haw*. In the sketch, Campbell, not recognizing the famous evangelist sitting in his chair, tells a series of Oral Roberts jokes, including one where Roberts was run over by a motorboat while walking on a lake with his pet duck. The other joke is a bit more elaborate. In it, Saint Peter greets Roberts at the gates of heaven, asking him, "Are you the real brother Roberts?" "Yes, I am," Roberts said. Peter then said that Jesus wanted to meet him. When Jesus saw him, he asked, "Are you *the* Oral Roberts." Oral answered, "Yes, I am." Jesus then said that the Father wanted to meet him. After finding out that he was talking to the real Oral Roberts, God the Father complained about a pain in his shoulder. When Roy Clark finally introduced Roberts to Campbell, Oral joked, "You know, I've placed my hands on many people during my ministry and prayed for them. I'd sure like to get my hands on you."[5]

There were other jokes. Oral explained to ORU students in early December 1972 that he ran into the comedian Jack Benny in the hallway at the NBC studios in Burbank. Benny wanted to tell Roberts about a skit he had recently performed on *Laugh-In*, just in case he hadn't seen it. In the sketch, which aired in October 1972, Benny walks up to a door labeled Oral Roberts, looks at the camera, and says, "What have I got to lose?" Benny, who was seventy-eight, knocks and asks, "Can you turn me into a permanent thirty-nine?" Without a reply, the door slams in his face. Benny, deadpan, says to the camera, "Maybe I ought to try Billy Graham."[6] There was another joke that when Roberts prayed at the 1976 Bicentennial, the Liberty Bell was healed. Johnny Carson had his own Oral Roberts joke. He said he recently dropped out of the Oral Roberts Golf Classic in Tulsa because every time he putted, the hole healed over. Oral started to receive mail from people wanting to enter the tournament. He had to write back that the event didn't exist.[7]

Oral saw no reason to be offended. For one, he said, the jokes kept him humble. They also, he believed, revealed something deeper. All their punchlines were about the same thing: healing. "You can't say our name without thinking of healing because there's a lot of it," he reflected.[8] Patti Roberts, when asked about the utility of appearing on secular TV shows, said that people know "what Oral Roberts stands for, they know what he is and by his just being on TV he is testifying for the Lord."[9]

Regardless of his ability to sell a punchline, Roberts's appearance on these comedy shows—especially on *Laugh-In*, whose reputation for off-color jokes may have offended, or at least puzzled, his conservative supporters—displayed a newfound confidence. After recounting his experience on the set of *Hee Haw* to the ORU students, he told them that he didn't mind being the butt of jokes as long as they didn't make fun of the Lord. Several years earlier, he would have never appeared on a show like *Hee Haw*, but he felt like God was so strong in his life at that time, that it would be all right.[10]

Laugh-In and *Hee Haw* weren't the only shows on which Oral appeared in the early 1970s. In 1970, he was on *The Dick Cavett Show*, and later that year, he and his son Richard went on *The Mike Douglas Show*. In 1971, he appeared on a Jerry Lewis telethon. In 1972, he was a guest on *The Tonight Show Starring Johnny Carson*, *The Mike Douglas Show*, *Dinah's Place*, and *The Today Show*, and was featured on an episode of NBC's *Chronolog*. The next year, he was on Dinah Shore's show again. In 1974, he was a guest on *The Merv Griffin Show*. In all these appearances, according to one of Oral's biographers, he "performed flawlessly. He admitted mistakes freely, confirmed the psychosomatic nature of much religious healing, and was calmly tolerant of contradictory opinions."[11]

The gamble—opening up on talk shows and laughing at himself—was paying off. "The Lord," he told ORU students in November 1972, "has given us favor with these people." He also bragged that his picture was hanging in the artist section at NBC studios right next to that of Bob Hope, who played golf with Oral in Tulsa earlier that May. He even had his own parking space next to Hope's and Dean Martin's.[12]

At the time, Oral's television shows aired on hundreds of stations in the United States and Canada, and ORU had $55 million ($344 million in 2021 dollars) worth of facilities, 1,500 students, and a nationally ranked basketball team. The Oral Roberts Evangelistic Association mailed out 400,000 letters a month, and Oral played golf at the exclusive Southern Hills Country Club; served on the board of the National Bank of Tulsa; counted the Oklahoma governor, David Hall, as a personal friend; and had shifted his church membership from the small and culturally marginal Pentecostal Holiness Church to the more mainstream and respectable United Methodist Church. In the mid-1980s, he was the head of a $120-million-a-year business with 2,300 employees, a 5,400-student university, and a medical school, and was in charge of a 2.2-million-square-foot medical complex. He wrote more than 130 books, and his publications were translated into more than one hundred languages. He was so well known that in 1980 he was recognized by 84 percent of Americans, among religious figures second only to Billy Graham and forty points ahead of the next most-recognized figure. In a career that spanned seventy years, he conducted more than 300 healing crusades in more than thirty-five countries and reportedly laid hands on over two million people for healing prayer.

In an April 1973 piece for the *New York Times*, religion writer Edward Fiske wanted to know what accounted for Roberts's popularity. In addition to the usual platitudes—charisma, intelligence, and shrewdness—Fiske argued that it was Roberts's ability to command personal loyalty. Comparing Oral to the other postwar religious giant, Billy Graham, Fiske concluded that Graham, though "obviously the dominant figure of the era," was an "impersonal force." Graham was a link between the nation's Calvinist heritage and its civil religion, which attracted mostly white middle- and upper-class evangelicals. Roberts, on the other hand, fostered a sense of personal closeness with his supporters, most of whom were lower- and middle-class remnants of the Midwest's and South's agrarian and Pentecostal tradition. For these people from the middle of the country, Roberts was an important symbol that upward mobility was possible.[13]

For the United States as a whole, Oral represented the cultural and economic shifts of post–World War II life. Little interested in electoral politics, Roberts's message shaped—and was shaped by—the consumer and therapeutic ethos of his age. Some of his favorite catchphrases—"Something Good Is Going to Happen to You" and "Expect a Miracle"—embodied his belief that God wanted people to live happy, healthy, and wealthy lives. Under Oral's watch, consumption and accumulation became spiritual disciplines rather than simply secular desires. This doesn't mean that Oral wasn't caught up in politics, however. Most obvious was his participation in the nascent culture wars, seen most clearly in his founding of

ORU, which was partially motivated by his desire to combat secularism and rebellious college students.[14] In addition to its conservative cultural politics, ORU was tied to changes in American capitalism after World War II, especially the public-private partnership of Cold War liberalism. In addition to his millions of supporters, whose donations were generally small, Oral drew money from three other sources: the federal government, wealthy businessmen, and private philanthropic corporations like the Ford Foundation.[15] As the Cold War liberal order collapsed in the late 1960s and early 1970s and American capitalism shifted to a finance-based model, Oral increasingly relied on "seed faith" to raise money. This type of fund-raising appeals almost exclusively to private donors to invest "seed capital," a concept that has become popular with entrepreneurs and venture capitalists and has continued to thrive in crowdsourcing websites like Kickstarter, Indiegogo, and Patreon. He also played a key role in the rise of the Sun Belt, a region of the nation that grew, thanks largely to government largesse, in influence and prosperity after World War II. When it was opened in 1965, ORU, with its modernist look and technological innovation, represented the promises often overlooked in states like Oklahoma.[16]

The height of Roberts's influence also coincided with the "age of evangelicalism" in the 1970s and 1980s. It was during these years that evangelicalism, especially after *Time* declared 1976 the "year of the evangelical," began three decades of unprecedented cultural and political influence.[17] These same years also witnessed Roberts's fall from grace. Some of the very traits that had made him successful, arrogance and self-assurance, eventually got the best of him. His success and prosperity, both institutional and personal, contributed to a sense of invincibility and the belief that prosperity was endless. His obsession with building his empire led him to measure success and abundance with brick and mortar. Beginning in 1977 and ending in 1989, Roberts's prohibitively expensive building projects, especially his 2.2-million-square-foot medical complex, the City of Faith, forced him to engage in increasingly manipulative fund-raising tactics. The perception, which was often justified, that he had abandoned preaching the gospel for wealth and the desire to keep the City of Faith open at all costs basically ruined his reputation. He continued to have a public presence, but it was never the same.

Oral Roberts was a giant in postwar American evangelicalism. This book is an attempt to demonstrate how and why a poor Oklahoma farm kid and son of a traveling Pentecostal preacher became one of the most significant figures in not only American religion but also American culture. The Roberts that will emerge in the following pages will both inspire and frustrate. He could be both humble and arrogant. He could be incredibly innovative but stuck in his ways. He could be a sincere disciple of Jesus Christ as well as a crass manipulator of people's emotions. He preached the importance of self-sacrifice while he owned several houses, luxury cars, gold jewelry, and finely tailored suits and had memberships at exclusive country clubs. He could be honest with his failings but was prone to destructive levels of self-deception. None of this should be surprising. Roberts's career lasted nearly seven decades. Through it all, though, he preached a simple and consistent message: that salvation through Jesus Christ offered freedom from sin, sickness, and poverty.

1

Teenage Runaway

ORAL ROBERTS WANTED TO START OVER. The first sixteen years of his life felt like torture. He stuttered, which made him the butt of family and classmates' jokes; attended ten different schools; and lived in devastating poverty. He knew that life had something better for him. Maybe running away would cure him of the debilitating social anxiety created by his stammering. He could escape the people who knew him, get away from his parents' strict rules, and pursue his dream to become a lawyer and governor of Oklahoma. Most importantly, though, he would be able to escape his family's cycle of poverty. "I'd had it with poverty," he later wrote. "Had I accepted it, my life would never have had a chance to amount to a hill of beans."[1]

Life as a teenage runaway was not all he had hoped it would be. There were definitely highlights. He was popular, a successful student, and a star basketball player. He also rarely attended church, drank alcohol, used foul language, committed "sexual indiscretions," slept two to three hours a night, and still stuttered. Then there was the persistent voice in his head. Ever since he was a child, his mother, Claudius, repeatedly told him the dramatic story of his birth and how she promised to give him to the Lord.

There was another thing Roberts could not escape: his family's history with tuberculosis. Claudius's father and youngest sister died of the disease. Oral pushed his body to the brink while he was living in Atoka, a town about fifty miles from his hometown of Ada. To provide for himself, he worked for the *Ada Evening News* and the widow of a district judge with whom he was living. In exchange for room and board, he woke up at 4 a.m. every day to build the fires in the kitchen and the other boarders' rooms. On Saturdays, he worked ten hours at a local grocery store. He was also a full-time student, played basketball, and kept an active social life. His body caught up with him in February 1935. At the Southern Oklahoma District Basketball Tournament, he lost consciousness while going up for a layup and hit the floor, blood running from his nostrils and mouth. His coach immediately picked him up and took him home to Ada, but the teenager was not particularly excited about this prospect: "Home to me was back to poverty, back to religious faith that found no place in me, back to dreaming with no way out."[2]

The Roberts's situation didn't always look so bleak. Before settling in Oklahoma in 1894, Oral's grandfather, Amos Pleasant Roberts ("Uncle Pleas"), and his brothers were some of the thousands of westward-moving Americans looking for land and opportunity. In 1871, Uncle Pleas, a former slave overseer at a large plantation in Alabama, moved with a twenty-wagon team of families to central Arkansas, where he started the town of Robertsville in Conway County and where Ellis Melvin Roberts was born on March 1, 1881. The family then drifted to Texas in 1890 and finally to Pontotoc County, Oklahoma, in 1894. The Roberts clan was well respected. Amos was a school superintendent, a justice of the peace, and was reportedly President Theodore Roosevelt's choice as a federal judge in Indian Territory, but he didn't meet the educational requirements.[3]

Claudius Priscilla Irwin was born on March 24, 1885, in Russellville, Arkansas, to Frank Irwin and Demaris Holton, a half-blooded Cherokee. While Ellis's father was on Roosevelt's short list for a federal judgeship, Claudius's father was an indebted sharecropper. Every summer her family lived on the credit doled out by a local merchant, using their cotton crop as security. When they finally sold their cotton, all the money went immediately to pay back the debt. This cycle of debt led Claudius to loathe the life of a farmer's daughter. She wrote songs to make life more bearable, including one about the greedy merchant, Lige Jackson, that kept her family in debt:

> I see a country farmer,
> His back is bending low
> A picking out his cotton
> As fast as he can go.
> He piles it in a rail pen
> Until the merchant comes
> To attach all his cotton
> 'Til he can pay him some
>
> Chorus
> "Then pay me, Farmer, pay me!"
> I hear Lige Jackson cry.

"Oh, Sir, I am not able
You've sold your goods too high."

Like her youngest son, Claudius dreamed of something better for her-self. She vowed that she would never marry a farmer. She wanted to marry a preacher instead.[4]

Ellis and Claudius were married on February 17, 1901. Ellis was a farmer. The early years of their marriage were not easy. They were poor and had two children quickly. Velma was born in 1902 and Elmer in 1906. Tragedy hit the young family when the six-year-old Velma, who was usu-ally a lively child, started to experience epileptic seizures. Because Velma needed constant supervision, Ellis and Claudius could not socialize. The lack of friends was devastating.

Their lives began to change in 1914 when a five-member team of Pen-tecostal evangelists, the Dryden brothers—Luther, Bill, and Dewey—and Dan and Dolly York, set up camp in Pontotoc County. Years later, Claudius remembered that Oklahoma was the perfect place for a Spirit-filled revival because it was "a melting pot for all kinds of people." The 1914 meetings were reportedly electric, so Ellis and Claudius decided to visit. Ellis found a spot close to the pump organ, and at the end of the night, Claudius realized that "these people had the kind of salvation" she wanted. Her husband was less impressed. He told her that he had seen all that he needed to see and that they were not coming back.

Ellis was sick all the next day. For a couple who had witnessed the Holy Spirit–filled meeting the previous night, his illness was surely a sign that God was speaking to him. As that evening's service drew near, he became restless and, despite his declaration that he would not go back, he wanted to go again. He told Claudius that he would go only if someone offered to harness his wagon. He probably was not expecting someone to actually do it, but his brother-in-law said he would harness the team. As Ellis and Claudius got within hearing distance of the revival, they could hear the song they learned the night before, "Open the Pearly Gates." That night's meeting began to have its desired effect. Ellis, who still had not accepted Christ as his Savior, began a rigorous study of the Bible. His studies con-vinced him of the truth of the Pentecostal message.

It was another year before Ellis and Claudius finally surrendered to the Lord. In the meantime, they continued to struggle with seeking salva-tion and caring for Velma. Watching other families on their way to church from their front porch on Sunday mornings, they felt sorry for themselves because they could not join them. Things began to look better when a Christian family moved in next door and, realizing the Roberts's situation and desire for Christian fellowship, began to visit them on a regular basis. Claudius described the visits as "an oasis in the desert." Ellis and Claudius spent many evenings on their front porch hoping to see the bobbing of the family's lantern as their wagon approached their home.

The next Dryden-and-York-led brush arbor meeting was held fifteen miles from the Roberts home in Ada. The distance and a sick Velma made attending the meeting seem impossible, but they were determined. When possible, they hired someone to watch Velma, or they took her with them, one going under the arbor while the other sat with her in the wagon. One evening they were able to get Claudius's mother to watch Velma, so they attended together. Claudius wanted to go forward to accept Christ as her Savior but held back because she believed that the husband, as the "first member of the family," should be the first to seek salvation. Since Ellis was not quite ready, he encouraged his wife to go ahead of him. On the way home, Ellis told Claudius, "I am glad you got saved. I am going to get saved, too."

Before he could receive his salvation, he had to confess to a neighbor that, twelve years earlier, he had killed one of his hogs. The man's hogs apparently tended to wander onto Ellis's property whenever it rained. Once on his property, they gorged themselves on corn. One day, Ellis had had enough, so he told his hired hand to drive a 300-pound hog toward him so he could kill it. As the hog drew closer, he hit it with what he assumed was the butt end of his cane knife but was the sharp end instead. With a sickening thud and squeal, the hog died. Rather than admit to his crime, Ellis and his hired hand threw the dead animal into a brush pile.

On his way to the brush arbor meeting twelve years later, Ellis ran into the neighbor, Bud Holiday. Ellis asked him if he remembered losing a hog. Yes, he did. "Bud," Ellis explained, "I am trying to get to God and I can't because that hog stands between me and God. If you will tell me the price of the hog, I'll gladly pay you for it!" Bud, who had become a preacher, told him not to worry about it. All was forgiven. If he would not let him pay for it, Ellis asked Holiday, could he at least promise to keep their secret? With this weight off his shoulders, Ellis could finally receive salvation. After he gave his testimony, Luther Dryden told him, "That is good preaching." Holiday, contrary to his promise, told the audience about the hog incident, but Ellis said he didn't mind because he knew he had been saved. When he arrived home that evening, his wife greeted him on their front porch, and he proceeded to preach to her for an hour and a half.[5]

Though it was just a little over a decade old when Ellis and Claudius joined its ranks, Pentecostalism had spread like wildfire across the world. On January 1, 1901, fourteen years before the couple experienced the baptism of the Holy Spirit, a small, radical holiness sect at Bethel Bible College in Topeka, Kansas, reported that some of its members had spoken in tongues. There had been sporadic reports of Christians speaking in tongues since they were first recorded in the book of Acts, but what was new was the significance given to tongues. Charles Fox Parham, the founder of Bethel and a former Methodist pastor who ran afoul of the denomination's hierarchy for his radical holiness views and anti-authoritarianism, argued that speaking in tongues was the "initial evidence" of the baptism of the Holy Spirit. Parham believed that any person who received the baptism of the Holy Spirit would miraculously be able to speak in a foreign language, an ability that was necessary to spread the gospel to the entire world before Christ's imminent return. Agnes Ozman, the first Bethel student to speak in tongues, allegedly spoke in Chinese, a language of which she had no prior knowledge. Other languages heard at Bethel were Swedish, Russian, Bulgarian, Norwegian, Italian, and Spanish.[6]

Parham's early attempts to spread his new doctrine were disappointing. There were a couple of problems. First, he struggled to convince people that speaking in tongues was the biblical evidence of the baptism of the Holy Spirit. Second, the press and some dissenters portrayed Parham and his students as religious fanatics. One dissenter recounted the events at Bethel on New Year's: "I believe the whole of them are crazy. I never saw anything like it. They were racing about the room talking and gesticulating and using this strange senseless jargon which they claim is the word from the Most High. . . . I do not believe their senseless jargon means anything." A snarky Topeka journalist attempted to reprint the words spoken by one of the students: "'Euossa, Eussa use, rela sema calah malah kanah leulla sage nalan. Ligle logl lazle logle. Ene mine mo, sah rah el me sah rah me.' These sentences were translated as meaning 'Jesus is mighty to save,' 'Jesus is ready to hear,' and 'God is love.'"[7]

Parham's luck began to change in late 1903 after a series of revivals in the small lead- and zinc-mining town Galena, Kansas, whose success provided him with enough financial resources to travel to Houston in 1905. Due to Parham's own racism and Houston's segregation laws, a Black student, William J. Seymour, had to sit out in the hallway during Parham's lectures. Seymour, the one-eyed son of former slaves, became convinced by Parham's teaching that speaking in tongues was the initial evidence of the baptism of the Holy Spirit. In January 1906, Seymour received an invitation to go to Los Angeles to pastor a small holiness mission in the city. He decided that this was a sign of God's will for him to spread the message of the baptism of the Holy Spirit. By April of that year, Seymour had secured a small mission building at 312 Azusa Street and begun holding revivals of his own. The meetings quickly became known for their rowdiness and, to the shock of many, their egalitarianism. Observers noted that Blacks, whites, Latinos, men, women, rich, and poor all participated equally in the daily meetings. When Parham visited his pupil in 1906, he was horrified by the interracial nature of the rambunctious Azusa Street meetings. Los Angeles papers also decried the cross-racial mixing and the bizarre behavior of the participants, describing "fanatical rites" that work them into a "state of mad excitement in their peculiar zeal." Despite this opposition, the Azusa Street revival lasted for three years and attracted the attention of people around the globe. Pentecostal revivals were soon reported in Canada, England, Scandinavia, Germany, India, China, Africa, and South America.[8]

Early reports painted Pentecostals as social and religious pariahs. One early critic compared Pentecostals to "savages" in undeveloped countries. Pentecostalism thrived among people who were susceptible to suggestion and in a "low state of culture." It made sense for speaking in tongues to happen in places like India and Korea because people there "are controlled largely by their feelings, which often break through all restraint and assert complete mental mastery." A person should safely assume, he continued, that such persons "would naturally expect less of this suggestibility and loss of rational control." He concluded that speaking in tongues was a reversion to primitive superstition and was a psychological maladjustment. This critique of Pentecostals was common. Contemporary observers and later historians contended that Pentecostalism attracted those modernity left behind, namely, poor white and Black people whose embrace of ecstatic religious beliefs and practices and rejection of respectability reflected their outsider status.[9]

Ellis Roberts was one of many Pentecostal preachers who had received no formal theological education. According to Oral, what his father lacked in education he more than made up for in hard work, an innate speaking ability, and "practical experience through the rough-and-tumble of life." He often spent hours poring over his King James Bible, concordance, Bible dictionary, and various commentaries in preparation for his sermons.[10] Ellis never regretted this lack. He voiced the opinion of many Pentecostals when he said that he would choose the anointing of God over education: "I'll choose God's power every time."[11]

Still, Ellis delayed becoming a pastor. He told Claudius that he didn't feel comfortable leaving her with the children, especially Velma, and even if he could preach, he was a poor public speaker. Finally, after some prodding from his wife—and God—Ellis decided to become a preacher, even if he had to preach barefooted, which he sometimes did. Before he could start preaching, he had to buy a Bible. As a young child, Velma destroyed the family Bible after Ellis threw it on the floor. With the family's last five dollars, he traveled into the local town with his brother, who was on his way to buy an expensive wood stove for his wife. On the way home, Ellis's brother bragged about the new stove and how much his wife would love it. When Ellis told his more successful brother about his five-dollar Bible, he was apparently unimpressed.[12]

Ellis also sold the family farm. The decision to sell his farm and to try his hand as a traveling Pentecostal pastor must have been agonizing. Though the farm was nominally profitable, Ellis now had children to feed—a second daughter, Jewel, was born in 1911—and the Pentecostal circuit was certainly going to be less profitable and consistent. He was determined, however, to follow God's call, so, in 1916, he sold the farm, paid off his debts, and purchased a buggy and a pump organ. Ellis could have had better timing. Shortly after the sale, oil was discovered on his former property. He may have missed out on the modest wealth his family and neighbors made, but he never regretted the decision, saying that the following years were a "period of great happiness."[13]

He was licensed to preach by the Pentecostal Holiness Church, but his job can be best described as a church planter. The denomination boasted few actual church buildings, so Ellis was tasked with holding brush arbors and, if enough people were converted, helping to build a crude structure, securing a new pastor, and then moving on to the next place. A brush arbor was a temporary structure. Since church buildings were scarce, communities would cut down saplings and trim them for poles and then lay a lattice of tree branches for a roof. For seating, they used two-by-twelve-foot pieces of lumber and, for lighting, coal lamps. If the meetings were successful, efforts were made to build a more permanent structure. Ellis was apparently good at his job. More than fifty people became pastors, evangelists, and Bible teachers under his tutelage.[14]

Despite his oft-stated frustrations with his father, Oral admitted that Ellis was a dedicated laborer for the gospel, often taking on tasks that few others would. His first pastorate was at a church in Sulphur, Oklahoma, which consisted of little more than "a few chairs placed in rows beneath some willow trees in the yard of one of the church members." The unglamorous position had been offered to younger ministers, but, according to Claudius, because "there wasn't much to offer a young preacher except the opportunity to work for the love of working for God," nobody but Ellis was willing to take the risk. His journey to the church on his first Sunday was arduous. He woke up with a fever, and his first ride dropped him off twenty miles from his destination. Discouraged, and wanting to escape the hot Oklahoma sun, he sat down in the shade of a tree and pleaded with God to send a car. If a car arrived to take him the rest of the way, despite feeling "sick in body," he promised God that he would preach that evening. He soon heard the rattle of a Ford Model T, which, despite the noise, "was music to Ellis' ears." That evening, nine young men accepted Christ as their Savior.[15]

Other experiences were a bit more harrowing. At one "church" in Center, Oklahoma, the Roberts clan arrived, only to find that the exterior and interior needed work. The weeds had grown out of control, and, on the inside, they found the bloody aftermath of fights between "rough cowboys" and the "roustabouts from the booming oil fields." The walls, Claudius remembered, were covered in blood three feet high. The family had to cut the weeds and scrub the walls to get ready, and the first few nights of the revival were less than promising. The attendance was good, according to Claudius, but nobody was converted, and the offering was inadequate to support the family. During the day, the family collected cotton, providing enough money for a few groceries but not for clothes. Ellis's shoes were so badly worn that he had to cut out cardboard soles every morning. Despite this slow start, Claudius said that it ended up being "one of our best revival meetings."[16]

The miracles continued. One night, just a few months before Oral was born, a neighbor boy came to the family's front door and asked Claudius to come to his house to pray for his dying brother. The child had flu and pneumonia and was not expected to make it through the night, but Claudius knew the child would recover. She was on her way when a loud thunderstorm popped up, drenching her; she was considering returning home when the storm suddenly stopped. Her trials were not over. When she looked around, she discovered that she was in the middle of a field, standing near a heavy-duty barbed-wire fence. It took her a great deal of effort to pass through the fence. Though she was several months pregnant, she lifted the strand of one of the wires and put her foot down on another so she could continue her journey. It was then that she asked God to give her new son black hair and blue eyes, a sign of her Cherokee heritage, and that if he healed the dying boy, she would dedicate her son to his work.[17]

Granville Oral Roberts was born on January 24, 1918, in Ada, Oklahoma. One of Claudius's cousins, Minnie Lewis, named the baby. "We'll name him Granville Oral," she told Claudius, "and we'll call him Oral."[18] He had long black hair and blue eyes. Claudius never doubted that he was going "to bring the gospel message to his generation." He later claimed that his first two initials spelled GO because God wanted him to "go" to the people with his healing message.[19]

Before statehood in 1907, Oklahoma was divided into the Indian and Oklahoma Territories, but there were essentially three different "Oklahomas" when Oral was born at the dawn of the 1920s. The oldest, obviously, was the indigenous Oklahoma. In 1830, President Andrew Jackson passed the Indian Removal Act, which, over the next twenty years, forced nearly sixty thousand members of the Five Civilized Tribes—Cherokee, Muscogee, Seminole, Chickasaw, and Choctaw nations—from their homelands in the southeastern United States to west of the Mississippi. Many of them settled in southern Oklahoma.

Another Oklahoma was white and southern. Oral's white ancestors—people like Uncle Pleas—were southern Democrats from Arkansas, Texas, and the rest of the old Confederacy. They brought with them their racial politics and cotton. Southern Oklahoma became part of the Cotton Belt, with all its economic and racial baggage. By the time Oral was born, the part of the family that settled in Pontotoc County was more likely to be tenant farmers than property owners. In the 1920 census, 60 percent of the county's residents performed some type of tenant work.[20] Even though Pontotoc County was a Democratic stronghold, the rural poor in the county made it one of Oklahoma's most reliable socialist regions in the early twentieth century. According to family tradition, some members of the Roberts family struck it rich when oil was found on their property.[21]

The third Oklahoma, the one to which Oral would later take his southern restlessness, was strongly northern Republican; its white migrants came from Kansas and the rest of the Midwest. It also had a sizable Black population; about one in ten voters was a Black homesteader. Compared to their southern counterparts, northern Oklahomans tended to be wealthier.[22]

Even when Oral was a baby, God could heal through him. When he was seven months old, Claudius fell ill with typhoid fever. A doctor gave a grim diagnosis. The moments when she was conscious, she believed that God would spare her. On the verge of death, she asked to see Oral. Her family, believing they were granting a mother her dying wish, complied. She miraculously started to feel better. Years later, she remembered, "God's healing power had touched my life."[23] There were moments, however, when God seemed to be absent. On March 1, 1921, the eldest Roberts child, Velma, died. She was only nineteen years old.[24]

God worked through the young Oral in other ways as well. He may have hated his family's poverty and resented his father for being so comfortable with mediocrity, but he claimed that he always had faith that God would provide for his family's material needs. One story he liked to recount was when his father was away holding a series of revival meetings and was not able to send money back home. The situation was so severe that the family did not even have food to eat, which was common for the family. According to Oral, his father was partially responsible for the family's ills. The unambitious patriarch had a habit of preaching a few revivals, collecting the money, and then sitting at home until the money or food ran out before preaching again. When Claudius, Oral, and Vaden, Oral's older brother by fifteen months, went to visit a neighbor, she offered them supper, but Claudius refused. They came to visit, not to eat, she explained. Vaden was not pleased with her answer. He believed that she should have asked him before deciding for everyone. Much to Vaden's frustration, after watching the family eat, his mother thanked God for his goodness. He grumbled under his breath that God hadn't been very good to him. Oral rebuked his brother, telling him not to let their mother hear him; besides, he said, "God will take care of us."

He may not have understood or even believed the words he was saying, but they were prophetic, nonetheless. When the trio got back to their house, they discovered that someone had generously left behind a box of food. In the box were a country ham, a sack of flour, ten pounds of lard, ten pounds of sugar, a sack of potatoes, and "lots of other good things," Oral remembered. An hour later, after Claudius finished cooking a massive meal, Oral turned to Vaden and said, "I told you God would take care of us."[25]

Being a Pentecostal pastor's kids made the Roberts children, especially Oral and Vaden, a favorite target for bullies. They liked to call the Roberts boys "holy rollers," a pejorative that critics used to mock Pentecostals' ecstatic behavior, which included rolling on the ground and shaking. The boys' encounters with bullies sometimes turned violent. In one instance, Oral remembered that one of their tormentors was at least six feet tall and five years older than the Roberts brothers, but Vaden was confident they could beat him up. His plan was for him to distract the bully while Oral sucker-punched him on his blind side. With the bully on the ground, Vaden and Oral jumped on top of him and continued to pummel him until he finally surrendered and vowed to never call them holy rollers again.[26]

The Roberts boys did their fair share of terrorizing. They gained a well-earned reputation as the "two meanest children in the county," Oral recalled. At one revival, Vaden nearly cut off another boy's ear because he refused to stop touching the Roberts boys' quilt. In another incident, Vaden drove a nail through Oral's hand. After discovering his brother driving nails into a stump, Oral wanted to drive one. When Vaden refused, Oral put his hand on the stump, prompting Vaden to say, "I'll nail your hand to this stump." Oral didn't think he'd actually do it. The boys caused quite the scene. When they both realized what Vaden had done, they started jumping and hollering, which drew the attention of their mother, who joined them in their jumping and hollering. Oral's hand was finally saved when an uncle, who initially thought the scene was hilarious, pulled out the nail with a hammer.[27]

Oral's social isolation was made worse by his stuttering. It was not until he started school that he realized how much his stammering could be a roadblock to success and social acceptance. He never had any problems learning the course material but nearly always failed at public speaking. His stammering also made him a target for bullies. In one instance, a gang of nearly fifteen boys chased him all the way home. After scaring away the boys, Claudius told her frightened and insecure son for the first time about the night she dedicated him to the Lord's service.

The torment didn't stop at school. His own family mocked him. While Oral was frail and insecure, Vaden was healthy and smooth-talking, making him the more popular of the two boys. Ellis and Claudius always had faith that Oral was going to be the preacher and the "one who was going to make his mark," but their family felt otherwise. When Ellis told one of his brothers that Oral was called by God to be a preacher, he responded, "Why, Ellis, have you lost your mind? Oral can't even talk." The family made their preference for Vaden known in other, more cruel ways as well. One time when the boys wanted to show off their newly purchased suits, the family oohed and aahed at Vaden. They made fun of Oral, saying, "Isn't he the funniest-looking thing you ever saw."[28]

Claudius had a more positive recollection of Oral's boyhood. His family mocked him, she admitted, but not for his stammering. Instead, it was because he was awkward with his hands and could not pick as much cotton or chop wood as well as others. One uncle believed that the ability to do this kind of work was a measure of a person's worth.[29] She also lauded his ability to speak in front of an audience. Starting when he was eight years old, at about the same time that Oral claimed his stuttering became a serious problem, he demonstrated uncanny speaking skills. Since the family was poor, Ellis and Claudius couldn't afford to give their children a regular allowance, so Oral took it upon himself to make his own money by selling newspapers. One day after seeing his nephew expertly hawking papers on a street corner, his uncle John Roberts, one of his naysayers, explained that Oral was outselling all the other boys and that he was "quite the talker." He went on, "I believe that boy will make a preacher like his father!"[30]

These features of Oral's childhood—the poverty, the stuttering, the bullying, and the overbearing religious parents—were too much for the ambitious young man. He knew that his decision to run away broke his parents' hearts, but, like his mother, Oral was stubborn. Before he left, his five-foot-tall mother brought her six-foot-one son to eye level and told him, "Oral, I made a vow to God concerning your life. I dedicated you to Him. Son, every night you are gone, I will rise from my bed and pray for God to bring you home." Even in his most wayward and hedonistic moments in Atoka, his mother's words stuck with him.[31]

At the time Oral collapsed on the gym floor in 1934, tuberculosis (TB) was on the decline in the Western world. After the German physician and microbiologist Robert Koch discovered TB's microscopic cause—mycobacterium tuberculosis—in 1882, humans were edging closer to discovering how and why the disease was spread. One thing they knew for certain was that it was highly contagious, which led to efforts to prohibit taken-for-granted actions like spitting in public. Race was another popular explanation. Oral's Native American heredity was assumed to be the culprit. When TB was first identified as a major health problem among indigenous Americans in the 1870s, Indian agents and physicians thought that susceptibility to TB was built into their bodies. Roberts himself observed this phenomenon. Traveling with his father on preaching tours, he noticed that Indians were especially prone to die from tuberculosis. The relationship between race and TB has largely been discredited. As is the case for so many others who get the active form of the disease, Oral's illness was a combination of genetics and environment. His mother's father and two of her sisters died of TB. Oral also grew up in a TB-friendly environment. By his own account, he often went without food, walked barefoot in the winter, worked in the cotton fields, and ran himself haggard in Atoka.

Death from TB is slow and painful. Starting with a wet, hacking cough, TB sufferers eventually drown to death in their own lungs. It slowly eats infected persons' lungs from the inside out and eventually causes their chests to fill with blood and the liquid remains of the lungs. When Claudius saw her son after his collapse, he was unrecognizable. She described him as a "poor, slim boy that looked like death itself." Oral's condition deteriorated quickly. He lost over 40 pounds, dropping from 165 to 120 (in one autobiography, he said he dropped from 150 to 120). His days and nights were spent in wracking pain and hemorrhaging. Ellis had to repaper the bedroom walls because Oral spit up so much blood.[32]

There was little doctors could do to help someone in Oral's condition. They could send him to a sanitorium, where it was assumed open air and rest could cure the disease and, perhaps most importantly, isolate him from the noninfected. His doctors could also change his diet. Oral's doctors put him on a strict diet of raw eggs beaten in sweet milk. This unpalatable mixture was easier on the digestion than solid food, and for patients like Oral, who had lost a dangerous amount of weight, the fat in eggs and milk would aid in healthy weight gain. The egg and milk diet didn't help the teen. In what was essentially a death sentence, the doctors advised Ellis and Claudius to send Oral to the Eastern Sanitorium in Talihina, Oklahoma. When the judge signed the papers sending Oral to the sanitorium, he said, "Ellis, I hate to do this. Putting anyone in the sanitarium in Talihina usually means he comes out dead. Oral deserves better than that."[33]

Prayer for the sick was and has remained one of the key pillars of Pentecostalism. Lying on his deathbed, Oral heard at least two different views on healing. The first was the one that had dominated American thought for much of the nineteenth century. This view held that sickness, pain, and suffering were expected features of life and that patience was the appropriate response to suffering. After all, not even Jesus's life was free of suffering. Miraculous healing might happen, according to this view, but it was the exception rather than the rule. This was also the age of "heroic medicine," which was founded on the ancient Hippocratic theory that sickness and disease were the consequences of an imbalance of "humors" within a person. The treatment was often worse than the disease. Balance was restored through purging, bleeding, or emetics, which usually involved ingesting mercury and opium. The discovery of anesthesia in the 1840s undermined the belief that pain was a necessary part of health. Under the umbrella of the divine healing movement, American Protestants began to make the case that sickness was never the will of God, and that healing was available to every person who had sufficient faith.[34]

With the doctors unable to cure Oral and death knocking at the door, prayer was the only thing left to try. Prayer for the sick was a mainstay for Ellis and Claudius. According to Oral, whenever his father finished preaching, his mother would meet the sinners at the "mourner's bench" and pray them through salvation and the baptism of the Holy Spirit and lay hands on the sick to pray for healing. Claudius's faith in God's healing power hit a snag in 1921 after Velma's death, but she always maintained that God could heal through prayer. While many told the seventeen-year-old that he would be healed if it was God's will, his parents reminded him that God called him to change the world and that to be healed, he first needed to have faith in Jesus.[35]

Finally, after years of rebellion and months of suffering, Oral Roberts accepted Christ as his Savior. The moment was dramatic. The first thing that happened was he "felt a warmth" flow into his body. And when he looked up at his father, who was praying over him, he saw a bright light envelop his father when "suddenly the likeness of Jesus appeared in his face." Instead of telling his father about his vision—the first of many visions of Jesus—he cried out, "Jesus, save me! Jesus, save me!" The frail, sickly teenager suddenly found the strength to get out of his bed, embrace his parents, and dance around the room celebrating the newfound presence of God in his life. He also had the strength to pen a letter to the Pentecostal Holiness Church's publication, the *Pentecostal Holiness Advocate*. He wrote that he had been saved and was ready to enter the ministry but that before he could enter the field, he needed prayer to overcome his infirmities.[36]

Seven words changed Oral's life. On the verge of death, his older sister, Jewel, who had also run away from home, told him: "Oral, God is going to heal you." It would take another sibling, Elmer, to finally take Oral to be healed. Elmer, who had never been particularly close to his younger brother and had never shown much interest in the Christian faith, was attending a series of healing revivals when he decided that his brother could also be healed. Borrowing a car from a friend, he drove to his parents' house, dressed his brother, and loaded him on a mattress in the backseat of the car for the eighteen-mile drive from Stratford to Ada, Oklahoma. Oral remembered feeling every bump in the road on the way to the revival. He also remembered hearing God's voice: "Son, I am going to heal you and you are to take My healing power to your generation." It was at that moment that God was going to heal him.[37]

Not much is known about the evangelist who prayed for the dying teenager, George Moncey, who has been described as an "elusive and shadowy figure." When he arrived in Ada in July 1935, the residents had never heard of him, and he reportedly left town in a cloud of controversy. No matter his obscurity or behavior, he changed Oral's life. Moncey later used Roberts's healing under his tent in his advertisements.[38]

Oral believed that someone told Moncey about his native ancestry because at some point during the service the evangelist approached the dying boy and said, "An Indian boy was healed here a few nights ago." The evangelist did not pray for Roberts until the very end of the evening, around 11 p.m. Laying hands on Roberts, Moncey said, "You foul tormenting disease, I command you in the name of Jesus Christ of Nazareth, come out of this boy! Loose him and let him go free." The next thing Roberts remembered was finally being able to breathe. He was then asked to take the microphone to testify. He also found out he was healed of stuttering. He spoke for about fifteen or twenty minutes. Preaching felt natural, he later said.[39]

Oral's first public retelling of his healing wasn't nearly this dramatic. This account of his healing came in the October 5, 1939, issue of the Pentecostal Holiness Church organ, the *East Oklahoma Conference News*. In this version, it was the flu, not TB, that made him collapse during the basketball game. He told the paper that at the end of sixty days, as he was nearing death, "I called in my school mates and gave them my books, and at the same time told them good bye, meanwhile my parents were praying for me—even whole churches—and at last I opened my heart, prayed with all the earnestness of my soul, and God saved me." Once his strength returned, he vowed to enter the ministry, but he lapsed in his faith after falling in with a rowdy crowd.

Not long after, he was bedridden again. Still, it was not TB but a nervous breakdown that kept him in bed for five months. There was also no dramatic healing or impromptu sermon at a George Moncey revival in July 1935. Instead, he was healed during family prayer in February. And, once again, God healed and saved him. This time his salvation stuck, and he entered the ministry immediately. He gave his first sermon in August 1935. A year later, he was licensed to preach in the East Oklahoma Conference of the Pentecostal Holiness Church. He bragged that he had already preached 600 times and that 400 people were saved, 125 were sanctified, 98 received the baptism of the Holy Ghost, 187 joined a church, and 69 were baptized. He had also performed five wedding ceremonies. The once sickly youth said he saw greater things ahead if he stayed true to Christ.[40]

2

The Discovery

ORAL HAD AN EXTENDED LIST OF QUALIFICATIONS FOR HIS FUTURE WIFE. Ten, actually. First, she had to be a Christian. Second, she had to be intelligent in both God's Word and the "world we live in on earth." Third, she had to support his life's calling and to "cooperate with it as part of her own commitment to the Lord." Fourth, she had to be attractive but not too attractive: "just a man's woman who has the ability and desire to be a full wife physically." Fifth, she had to want a family. Sixth, she had to be industrious and a good housekeeper. Seventh, she had to be even-tempered, "not given to fits of rage or jealousy or impatience." Eighth, she had to be able to carry on a conversation. Ninth, she had to have a backbone, willing to stand up to him if he was wrong or if he lost his temper. Finally, she had to want a lifetime commitment. "When I marry her, it must be a done deal."[1]

Evelyn Lutman was born on April 22, 1917, in Warsaw, Missouri. Her birth father, Edgar Lutman, was a local merchant when he married Evelyn's mother, Edna Wingate, but his alcoholism tore the family apart. After years of abuse, Edna was granted a divorce. Evelyn was four, and her sister, Ruth, was two. Except for a brief glimpse of him walking down a Missouri sidewalk when she was twelve, Evelyn never saw her father again. Her only contact with him was a brief correspondence when she was in college. Her biggest regret was that she never got the chance to talk to him face-to-face about Jesus before he died of tuberculosis.

After the divorce, Evelyn and her sister were given to the custody of their maternal grandparents in the Missouri Ozarks. They moved back in with their mother when she remarried. Edna's second husband, Ira Fahnestock, offered the loving and stable environment that the five-year-old Evelyn needed. Their life changed when a neighbor told Ira that an old woman named Granny Hubbs was causing a scene at a nearby revival. More interested in observing the eccentric old woman shout than hearing the gospel, the Fahnestock family decided to go. Granny Hubbs was apparently an effective preacher. At the end of the weeklong revival, Edna and Ira walked away as born-again Christians.

According to Evelyn, their lives changed immediately. Her stepfather "had an insatiable hunger for God" and forced the family to attend any Christian meeting that was held nearby. He was also a voracious reader. Most notably, he subscribed to Aimee Semple McPherson's monthly magazine, *Bridal Call*, whose message often made him cry tears of joy. Just a few months after his conversion, Ira moved his family to Coffeyville, Kansas, because he heard reports of people speaking in tongues there. The plan was to stay there until he received the baptism of the Holy Spirit and then return to their farm in the Ozarks. One year later, the family returned to Missouri. Like Ellis, Ira became an itinerant preacher for the Pentecostal Holiness Church after his Holy Ghost baptism. Ira wanted to be a full-time preacher for the denomination, but, just as with Ellis Roberts, it was nearly impossible to support a family on a pastor's salary.[2]

It was even more difficult during the Great Depression. Life for Oklahomans like the Roberts and Fahnestock clans, people whose ancestors migrated to the state in the late nineteenth century, had been in decline since the First World War. A combination of falling international markets for wheat, corn, and cotton; mineral depletion and soil erosion; pests; drought; and mechanization meant many of these yeoman farmers lost their land as acreage was consolidated into large farms. This situation turned nightmarish during the 1930s, as collapsing crop prices and a series of environmental disasters, including the worst drought of the century, crippled the region's economy. In eastern Oklahoma, where the Roberts and Fahnestock families lived, cotton acreage had shrunk to half its former size by 1939, losing nearly 12.5 million acres to other uses. Even reliably stable industries—oil, transportation, and construction—declined. Oklahoma's unemployment rate, 29 percent in 1933, was higher than that of any other state in the South or northern plains. It was second only to Arkansas's 39 percent that same year. Thanks to government aid, the Oklahoma number declined to 22 percent by 1937.

Government relief programs, however, didn't totally erase Oklahomans' suffering. Grants averaged from $10 to $12 a month, half the national average, for a family of four in 1934 and 1935, the peak years of government assistance. Up to 90 percent of the population in eastern Oklahoma collected relief payments in 1934. Things improved a bit in 1935 after the passage of the Works Progress Administration (WPA), when the average wage for the unemployed reached from $30 to $50 a month, but families that were forced to stay on the government dole saw this number cut in half as federal funds were reduced. Welfare analysts estimated that an urban family of four needed a minimum of $60 a month for subsistence living.[3]

Much to Evelyn's embarrassment, Ira was one of many Oklahomans who found work through the WPA. Though Evelyn never mentioned how much her stepfather received in federal aid, it is likely that he never received enough to support his family. As a child, Evelyn declared that she would never marry a pastor because it was a life of grinding poverty. On their travels during the Depression, Ira, Evelyn, who played guitar, and Ruth, who played violin, were usually only given food as payment. She decided that she was going to prepare for a better life for her future children.[4]

Evelyn would have preferred to be a missionary, but if she couldn't do that, being a schoolteacher was the next best thing. She was fascinated with blackboards. Whenever she could get away from chores, she could be found improvising blackboards, for instance, using matchsticks to write on the ground. Her grandparents supported her plans, emotionally and financially. Her grandmother told her that since she was going to be talking for a living, she had to learn perfect grammar (using slang was unnecessary and unladylike) and needed to get the best education she could. Her grandfather loaned her money to cover expenses at Northeastern State Teacher's College in Tahlequah, Oklahoma, and later helped her to borrow money from a bank so she could attend classes at Texas College of Arts and Industries in Kingsville, Texas.[5]

Oral and Evelyn met in August 1936 at the annual Pentecostal Holiness camp meeting in Sulphur, Oklahoma. Camp meetings were exciting events on the church calendar. Families would travel together, set up camp, and attend worship services. Camp meetings served two primary purposes: revivalism and evangelism. Revivalism was aimed at people who were already involved in a church. The hope was that church members would renew their spiritual commitments. Evangelism was aimed at people who had no church commitment. Outsiders gathered on the fringes of the camp and observed the meetings from a safe distance. To the chagrin of some, camp meetings also served important social functions.[6]

Oral and Evelyn met in the orchestra pit during the first evening service. For Evelyn, it was love at first sight. That night, she wrote in her diary that she had met a "tall and handsome man," and that his name was Oral Roberts. She intended to make him her husband. She then showed the diary to her mother, who, reflecting the anti-indigenous racism rampant in Oklahoma, asked her love-struck daughter if she knew that Oral's mom was an Indian. "Mama, I'm not going to marry his mother," Evelyn responded. The only impression she seemed to have had on him was that she had a terrible singing voice. While listening to her sing a solo one night, he told the person next to him, "That's a pretty girl up there, but she sure can't sing."[7]

The following night, Oral was running late, and when he finally sat in his seat, Evelyn was already tuning her guitar. The usually dapper Oral asked her how his hair looked. "You look very nice," she replied. They sat next to each other the rest of the week. Much to Evelyn's disappointment, Oral never asked her out on a date. A woman, she later wrote, couldn't just go up to a man and say, "I want to marry you."[8]

When Oral met Evelyn, women were the last thing on his mind. As a young, up-and-coming preacher, he was singularly focused on God's calling for his life. For nearly a year he had been a preacher for the Pentecostal Holiness Church, often working alongside his father. In June, he was elected secretary of the Pentecostal Young People's Society in the East Oklahoma Conference. Roberts went to the Sulphur meeting with one goal: to receive the baptism of the Holy Spirit. He was frustrated that he had been preaching on the importance of speaking in tongues for a year but had not yet received the baptism himself.

Oral and Evelyn didn't have any contact with each other for two years after their first meeting. Evelyn moved to the Rio Grande valley in Texas to teach, where she dated other men. One suitor, who was ten years her senior, seemed to have asked her to marry him simply because she was around. He told her that he was "at the age" when he needed a wife, that he would provide for her, and that he wouldn't get in the way of her faith. Another man was on his path toward becoming a successful businessman. He also promised to provide for her. She explained to these men that she enjoyed their company but that she was not the woman for them. They needed to find women who would give them the love and support they needed.

She also backslid. She never lost her enthusiasm for going to church and Sunday school, but she also wanted to fit in. When she was living with her parents, she never went to dances or movie theaters and never drank or smoked. When she was away, however, her favorite activity was dancing. She started going to movies as well. These indiscretions weighed heavily on her heart. Her guilty conscience led her to write a letter to her home church asking it to take her off the membership roll because she had "wandered away from the Lord and have done things a church member shouldn't do."⁹ These infractions may seem inconsequential, but they were serious offenses in the rigid Pentecostal world in which Evelyn and Oral lived. The Pentecostal Holiness Church forbade members from holding memberships in secret societies, social clubs, and political parties; being involved in activities and "places of worldly amusement" like baseball games, picnics, circuses, dance halls, and county and state fairs; and dressing immodestly and consuming, producing, and selling alcohol and tobacco products. It did, however, leave room for members to participate in legal efforts "on the part of labor to prevent oppression and injustice from capitalism." Church picnics and other social events that promoted "fellowship among the members" were also acceptable. Any person who violated the denomination's rules of conduct could be ousted from a congregation.¹⁰

After the Sulphur camp meeting, Oral moved to Westville, Oklahoma, where Ellis had been assigned a pastorate. It was while living here that Oral first told his friend, Frank Moss, about his ten requirements for a wife. Moss attended church with Evelyn's parents in Westville. Ellis was their pastor.

Oral spent the two years after his first encounter with Evelyn making a name for himself as a fiery and ambitious preacher in Pentecostal Holiness churches. He was described as "studious, zealous, and fervent," and as a "wonderful evangelist working in the interest of lost souls and the church." His own reports from the evangelistic field were equally encouraging.¹¹ He also demonstrated that he could be a trusted gatekeeper for the denomination's interests. He scolded other Pentecostal youth for their spiritual immaturity and lack of focus. All too frequently, they would "hoist the flag of Holiness and lift up the standard of clean living for young people," only to give up with the first hint of trouble or simply lose interest. He also took shots at educated clergymen who relied more on Thomas Paine and Robert Ingersoll than on the Word of God and the Holy Spirit for their beliefs and sermons. For their part, laypeople weren't praying or reading the Bible but instead were going to movies, getting divorced, reading rotten literature, and taking advantage of others to get rich.¹²

Rebellious youth and heretical pastors were easy targets, but there is evidence to suggest that Roberts was caught up in a generational conflict within the Pentecostal Holiness Church. Since its formal establishment in 1911, the denomination had grown into a stable organization with a paid bureaucracy and a class of professional clergy, which jealously guarded its power. Older pastors were apparently frustrated with some of their juniors.

One worried that the church was "playing up" its young preachers to the detriment of the denomination, and the young preacher who grew a "big head" would inevitably fail.[13]

Roberts criticized pastors who inadequately supported evangelists. It is hard to know how Oral's superiors responded to one article he wrote in the *Pentecostal Holiness Advocate*, "Relationship of Pastor and Evangelist," but it wouldn't be surprising if it ruffled a few feathers. The Pentecostal Holiness Church had a rigid hierarchical structure, and, coming from a twenty-year-old evangelist, the piece reads as fairly presumptuous. In it, Roberts offered to "outline a general working policy of cooperation between the pastor and evangelist." The article reveals a young evangelist who was ambitious, arrogant, and entitled. Pastors had an obligation to treat evangelists as equals, give them a nice place to stay, advertise for them, and prepare their flocks "for the coming revival." On their end of the relationship, evangelists had a responsibility to support the local pastor.[14]

Roberts also tried his hand at book publishing. In early 1938, the Pentecostal Holiness Church publishing house, based in Franklin Springs, Georgia, printed his first book, *Salvation by the Blood*. The book's main theme, the atoning blood of Christ, established Oral as an effective communicator. A July 1938 advertisement described it as a "sermon worthy of distribution."[15] He seemed to have let the attention go to his head; in an attempt at a romantic gesture, he sent Evelyn an autographed copy of *Salvation by the Blood* for her twenty-first birthday. On the inside cover he wrote, "I trust it will bless your soul."[16]

By this time in his career, Roberts was ready to find a wife. Evelyn wasn't the first Lutman woman he pursued. With Evelyn attending school and teaching in Texas, Roberts started dating her sister, Ruth. But the dates must have been awkward. Oral only wanted to talk about Evelyn. Mutual friends were also whispering in his ear. Though he only had the vaguest recollection of her, they told him that Evelyn was the perfect match for him. She was smart, a good musician, an excellent cook and housekeeper, even-tempered, and beautiful ("not in a superficial way but with an inner beauty because of her character and her devotion to the Lord," Oral later wrote).[17]

Their courtship started in early 1938 and happened primarily through letters and *Salvation by the Blood*. The correspondence seemed to be going well until Oral mentioned that the two of them "may spend the next fifty years" of their lives together. They had only exchanged a handful of letters and had only met once, so naturally Evelyn was taken aback.

She told him that she had no intention of living in a parsonage "raising a bunch of preacher's children." Oral's response was quick; he sent it air mail: "You needn't worry, if you think I would want to spend the rest of my life with you, you are badly mistaken." Both immediately regretted their harsh words.[18]

They quickly patched things up, and in September 1938, Oral and his mother drove to Texas to meet Evelyn. This meeting was more memorable than their first. It was recess time when he drove up to her school. The children excitedly began clapping their hands and yelling, "Miss Evelyn, your boyfriend is here." Roberts must have been a striking figure. He showed up in his new Chevrolet coupe and was wearing a light gray suit. "He took my breath away," Evelyn remembered. Oral was equally enamored. As he watched her read a story to the children, he thought, "She is even more lovely than they told me." That night, they stayed in the boarding house Evelyn shared with other single teachers. When they got there, Oral was excited to discover that Evelyn played piano.[19]

The next step was to meet Evelyn's maternal grandparents, the Wingates. Though he eventually won them over, Oral didn't make the best first impression. Mrs. Wingate noted how thin he looked—he was six feet one and weighed 150 pounds—and asked Evelyn, "Is he a mama's boy?" Evelyn, slightly offended by her grandmother's remarks, said that, yes, he was thin and asked, "what's strange about a boy loving his mother?" She was also leery of her granddaughter marrying a preacher. Considering her success as a teacher—she made eighty dollars a month to Oral's forty dollars—she hoped that Evelyn would marry a businessman or school administrator, someone who could better provide for her. Her grandfather appears to have been easier to win over. After Oral told him that he had worked on farms his entire life, Mr. Wingate told Evelyn, "That young man will do. He's been a farm boy."[20]

It was on a fishing outing that Oral discovered that Evelyn met his ten qualifications. She was intelligent and easy to be with, and wasn't intimidated by him. Perhaps most importantly, they talked easily about Oral's ministry and their mutual life plans. The conversation was so natural that it felt as if they had been together every weekend for months. Back in his car, Oral proposed, but before she could answer him Evelyn had to confess that she had backslidden. She told him that a minister deserved a wife "who is living just as close to the Lord as she can." Roberts told her that he had checked up on her and that any person who loved the Lord as much as she did "can't stay away from Him very long." Later that day, Evelyn had a chance to rededicate her life to God when the two attended a local Assemblies of God camp meeting. When it came time for the sinners to walk the sawdust trail, Oral stepped out of the way for her to pass. After five minutes of prayer, Evelyn remembered, "It seemed He was so much more wonderful to me this time than He was when I was first converted." On the drive home, Oral told Evelyn that he was now sure he wanted to marry her.

The original plan was to get married the next June, once Evelyn finished out her teaching contract, but Oral didn't want to wait. The loneliness of his evangelistic obligations, and probably more than a little sexual desire, prompted him to write to her nearly every day. He eventually asked her to move their wedding to December, but Evelyn was hesitant because the school board didn't employ married teachers and she was worried she would have to resign. To her delight, the school board told her she could get married and finish out the school year. They also promised to write her a positive letter of recommendation.[21]

After securing a pastor—Oscar Moore—and a church—Ellis's church in Westville, Oklahoma—Oral realized that he didn't have the twenty dollars required to pay for the wedding. One way he tried to save money was to cut back on his favorite soft drink, Dr Pepper. He limited himself to three bottles a week, each costing five cents. Two for himself and one for his host pastor. When this didn't result in enough savings, he went to a bank for a loan of twenty dollars, but he left the bank with only eighteen dollars. The banker took two dollars for interest in advance. With the remaining eighteen, Oral paid five dollars to Moore, five dollars for the marriage license, and three dollars for flowers. He still didn't have enough money to pay for Evelyn's wedding gift, which was ten dollars and sitting in layaway. Evelyn gave him the money for the present. They were married on December 25, 1938.

Because Oral had preaching responsibilities and Evelyn had to fulfill her contract, they had to go their separate ways after the nuptials. They spent only one weekend together in March, but it was memorable. Their first child, Rebecca Ann, was born nine months later on December 16, 1939.[22] The first two years of their marriage were physically and mentally exhausting. In early 1940, Oral served as chairman of the Conference Committee on Education and Publication, and a year later he was on the finance committee. His responsibilities took him out of eastern Oklahoma and into the eastern United States and Canada.[23]

During these same years, Oral's passion for education began to emerge. Oral grew up in a religious and social atmosphere in which scholarship was suspect because it was assumed to be a distraction from evangelism or, worse, a destroyer of faith. There was also a class element to this anti-intellectualism. Early Pentecostal saints reserved much of their vitriol for mainline clergy, whose education and cultural elitism alienated them from ordinary believers and led to spiritual bankruptcy. Aimee Semple McPherson attacked "present day Sauls" for striding "along on their high horses of earthly knowledge, theology, formality, and ceremonial and clerical dignity, breathing out threatenings against the despised Pentecostal people."[24] Another observer reserved special vitriol for Methodist bishops, equating them with the antichrist. To become a Methodist pastor, said this writer, "a man is obliged to pass through their human institutions by way of a course of unnecessary study, paying out a good sum for books and then devoting much time to packing his head with human wisdom."[25] This isn't to say that they outright condemned education, but it needed to be the right type. Its sole focus was on the mastery of the King James Bible and evangelism. At its founding convention in Hot Springs, Arkansas, in 1914, the Assemblies of God, which went on to become the largest Pentecostal denomination in the world, noted that one of its greatest concerns was to create a Bible training school. In 1914, there were approximately ten Pentecostal Bible schools, which were typically tied to a local church to meet the needs of a population that lacked a formal education. By 1930, there were twenty such Bible schools.[26] The Pentecostal Holiness Church took a more moderate position on education. In 1933, it founded Emmanuel College in Franklin Springs, Georgia.[27] Twelve years later, the editor of the *Pentecostal Holiness Advocate* and eventual ally and then naysayer of Roberts, G. H. Montgomery, argued that the denomination needed to start its own seminary.[28]

Though Oral's status as a high school dropout didn't seem to matter in Oklahoma, it made him something of an outsider in the East, where many of the Pentecostal Holiness pastors and leadership had attended Emmanuel. Always the astute observer, Roberts became a vocal supporter of the small college. While preaching in Virginia and Canada in late 1940, he attempted to raise seventy dollars to furnish a room in Emmanuel College's new dormitory. Early on he was an innovative fund-raiser. He initially tried to fill seventy dime folders out of his own pocket but soon realized that would take too long, so he took his appeal to the churches. The decision to use the folders and to ask for dimes was a stroke of genius. By asking people to fill the sleeves with their own money, he was encouraging them to reach a tangible goal. They could see the folders slowly filling up. A dime also wasn't very much money. His decision to help the college was undoubtedly political, but it was also a sign that even as a young evangelist he was interested in "making it possible for others to go and receive a Christian education in a college where each teacher is baptized with the Holy Ghost and fire."[29]

The successful fund-raiser planted in Roberts's mind the relationship between giving and receiving. When he first launched the fund-raiser for Emmanuel, the devil spoke in his ear, telling him that people would give money either to the college or to Oral. They wouldn't do both. At a meeting in Norfolk, Virginia, he received, he said, "as much as if I had not raised this amount for Emmanuel." Likewise, at a meeting in Ontario, the church paid him the "largest offering they had ever paid anyone before." He wished other evangelists would adopt this fund-raising tactic because "God will bless them for it, and they will not lose financially."[30]

The nomadic lifestyle of an evangelist was fine for a single man or even a husband and wife but not a growing family. The accommodations were oftentimes less than ideal. Oral, Evelyn, and Rebecca were either graciously welcomed or treated like a burden. During one revival in January 1940, the temperature was four below zero, but the family stayed in a dilapidated house that "let the wind through" and had heat only in the kitchen and living room. To stay warm in bed, the one-month-old Rebecca slept between her parents. It had no indoor plumbing, so they had to run through the bitter cold to the outhouse. The food, however, was excellent. Breakfast usually consisted of hot biscuits, country ham, and cream gravy or eggs.

The family finally felt what it was like to have their own home in November 1941 when Oral accepted his first pastorate. The church, in Fuquay Springs, North Carolina, was a good place for Roberts to start his new role as a pastor. The position offered numerous advantages, most notably higher pay, a sense of stability, and, for Rebecca, a bed of her own. Adjusting to her own bed proved to be difficult. Rebecca couldn't sleep unless she was touching Evelyn. Oral, annoyed that Evelyn was spoiling the child, told her to stop holding her hand. Unable to hold her mother's hand, Rebecca cried until Evelyn secretly stuck out her foot so she could clutch her big toe. Rebecca would then fall asleep.[31] Oral appears to have been well liked by the townspeople, who remembered him as handsome, charming, and excited to spread the gospel.[32]

Young and full of energy, Oral and Evelyn canvassed the community, going door to door to ask people about their religious affiliations. As a pastor, Oral made it a practice to visit the members of his church whether they invited him or not. One way he tried to break down the barrier between his parishioners and him, Evelyn recalled, was to raid their refrigerator, asking the "lady of the house" if she had any "beans, corn bread, and buttermilk." On Saturdays, he was a street preacher. In order to draw a crowd, he would put a loudspeaker on top of his car, drive to a busy street corner, park, and play records until an adequate crowd gathered. Evelyn sometimes sat in the car and managed the music and loudspeaker while also caring for Rebecca.[33] Oral also hosted a number of successful revivals. His goal was to make the church a "beehive of spiritual activity."[34]

In July 1942, Oral left the seemingly ideal situation in Fuquay Springs to accept another pastorate in Shawnee, Oklahoma. The reasons for his departure aren't totally clear. One of Oral's biographers claims he may have been motivated by the refusal of the church's founder, J. M. Pope, to align it with the Pentecostal Holiness Church, something Roberts, who was still a company man, wanted to do.[35] If so, then Pope had a change of heart almost immediately upon Roberts's arrival. A 1942 article in the denomination's newspaper said that though the church was interdenominational, Pope planned on transitioning it to membership in the denomination.[36] The more likely reason for the move was that Oral and Evelyn wanted to return to Oklahoma.

The years in Shawnee were fruitful. Under Roberts's leadership, the church grew from forty-two to ninety-five members, and its yearly revenues, from $1,700 to $8,700. He broadcasted a radio show, *The Gospel of the Cross*, over two radio stations, in Shawnee and Ada, respectively. He continued his education by enrolling at Oklahoma Baptist University, doing so secretly, fearful that his superiors would disapprove his enrollment at a Baptist institution. A second child, Ronald David Roberts, was born on October 22, 1943. Oral resumed his work with denominational causes, serving on the Education and Publication Committee of the East Oklahoma Conference and championing Emmanuel College.[37]

Above all, Oral was restless. "My blood craves action," he wrote in 1943. "I desire advancement! My spirit calls for progress! Thank God for the glory of the past! But let's do better tomorrow!"[38] Starting that same year, Roberts was able to channel his energy into helping to establish Southwestern College in Oklahoma City. The impetus to open a school in the West was the un-Christian atmosphere of public schools. There was a disturbing trend of young girls being forced to dress immodestly in their physical education classes. They had been compelled to wear shirts or slacks "while young men looked on," Oral chronicled. At the time, it was nearly impossible to change state laws to conform with Christian principles, so the only option was to start a "school where the environment contributes toward holiness rather than permit [students] to be consumed by the worldliness of the present state school system." Roberts apparently wasn't alone in his desire to see a Pentecostal college opened in Oklahoma. His Shawnee church raised $1,307 for the cause in one service. Though he was slowly growing frustrated with the denomination, Roberts remained loyal. Not only was he on the educational board, but he also assured members that the new school would be maintained by and serve the interests of the Pentecostal Holiness Church.[39]

At this same time, many leaders in the Pentecostal Holiness Church were becoming concerned about the ambitious young man in their ranks. Roberts, they believed, was becoming presumptuous, but they couldn't deny that he was successful and passionate. As long as he continued to conduct himself properly and preach correct doctrine, they could tolerate him. Evelyn remembered that the denomination's superiors thought her husband was a nuisance. Whenever he had an idea that he thought might benefit the denomination, he brought it up at the denomination's conferences. In one particularly hostile instance, Oral said he didn't think it was proper for church deacons to work on Sundays because "God gave us six days to work, and He didn't intend for us to use God's Sabbath for work." She feared that some of the ranking members wanted to cut the know-it-all's throat.[40]

In summer 1945, Oral once again uprooted his family to accept a pastorate in Toccoa, Georgia. He only made it to the end of the year before he returned to Shawnee. The choice to leave doesn't appear to have been wholly voluntary. Though he was well liked by his parishioners, the denominational conference in Georgia wouldn't accept him, according to Evelyn, because he was from out of state.[41] There was likely something to her claim, but it's also possible that this was simply an excuse to get rid of Roberts, who was beginning to bristle under the authority of the denomination.

The Roberts clan returned to Oklahoma, where Oral re-enrolled in classes at Oklahoma Baptist. Back in Shawnee, Evelyn went to work at a five-and-dime general store because Oral's salary wasn't enough to make ends meet. Like many Pentecostals, Oral had traditional views on how the family should function. Every morning she left for work, Evelyn left Oral's lunch in the refrigerator, but after a few days she realized that the lunches had gone untouched. When she confronted her husband, he told her that "*no* man wants to eat his lunch at home with his wife at work. I didn't want you to go to work. I don't want you to work now. You must believe with me and God will supply our needs." That was the last time she ever held a job outside of the home.[42]

Oral remembered the years between the beginning of his preaching career in 1935 and the year he started his independent healing ministry in 1947 as some of the most miserable of his life. Underneath his brashness and ambition was a deep sense of insecurity. It was the type of insecurity that young persons trying to find their way experience. Desperate to please his elders in the Pentecostal Holiness Church, he modeled his teachings and preaching style after theirs, which meant, for him, that he wasn't following God's command to heal the sick. God's nudging voice that he was supposed to heal the sick started to haunt Roberts when he moved to Enid, Oklahoma, in 1946.

This is not to say that there weren't periodic miracles in his life. The one he talked about most often happened when he was in Toccoa. One day he received a phone call that an elder at the church, Clyde Lawson, had been involved in an accident. When Oral arrived on the scene, Lawson was holding his foot in pain. The toes of his foot had been crushed by a heavy motor that he had been carrying. Without thinking, Roberts knelt down and prayed for the foot. The pain was soon gone and the foot was healed. Oral's friend Bill Lee asked him if he had that healing power all the time because, if he did, he "could bring a revival to the world." All Roberts could say was, "Bill, I wish I did."[43]

Roberts believed there were two reasons for the absence of miracles in his ministry. One was that it simply wasn't the right time. He always knew that he was going to pray for the sick, but he hadn't received the anointing of God. He also did whatever he could to drown out God's voice by throwing himself into his work. Indeed, he was something of a workaholic. In addition to pastoring his church in Enid, he was taking classes at Phillips University, a Disciples of Christ institution, and teaching one day a week at Southwestern College. He estimated that he was working eighteen hours a day, which left him too exhausted to even think about God's calling for his life.

The second reason was external. At the time he started preaching, divine healing wasn't emphasized in the Pentecostal Holiness Church, at least according to Roberts. Some leaders even doubted that God wanted to heal the sick. Average members of the denomination were also unconcerned with healing. They were more worried with their "common little problems" like crops, in-laws, and jobs.[44]

The absence of miracles wasn't the only irritant. There was also the matter of money. While in Enid, Roberts started to feel the financial pressure of raising a family. The first sign that there was going to be trouble was the parsonage. When they arrived in Enid, there was none. The house usually reserved for the pastor wasn't available, so Oral, Evelyn, and their two children moved in with another family with four children of their own. The living quarters were tight. The house had only five rooms, two of which were bedrooms and one a bathroom. After a few weeks, Evelyn had had enough. She threatened to take the children and move in with her mother until Oral found a house. He asked her for two more weeks.

With the two weeks coming to an end, Oral knew he had to act quickly. Since the church board was unresponsive, he took his appeal directly to the congregation. This is apparently when he first started to use the language that would eventually become seed faith. Without telling Evelyn, he decided to use his weekly salary as a "seed." He asked the congregation to follow his lead and to give sacrificially, telling them, "the greater the sacrifice, the greater the blessing."

Pledges began pouring in. The first was from a German farmer who, in broken English, promised to give $500 for a down payment on a house. A widow pledged $100. The climax came when a wealthy contractor asked what would happen if he offered $1,000. Though he later told Roberts that he meant it as a hypothetical question, Oral told him that he gladly accepted the money and that the contractor should view his pledge as "one of the greatest opportunities" of his life to learn "the joy of giving and receiving God's blessings of return." The contractor gave Roberts the check.

Evelyn wasn't nearly as excited as her husband. She was disappointed that he had pledged away his week's salary. The idea to give away the money may have seemed right in the moment, but she told him he would regret it when they had to buy groceries. She was the one, however, who had to eat her words. At four o'clock the next morning, a local farmer who had recently rejoined the church knocked on the Robertses' door and offered them four $100 bills. "As a farmer," he told a sleepy-eyed Oral, "I know I have to sow seed first before I can expect a harvest. The Lord said to give these to you as seed money." The family finally had enough money to find its own parsonage.[45]

Oral also had to fight to get a fair salary. In Enid, the church paid him $55 a week, which made him one of the three highest-paid Pentecostal Holiness ministers in Oklahoma. The average salary in the East Oklahoma Conference was $942.76 a year ($14,500 in 2021 dollars). At $55 a week, Oral's was over $2,000 annually ($30,800). The salary, however, was well below the national average, which was $3,000 in 1946, and wasn't enough to support the Roberts family. The family's furniture was falling apart, and they often had to return food to the shelves while standing in the grocery line. With his family living paycheck to paycheck, he approached the board for a raise. The board, however, wasn't about to start shelling out money to the already highly paid pastor. They asked Oral to submit a list of necessities that required a raise; his list included two haircuts a month.[46]

Evelyn remembered that Oral began having nightmares about suffering humanity. "He heard its screams of fear and misery, its sobs, its wails of frustrations," she recounted. It became obvious to her that something was wrong. She often woke up in the middle of the night to find her husband walking around their room or kneeling in prayer. He never admitted anything was wrong and simply told her he was praying. After finding him sobbing and praying in the corner of the bathroom, she finally convinced him to open up about what was bothering him.

This was apparently the first time she heard about God speaking to Oral on the day of his healing. It all made sense to her now. The years of frustration, the sleepless nights. They were all behaviors of a person who knew God's plan for his or her life but didn't know when or how to start.[47]

It was also at this time that Roberts made what he considered his "greatest discovery." The bulk of his morning devotions were dedicated to the Gospels and the book of Acts, but he also had made it a habit to open the Bible to a random spot and read a few verses. One morning as he was rushing out the door to go to class, he grabbed his Bible, opened it, and read 3 John. The second verse caught his eye: "Beloved, I wish above all things that thou mayest prosper and be in health, even as thy soul prospereth" (KJV). He was floored. Even though, by his own estimation, he had read the entire Bible over a hundred times, he had never paid much attention to this verse. The words for him were "beautiful yet they had something more than beauty. They had gripping power."

He then asked Evelyn to read the verse. She was as surprised as her husband. She even asked him, "Is this verse in the Bible?" And if it was, how was it possible that he had never read it before? He didn't have an answer for her. When he asked her what she thought the verse meant, she said, "Well, I guess it means what it says." That meaning became the pillar of Roberts's long career. The writer of 3 John expressed God's desire for his believers to prosper in mind, body, and spirit. He had found "that there was a true scriptural basis for believing that God wants man to be happy, normal, healthy, strong, and prosperous."[48]

That same morning, he asked Evelyn, "Do you believe God will give me a new Buick?" No, she said. What if he really believed God was going to give him a new Buick? Would she believe him then? Still no. Evelyn may have been surprised, but Oral wasn't when their neighbor, Mr. Gus, looked over the fence and asked Oral if he needed a new car. Mr. Gus, who owned a Buick dealership, told Roberts to visit him at work the next day and they would talk about replacing Oral's beat-up car. When Oral arrived, Mr. Gus told him that he wasn't a member of Oral's church—he wasn't even a Christian—but that he was impressed with the young preacher, who he believed was going to "do something unusual in the world." He wanted to help strengthen Roberts's faith by giving him a new car. Roberts told him that he would be sure to use the car for God's glory.[49]

When he told Evelyn about the car, he made sure to remind her of the fifty-five-dollar seed he had planted to get a parsonage. On their way home from the dealership, Evelyn told Oral to stop the car and get out of it and, with her, to put their hands on the car. The car was not just a new Buick, she said: "It represents what God will do when we obey and take Him at His Word. Let's just praise the Lord." The Buick showed how, in Roberts's mind, there was a relationship between the physical and the spiritual. "It was a *physical* machine," he wrote, "but it was a *spiritual* moment."[50]

A new car was great, but there still weren't any signs of God's miraculous healing power in Oral's life. Nearing thirty years old, Oral was reaching a point in his life at which he had to make a decision for the future. Sitting in a sociology class at Phillips University, he heard the same voice that spoke to him in 1935. The professor was talking about the origin of *Homo sapiens* when he said it was a scientific impossibility for Eve to have been made from Adam's rib. The professor's remark shook Oral to his core. As he and the rest of the class sat there in stunned silence, Roberts heard a voice: "Son, don't be like other men. Don't be like other preachers. Be like my Son, Jesus Christ, and bring healing to the people as he did." Oral stood up and walked out of the classroom.[51]

To make sense of the experience, he began a monthlong period of fasting and thorough study of the four Gospels and the book of Acts as though reading them for the first time. He came across John 14:18-21, in which Jesus told his disciples that even though his death was imminent, he was going to send them "another comforter which is the Holy Ghost." Oral's mind went back to the moment he experienced the baptism of the Holy Spirit twelve years earlier at the Sulphur camp meeting. The power to heal the sick had always been there, but he hadn't acted on it.

Now that he knew the power to heal the sick was accessible to him, he became even more critical of the "denominational church world." The book of Acts, he came to believe, made it clear that miracles of healing were not the exception but the rule in the early church. He was struck with the contrast between the early church and the modern one, whose neglect of God's healing power had made it weak. What was needed was a new revival. But this revival couldn't happen within the denominational church world. Oral was getting closer to recognizing that he could have the greatest impact outside of the Pentecostal Holiness Church. His superiors told him to settle down and be content.[52]

Oral was basically a shut-in during his monthlong fast. The time he would have spent eating he spent praying, and the time he would have spent counseling parishioners he spent locked in his office. The fast was taking a serious physical toll on his body, but he felt he was getting closer to God and to understanding his purpose in life. That is, until a mysterious evangelist appeared in Enid. This evangelist apparently "had a wonderful understanding of the Scriptures that teach Bible deliverance" and an impressive "boldness in commanding sickness to leave the bodies of people," but he was also greedy. Roberts was horrified to witness the way he shamelessly begged people for money for half an hour. As Roberts was leaving the revival, the devil told him he knew the real reason he wanted to start a healing ministry was to make money.[53]

Oral was reaching a breaking point. With the exception of the money-grubbing evangelist, everything seemed to be coming together. The only problem was that God hadn't given him any specific directions. He decided he had to have it out with God. He locked himself in his office, lay prostrate on the floor, and pleaded with God. Suddenly, he heard the words, "Get on your feet." Then, "Go get in your car." "Drive one block and turn right." As he turned right, the voice spoke again: "From this hour you will heal the sick and cast out devils by my power." When he got back to the parsonage, he burst into the door and told Evelyn that the Lord had spoken to him and that she should make him a meal.[54]

In April 1947, Oral began holding healing services at his church in Enid every Sunday at 2 p.m. The first several services appeared to have gone well. After eight weeks, there were three hundred reported healings and ever-growing crowds. Membership at the Enid church was at an all-time high, and they were "sending out a considerable supply of anointed handkerchiefs." There was some opposition from "doctors, lawyers, druggists, preachers, merchants, and others," but a surprising number of physicians and "professional men" sent notes of congratulations. Local pastors, however, didn't support the healing services. Oral attributed their opposition to the Pentecostal nature of the meetings. One pastor said he'd help at the services if people stopped speaking in tongues. Compromise, Roberts said, "is not in our nature."[55]

The results had been promising, but Oral wanted more. Wanting to know that the healing services at the church were the beginning of his healing ministry, Roberts reserved the Educational Building in downtown Enid for May 25, 1947. He asked God to provide three things at the service: an audience of one thousand, enough money to cover the rent for the auditorium and advertising costs, and enough healings to convince others and himself that he had been "called of God in this special ministry." He promised God that if all three requests were granted, he would resign his pastorate and start an independent healing ministry.

The meeting was electric. The song leader, Gilbert "Gib" Bond, one of Oral's childhood friends, remembered that after Oral delivered his sermon, "If You Need Healing, Do These Things," which would eventually be heard and read by millions, he called people forward to be healed. People charged to the front, according to Bond. Oral jumped off the stage to meet people as they came forward. "It was like the world exploded," Bond wrote in 1979. "God had confirmed His call on Oral's heart. He knew where he stood." When the numbers were tallied, there were 1,200 people in the crowd; the expenses, plus a little extra, were raised; and over 100 sick people were prayed for.

News of the successful revival spread. Roberts received requests from eight states and Canada to hold similar meetings. Others saw the meeting's success as an opportunity to strike it rich. Gib Bond, along with another friend, approached Roberts and told him that they wanted in on the racket. They were convinced that Oral was only interested, like so many other evangelists, in money. The offer horrified Roberts because it was God's anointing, not trickery, that was behind his desire to pray for the sick.[56]

Things began to move quickly in June 1947. Oral resigned his pastorate, and he and Evelyn decided to move to Tulsa. And he jetted off to hold revival services in the eastern United States. Evelyn's biggest concern wasn't the financial risks, which were admittedly serious, but what Oral's new life would mean for his family. Though he was frustrated with his life as a pastor for the Pentecostal Holiness Church, at least it kept him home most of the time. His new career as an independent evangelist meant he'd be traveling a great deal. She knew instinctively that it would be a life that would oftentimes be lonely. As she was seeing him off on the plane trip—the first he had ever taken—that would take him to the East Coast, she thought, "I'll probably be doing this the rest of my life. While we are both young, we should be together, but we have to be apart."[57]

Oral quickly learned that he could depend on Evelyn as a source of strength and stability. In November 1947, Oral held a crusade in Chanute, Kansas. The crowds were enthusiastic, and people were being converted and healed, Roberts remembered, but there was one major problem. The evening offerings were not even enough to pay rent on the auditorium. This was not the first time Oral and Evelyn had faced financial stress, but this was the first time he became noticeably upset over the situation. When Evelyn tried to encourage him, Oral replied that if God wanted him to continue in the ministry, he would need to provide the funds. As he stood brooding, Evelyn took the stage and scolded the audience for not supporting her husband. Cowering backstage, Oral felt emasculated. The devil said to him, "Well, you have sunk pretty low. When you have to let your wife take the offering, it's time you gave up." Despite Oral's doubts that Evelyn would succeed, the crowd responded by donating the $300 needed for the rent. One woman offered to cook "the best fried chicken they have ever eaten." Evelyn responded that there was nothing Oral liked more than fried chicken. That night, Evelyn did more than just raise money. She also proved that, Oral said, "God had given me a helpmeet."[58]

Things would hopefully be better in Tulsa. The city was growing into one of the most prosperous cities in the Midwest. Its economy relied on two major industries: oil and aviation. The combination of these two industries made it a prime candidate for war and postwar production. American Airlines, one of the nation's biggest airline companies, expanded service to Tulsa in 1936. Five years later, the government awarded a contract to Douglas Aircraft for war production. In 1945, American Airlines established a permanent facility in the city and took possession of Douglas's plant, reopening it in 1946. According to census data, Tulsa's population in 1940 was 142,157. The next two decades witnessed more growth. The 1950 census reported 182,740 citizens, and the 1960 census reported 258,271 citizens. According to one of Oral's biographers, it was a city where "men were judged by their accomplishments and not by their pedigree." Oral would soon become one of Tulsa's most valued citizens.[59]

3

Venture into Faith

ORAL'S NEW MINISTRY ENDED ALMOST AS QUICKLY AS IT HAD BEGUN. For several weeks, starting in May 1947, he had been attracting large crowds to healing services in Tulsa. Pentecostals from all over the Midwest came to witness the young fiery preacher heal the sick. But not everyone was happy. These meetings were loud, often went past midnight, and caused traffic congestion. As the meetings continued into August, neighbors complained that the combination of the heat and noise was making their lives miserable. One woman said that an attendee parked his car in her yard for several hours while he attended the services. Neighbors appealed to the city council to shut down the raucous meetings, or at least enforce the city ban on public address systems that interfered "with the peace and quiet of others." After receiving no help from the city council and only a promise to turn down the loudspeaker, cab driver Bill Doyle took matters into his own hands. Tired of the noise, especially since it was disturbing his ill wife, he fired four bullets into the tent. One bullet missed Oral's head by inches. The charge against Doyle, illegally discharging a firearm, was dismissed.[1]

Roberts believed that this incident made him an overnight sensation. Within twenty-four hours, he was known in the press as the "man praying for the sick." Though there's no evidence that the shooting gained any attention outside the Tulsa newspapers, news spread quickly in the Pentecostal world. In the first six months alone, he answered approximately 25,000 letters, mailed 30,000 anointed handkerchiefs, distributed 15,000 copies of his book *If You Need Healing—Do These Things* (1947) and 90,000 copies of *Healing Waters* magazine, mailed 100,000 gospel tracts, conducted ten major healing campaigns, personally prayed for 50,000 sick people, led 7,000 people to Christ, delivered 200 sermons, and preached to over 150,000 people. One of his sermons even averted a prison break when one of the conspirators, presumably not one of the prisoners, was saved at a service.[2]

He continued this breakneck pace for the next several years. In 1951, Oral preached to 1.5 million people at eleven major healing campaigns (an average of 10,000 per night), sold nearly 48,000 copies of *If You Need Healing* and 12,000 copies of *The Fourth Man*, printed 1.1 million copies of *Healing Waters*, received 208,000 letters, mailed out 108,000 prayer cloths and 458,000 gospel tracts, and broadcasted his radio show on 114 stations.[3] These numbers increased every year. In 1953, he printed 1.5 million copies of *Healing Waters*, sold over 55,000 copies of *If You Need Healing* and 19,000 of *The Fourth Man*, preached to 1.5 million people, received 280,000 letters, and mailed out 140,000 prayer cloths.[4] After one decade on the revival circuit, he had conducted 147 campaigns, preached to more than 8.5 million people, preached 1,706 sermons, prayed personally for the healing of 500,000 people, and led 3 million people to Christ.[5]

When Oral first arrived in Tulsa, he believed he had made a mistake. He was certain that God had called him to be a healing minister and that he was supposed to move to Tulsa, but, after a day of looking for a house, it looked like a dead end. With only $25 to his name, Roberts didn't have close to enough money for a down payment. Discouraged, and with nobody to turn to because every other person in his life was also poor, he cried out to God, "I feel like you want me to come to Tulsa, but every door has closed in my face." But as so often happened, God intervened. His friend, Oscar Moore, offered to sell him his house for $6,000. He gave Oral one year to make the $3,000 down payment. Roberts didn't tell him he had only $25.[6]

The disappointment didn't last long. Steven Pringle, a local Pentecostal Holiness pastor, asked Oral to guest-preach under his tent for six days in May 1947, a guest spot that stretched to nine weeks and almost led to Oral's murder, as related in the first paragraph of this chapter. After the August shooting, Oral started receiving letters from all over the country. Some asked him to visit their city, some offered to pay his airfare to come pray for them or loved ones, and others simply asked him to meet them at the Tulsa airport. The volume of correspondence was overwhelming. With only the two of them, Oral and Evelyn, it was impossible to keep up. Three young women who were at the Pringle meetings volunteered to transcribe Roberts's responses. The extra help must have been nice, but they were working from the Robertses' dining room, a space too small for the volume of mail and five adults. Oral moved the base of operation from the dining room to the garage and hired more stenographers, whom, thanks to an influx of cash, he was finally able to pay. It didn't take long before the garage became too small, so they bought a new house and turned the old one into their business office.

With the Tulsa operation quickly growing, Oral set his eyes on the nation. When he started his healing ministry, he still held his campaigns in municipal auditoriums or churches, but these spaces were inconvenient. For one, they were too small. With his rising popularity, he anticipated that he would need a space that could fit several thousand people. There was also the matter of the length of the campaigns. It was often difficult to rent auditoriums for any significant amount of time. If he was going to rent one, Oral wanted it for at least a week. Auditoriums or churches, since they were owned by other people, could be given to someone else without notice. Auditoriums, Oral lamented, often closed down religious meetings for "wrestling matches, shows, and most anything else that comes along."[7] Though a church might not shut down a crusade if something more attractive came along, it was still someone else's turf. For Roberts, who wanted to leave behind the world of sectarianism and wanted his crusades to be interdenominational, a church-hosted campaign might have given off the appearance of favoritism.

Oral's solution to these problems was a tent. He had been healed of TB and stuttering in a gospel tent, and the crowds he drew in Tulsa convinced him that a tent was the best move. He first began asking his supporters for money to purchase a "tent cathedral," which would seat 2,000 people, in early 1948. All he needed was 2,100 people to give $10 each to cover the cost of the tent, 2,000 folding chairs, an electric organ, a portable stage, and a semitruck. The $21,000 ($261,700 in 2021 dollars) price tag might have seemed steep, but it was worth it, he told supporters. Carnivals had the best equipment money could buy, and all they offered was "cheap, gaudy, and sinful amusement." The gospel of Jesus Christ, on the other hand, "is the only saving and healing power known to man."[8] He eventually purchased a 3,000-person tent. In the end, the tent, electric organ, grand piano, folding chairs, portable platform, sound equipment, two new trucks, and two accompanying 32-foot semitrailers cost $60,000 ($747,800).[9]

The tent was a wise move. The first major tent campaign, held in Durham, North Carolina, in June 1948, was consistently filled to capacity. At the concluding service on June 29, an estimated 7,000–9,000 people crammed together to watch Roberts preach and heal the sick. The crowd was packed so tight that the standing room extended to one hundred feet outside the tent.[10] He closed out the year with meetings in Granite City,

Illinois; Minneapolis; Ada, Oklahoma; and Dallas. While his greatest popularity was in the South, no part of the United States was left untouched by Roberts. He held crusades in New York, Los Angeles, Oakland, Seattle, St. Louis, Chicago, Detroit, Baltimore, Washington, DC, San Diego, Milwaukee, and Denver.

It didn't take long for Roberts to realize that the first tent wasn't big enough. In early 1949, he ordered a 4,500-person tent. Not even one year later, he upgraded again to a 7,500-capacity tent. After a violent storm in Amarillo, Texas, destroyed this tent in September 1950, he ordered one that would seat 10,000. In 1952, he ordered a 12,500-person tent. By the end of the decade, crowds as large as 15,000 filled his tent.[11]

It took a few years of trial and error, but, by the mid-1950s, Oral's campaigns followed a similar pattern. Preparations often started a year in advance with Collins Steele, Roberts's equipment manager, scouting out physical sites for the crusades. Six months in advance, Bob DeWeese, Roberts's associate evangelist, visited the area to start negotiations with the sponsoring churches. Early on, the pastors willing to sponsor a Roberts crusade were sparse, with only three or four agreeing to cooperate. But by the mid-1950s, that number was often in the hundreds. At a 1957 crusade at Los Angeles's Hollywood Bowl, four hundred pastors served as sponsors. The relationship between the Roberts ministry and local pastors was mutually beneficial. For many of the pastors, the opportunity to be seen on the stage with Oral Roberts couldn't be passed up, especially as tens of thousands of people filled the tent. There were also financial incentives. Always aware of the dangers of financial chicanery, Oral dedicated one night of each campaign to raising money for local churches, which would be split evenly among them. Though it would have been impossible for him to personally meet every minister, considering the hectic schedule associated with running weeks-long campaigns, Oral tried to become a personal presence. One way he did this was to host ministers' banquets. In Jacksonville in March 1949, he hosted 116 ministers and their wives to a fried chicken dinner in the banquet hall of a local hotel. For Oral, the pastors supplied an audience and cheap (free) labor.[12]

It wasn't just the pastors Oral tried to win over. Roberts had to make sure he had the approval of local officials, who had the authority to deny permits for tent revivals, which were sometimes held on public grounds. Whenever Oral was planning a crusade, he told his lieutenants to make sure that every bill was paid and every local regulation was followed. This reputation often endeared him to local political leaders, who, like the pastors, knew that being seen with the charismatic and photogenic evangelist was a smart publicity move. The mayor of Jacksonville made Oral an honorary citizen and gave him a key to the city. He also said Roberts's prayers delivered him from cigarettes.[13]

Sometimes, through no fault of his own, Oral left disaster in his wake. In April 1952, members of the Grace Baptist Church in Roanoke, Virginia, came to blows over Roberts's healing message. The church's pastor reportedly called Oral's services a "healing racket" and said any person who had "taken part or believed anything that Oral Roberts preaches" could "get out and stay out." Both sides predictably accused the other of starting the violence that broke out. The fighting was serious enough that eight policemen and a lieutenant were required to separate the warring factions.[14]

The crusades, which lasted seventeen days in 1950 and were reduced to ten in 1954, were generally all-day affairs. They began at 2 p.m. with Bob DeWeese leading a "faith-building" service. At these meetings, attendees heard a message on faith and received a healing card, which was required to be in the healing line at the night service. Healing cards, which were coded by colors and letters to determine the sequence in which they were called and were handed out on a first-come, first-served basis, could only be received at these afternoon meetings. With hundreds, and eventually thousands, seeking healing at Roberts's campaigns, the cards were essential for maintaining order, the ministry argued. Those who entered the healing line had to show their prayer card and sign a release that acknowledged that prayer didn't guarantee healing and that the ministry reserved the right to publish the results of the healing. At one meeting, Oral told the crowd that it would be "un-Christlike" to step into the line or to jump ahead. Roberts didn't do private prayers, but he always made the greatest effort to pray for every person who wanted it before each campaign was over.[15]

DeWeese arrived again at the tent at 7:15 p.m. to sell songbooks for twenty-five cents apiece. He then met with the sponsoring pastors under the platform for a brief prayer before leading the crowd in singing classic hymns like "Leaning on the Everlasting Arms" and "Blessed Assurance." The audience was offered another chance to buy Oral's books, and then DeWeese or a sponsoring pastor appealed for more money before the evening's offering. At five minutes until eight, Roberts finally jumped on the platform to be introduced by DeWeese. Early on, Roberts's sermons lasted for an hour, but they were reduced to thirty minutes by the end of the 1950s. When he finished the sermon, he asked penitent sinners to come forward to receive salvation.

Before the healing line formed, Roberts entered the invalid section of the tent, where the most serious cases, usually as many as thirty, were admitted. The invalid tent was grim. One United Press story from 1958 reported: "Ambulances pulled up to the doors to discharge children with grotesquely twisted arms and legs, hollow-eyed victims of palsy, of cancer, of rheumatic fever and polio. The saddest cases were brought into a ward-like special room safe from the eyes of others."[16] Oral later remembered that some of the people made his flesh crawl and that he was afraid they were contagious.[17]

With Roberts in the invalid tent, DeWeese took the evening's offering. The money collected at this time was set aside for campaign expenses, which averaged between $15,000 and $35,000 in the 1950s. The ministry suggested that everyone give fifty cents. In 1953, the average amount was fifteen cents.[18] Any money left over was given to the sponsoring churches, and any deficit was eaten by the Roberts organization. Even at the peak of his popularity as a traveling evangelist in the mid to late 1950s, Oral often lost $2,000–$3,000 funding a crusade.[19] During the last Saturday evening's collection, the audience gave to the "love offering," the money set aside for Roberts's personal use. This was usually the most generous offering of the campaigns. At the beginning of his independent career, Oral took two love offerings during the long campaigns, but he reduced this number to one in the early 1950s. The average love offering, the amount of which was usually kept secret, may have been about $5,000 in 1958. Oral also requested money for special projects, which ranged from purchasing tent equipment to sponsoring television broadcasts.[20]

The climax of every meeting was the prayer line. Those with prayer cards waited anxiously as DeWeese called those holding certain cards to form a line to Oral's left. Oral, who had taken a seat on the platform, having removed his coat and rolled up his shirt sleeves, finally called the people forward for prayer. Nearly all accounts, friendly or otherwise, portray the healing line as electric. Observers were especially impressed with Roberts's hold over the audience. Even when the healings seemed too good to be true, according to one Los Angeles reporter, "the faces of those who believe and who considered themselves healed were beautiful to watch."[21] By the end of a weeklong revival, Oral was exhausted. Evelyn said that he often lost five pounds during the week, but that it didn't take long to fatten him back up; she explained she would "feed him biscuits and sorghum molasses" as soon as she got him back to Tulsa.[22]

Oral believed that his message of divine healing tapped into something that Americans needed. He would never become a cultural warrior as would some of his contemporaries, but when he looked around him, he saw a culture that was sick. In fall 1948, he noted that, despite the "finest medical care in the history of mankind . . . we have more sickness, more new diseases, and more human torment than ever before."[23] About one-tenth of Americans were "psychotic," and an even higher number—he predicted it was in the millions—had no peace of mind "but [were] torn with 'inner conflicts' and deep-rooted sorrows." All of this brokenness added "up to the derangement of humanity by the power of Satan."[24]

He later wrote that humanity suffered from feelings of insecurity and nakedness. Insecurity was "caused by the rise and spread of Communism, that godless beast of human enslavement, that evil philosophy of the devil, that demonized forerunner of Christ." Nakedness was caused by the explosion of the hydrogen bomb. The awesome power that the bomb represented made the average American realize that "there is no place on earth to which he can flee [the bomb's] fire power. He is like a naked child lost in the night."[25]

Roberts wasn't alone in believing that the immediate postwar generation was in serious trouble. He consistently featured articles in his monthly magazine that pointed out the United States' moral, physical, and spiritual decay.[26] There were countless other prophetic voices, but none were as important as Billy Graham, who, even more than Roberts, got wrapped up in the nascent culture wars. Graham catapulted to national fame after his September 1949 revival, "Christ for Greater Los Angeles." For several weeks, Graham warned Angelenos of the desolation to come. Their city, in particular, was wicked and needed to turn toward God. He reported on the decay of the nuclear family, denial of God and God's moral law, crime waves, sexual immorality, and juvenile delinquency. On the global scale, the Soviet Union had successfully tested an atomic bomb, putting the world closer to total destruction than ever before. Graham's message was clear: the world was broken and needed to be fixed.[27]

That there was such decay wasn't necessarily a surprise. The world's dire conditions were also signs of Christ's imminent return. Many believed that the world would inevitably get more violent before Christ's second coming. Roberts told a South Carolina audience in 1953 that God was "widening the chasm between the good and the bad as he readies His people for the second coming of Christ."[28] This inevitability, however, wasn't an excuse for laxity. Rather, it made Christians' participation in the postwar world all the more important.

Christian history gave postwar evangelicals reason to be optimistic. The level of human misery, according to Roberts, was evidence of Satan's power, but the Bible promised that "the spirit of the Lord shall raise up a standard against him."[29] The recent past demonstrated that God sent revival when humans needed it most. In the United States, evangelicals looked to the First Great Awakening in the 1730s and 1740s, the Second Great Awakening in the early nineteenth century, and Dwight Moody's urban revivals at the end of the nineteenth century. These revivals gave mid-twentieth-century evangelicals hope that their generation was next.[30]

Roberts placed the growth of the "sign-gift ministries" at the center of this end-times drama. The previous generation of Pentecostal saints, led by people like Aimee Semple McPherson, Charles S. Price, and Raymond T. Richey, had started the work. Their ministries had awakened the world to God's healing power; however, it was ministries like Roberts's and other healing evangelists like William Branham, Jack Coe, and A. A. Allen that would complete it. Oral likened himself to John the Baptist. Like John, God chose Oral to prepare the way for Jesus's return. God tasked him with "coming through the wilderness of man's sin preaching for deliverance and that men shall know that Jesus is coming soon."[31] Roberts would succeed where the "established churches" had failed. "No longer," he said in 1948, "can we depend on our Church forms, our special music, our educated ministry, our fine church machinery to bring in the masses to God. We must have the 'power and demonstration of the Holy Spirit.'"[32] He had to look no further than his own success as evidence, remarking, in 1953, that he "didn't know the hunger for Bible deliverance there is in the world today. People want something real, something they can feel, and Bible deliverance is God's answer."[33]

The end may have been near, but Roberts still had his mind on earthly matters. In July 1948, he founded Healing Waters, Inc., as a nonprofit religious organization to run the day-to-day operations, which mostly included handling mail and distributing literature. By the end of the following year, Roberts needed to find a new space for Healing Waters, which by then had thirty employees and was still operating out of the cramped quarters of the former Roberts residence. He initially went looking for office space to rent, but, as he told it, every door was shut in his face. Then he remembered a vacant lot he had found in May 1947 during a preliminary visit to Tulsa. Thankfully, the lot was still available. When Roberts set foot on it, he knew that he "was standing on holy ground."

With the profits from his book *If You Need Healing*, Oral had enough money for a down payment on the lot, about $5,500, or half the asking price. The lot's owner told Oral that he would have to act quickly if he wanted it because an oil company was also interested in it. Roberts preferred to borrow money from banks, but since he knew no banker would give him a loan for an unimproved lot, he turned to a friend, who misunderstood Oral and gave him the full $11,000. When he told his generous friend that he had sent too much money, he told the evangelist to keep it and to pay him back when he could.

Borrowing money for the new building proved to be more difficult. Banks would not loan him money until he could prove that he could pay them back, which they suggested would take four to five years. Roberts once again turned to friends for help. This time it was Lee Braxton, a wealthy North Carolina businessman and civic leader. By the time Braxton met Oral in 1949, he was a forty-five-year-old retired millionaire.

Braxton first heard of Roberts after a friend recommended *If You Need Healing*. After reading it, he was intrigued and decided to fly to Miami in January 1949 to witness the evangelist firsthand. What he saw at the meeting convinced him that Roberts was "a man of vision." When a mutual friend introduced them, Roberts, after hearing that Braxton was chairman of a bank and a businessman, decided to tell him about his problems with the banks in Tulsa. Braxton initially told Roberts that he would have to think about it. Two months later, after attending a rally in Jacksonville, Florida, Braxton agreed to fly to Tulsa to investigate Oral's work. He likely saw a kindred spirit in Roberts. Like Oral, he ran away from home as a teenager in order to escape his family's poverty, rebelled, and experienced a dramatic conversion episode when he was seventeen.[34]

As soon as Braxton saw the cramped quarters of the Healing Waters office and read some letters, he agreed to help. Roberts hoped that Braxton's experience as a businessman and banker would win over the skeptical creditors, but Roberts received the same answer: no. One banker was particularly rude, putting up his feet on his desk and blowing cigar smoke in Roberts's and Braxton's faces. Braxton told Roberts that if no bank in Tulsa would help, his bank in Whiteville, North Carolina, would. Perhaps knowing how the Tulsa banks would respond to an outside bank interfering in local business, Braxton instructed Roberts to tell his banker that he was no longer interested in his money because it was coming from a North Carolina bank. His banker said Braxton could keep his money in North Carolina. "This bank will take care of you," he told Roberts.[35]

When the building was finished in fall 1949, it housed the Healing Waters business offices and a printing plant used to publish *Healing Waters*, religious tracts, *If You Need Healing,* and a songbook. Roberts, who had started calling himself a "middle-man for God," spent $250,000 ($2.9 million in 2021 dollars) for the lot, the building, and the printing press. He was understandably excited. "It never occurred to me," he told a local newspaper, "that I'd be able to go so far and do so much. That's when I look at this fine building and review the success we've had—I feel compelled to tell the whole world that faith in God can do anything."[36] It didn't take long for Healing Waters to outgrow this building. In 1954, it underwent a $400,000 ($4.6 million) upgrade.[37]

The Healing Waters office wasn't the only thing Lee Braxton felt needed to be improved. Braxton's real passion was expanding Oral's radio show, also called *Healing Waters.* When Braxton first told Oral he needed to expand his show, the evangelist said he didn't have enough money and was already too busy juggling all his other responsibilities to work on the radio show. At the time Braxton joined Roberts, *Healing Waters* was heard on only twenty-five stations and reached an audience of two million. Braxton wanted *Healing Waters* to be heard on one hundred stations by 1950.

Though Roberts didn't secure one hundred stations on time, Braxton brought an important energy and innovation to the Roberts organization. His plan to raise the $13,000 ($149,930) a month required to keep the show on the air was simple. He proposed to have an individual or church sponsor the program in its area for several months with the hope that local listeners would then make the program self-supporting. Braxton's scheme worked. A little over one year later, he reported that the program had increased to ninety stations and that so many people were interested in the program that his "desk was covered with mail."[38]

Braxton's other idea to raise money was to reach out to businessmen. In March 1951, he invited "fifty individuals, business and professional men" to meet in Tulsa at the Healing Waters headquarters to discuss Oral's radio ministry. Those interested had to pay for their own transportation to Tulsa, but Roberts promised to cover meals and lodging while they were there. Braxton had high hopes for the meeting, saying, "It may finally result in a million souls being saved before Jesus comes."[39] The meeting, held in June, was a success. All in attendance agreed that "radio is the best means of reaching the masses of people with this powerful message of Bible deliverance." They set a goal of carrying *Healing Waters* in all forty-eight states—it was only in thirteen at the time—and on 200 stations.[40] In October 1953, Healing Waters won a major victory when Roberts negotiated a contract with the ABC radio network that doubled the number of stations that carried the radio program from 200 to 400. Braxton estimated that after the addition of the ABC stations, approximately 20 million people could now listen to Roberts's weekly half-hour show.[41] For the remainder of the decade, this number fluctuated between 300 and 500 stations in the United States and Canada.[42] The radio also exposed Roberts to an overseas audience. In 1953, Radio Luxembourg, which reached an estimated 31 million people in Europe, started to transmit *Healing Waters*. A 1956 listing included stations in countries in Africa and Central and South America and in cities in New Zealand, India, and Australia.[43]

With radio secure, Oral started looking for other ways to spread the gospel, even if it meant violating Pentecostal prohibitions against movie viewing. *Venture into Faith*, filmed and released in 1952, has a simple plot. It follows the story of the Collins family, Jim and Ruth and their TB-stricken son, David. In the film, Ruth visits the Oral Roberts tent after a neighbor tells her about the miracles she witnessed there. Convinced that the sick could be healed through prayer, Ruth gets a bullheaded Jim, who saw little benefit in religion or faith healing, to go to a meeting with her. Watching Oral preach, Jim was impressed by Roberts's moderation and size, describing him as a fullback rather than a preacher. Roberts didn't preach fire and brimstone and left room for medical treatment in healing, but Jim left disappointed after a man sitting next to him, who had traveled over one hundred miles to see Roberts, wasn't going to be able to take his son to the front for healing because his healing card wasn't called. Jim, like many of Oral's critics, believed that the healing card technique was manipulative and crass. He is eventually won over after reading *Healing Waters* and having a discussion with the family's pastor, who testified that God still heals the sick. Predictably, David is then healed of TB at Roberts's hand. The film ends with Roberts visiting the Collins home to meet David, where he also leads Jim to salvation.[44]

Venture into Faith, produced on an $80,000 ($839,000) budget, was made chiefly for evangelistic reasons. The plan was to only show it in churches and auditoriums, never in commercial theaters. Lee Braxton hoped it would "reach thousands of people who might not otherwise" hear Oral's message of Bible deliverance.[45] The film was a success. Ten thousand people came to its premiere in Portland, Oregon, in September 1952.[46] Within one year, it was reported that thousands had been saved after seeing the film.[47] By 1954, a German version was being dubbed; the movie had been shown 2,131 times to 500,000 people in the United States and all over the world; and it had netted 22,258 conversions. The Roberts organization had also received requests to have the film translated into Greek and Spanish.[48]

Not every part of the film works. The acting is often wooden and the script is predictable, but it does work as an advertisement for the public face of the Oral Roberts ministry. The film does a number of important things. First, it portrays faith healing as rational. Though Jim Collins's job is never revealed, it's clear that his family lived in relative middle-class comfort. Rather than the poor, uneducated image of the faith-healing world in popular culture, the Collins family was portrayed as thoroughly respectable and, perhaps most importantly, reasonable. Jim's skepticism of faith healing was overcome only after firsthand observation and reading testimonies in *Healing Waters*. The only character who can be described as fanatical is the one *opposed* to faith healing. When this character, an annoying neighbor, finds out that Jim and Ruth are taking David to the Oral Roberts crusade, she scolds them about the phoniness of faith healing, calling Roberts a "so-called healer" and telling them that if they take him, they would be the laughingstock of the neighborhood.

Venture into Faith also wants the viewer to know that Roberts supported medicine. Healing ministries like Roberts's raised serious concerns that they were encouraging people to reject lifesaving medical treatment or that they allowed sick people to mix with healthy people. The healing line at the end of Roberts's services created concern that they were threats to the public good. The American Medical Association (AMA) issued a warning in 1956 that, though there were cases of psychosomatic healings, faith healers had a tendency to be irresponsible when they allowed diseased people to mingle freely with healthy people and that there was always the risk that people might abandon medical care.[49]

The AMA had reason to be concerned. Since the early twentieth century, Pentecostals had had an antagonistic relationship with medicine, believing that Christians who consulted a physician had weak faith. In a 1907/1908 issue of the Azusa Street Mission's paper, *Apostolic Faith,* the editor responded to the question, "Do you teach that it is wrong to take medicine?" with a direct answer: "Medicine is for unbelievers." Christians should rely solely on prayer for their healing.[50] Early Pentecostals were bombarded with stories not just of God's miraculous intervention in response to the faithful's prayers but with horror stories of doctors' visits gone wrong as well. Their antipathy for medicine shouldn't necessarily be read as "antiscience." Much of their frustration came from medicine's ineffectiveness and the ways physicians lined their pockets by selling fraudulent cures that often caused more harm than good.[51]

Oral was at the forefront of projecting the new image of Pentecostals as both practitioners of faith healing and believers in medicine. As medicine continued to improve throughout the twentieth century and as Pentecostals entered the middle class, their rejection of medicine became harder to justify. Midcentury leaders like Roberts, rather than seeing prayer and medicine as opposing forces, began to argue that they worked hand in hand. In September 1948, he wrote that he had the "highest respect for the highly skilled men and women who are devoting their lives for a healthier world" and that there was "no conflict between God's healing power wrought through faith and prayer and the doctor's efforts to bring a cure through earthly means." Indeed, many "fine doctors" had honored him at his meetings, and many doctors agreed that "they cannot heal, they only assist nature. Only God can heal."[52]

Roberts's early success didn't sit well with everyone. Surprisingly, it wasn't the media or cultural elites that criticized him, at least not yet. Most of the early press coverage treated Roberts like a curiosity, not a threat. The negative press would really grow with the premiere of Roberts's television show in 1954, which catapulted Roberts to national prominence. His first exposure in the national press was actually somewhat ambivalent. In May 1951, *Life* magazine blandly described Oral as the "loudest and flashiest revivalist to appear since Billy Graham."[53]

His fiercest opponents came from within his own denomination. The explosion of the healing revival at the end of the 1940s caught many denominational leaders by surprise. The shock wasn't necessarily divine healing but the popularity of strong-willed independent evangelists in their midst and their growing influence among pastors and laypeople. Denominational leaders were in a tough position. On the one hand, they were well within their right to try to contain the revival. Most of the early evangelists held ministerial credentials, with the Assemblies of God being the most common. On the other hand, if they came down too hard, they faced possible rebellion within their ranks. The evangelists' supporters in the pews were fiercely loyal. The Assemblies of God made moves to control the revivalists in the early 1950s. It emphasized the importance of local pastors and the availability of prayer for healing at local churches and, in 1951, asserted authority over the private businesses operated by the denomination's ministers.

Open hostilities started in spring 1953 when the Assemblies of God went after Jack Coe, its most popular pastor. In its letter of censure, the Texas district of the Assemblies of God accused Coe of insubordination, dishonesty, financial misdeeds, and antagonizing civil authorities. Coe believed that the attack on him was the result of the denomination's denial of faith healing mixed with a little jealousy. Any hope for compromise was dashed when Coe accused church leaders of "formalism and unbelief" and called for their ouster.[54]

That same year, the conflict between Oral and the leaders in the Pentecostal Holiness Church came to a head. For years, the denomination seemed unsure of how to handle Roberts. Denominational leaders were some of his most enthusiastic supporters early on; they especially liked that there was usually an increase in church membership after Oral left a town, but, as Bob DeWeese later put it, denominational hierarchies don't usually approve of people they can't control. For his part, Oral, who had learned about the intricacies of denominational politics as a young man, did his best to appease the leadership. He always encouraged people at crusades to stay in their local church or to find a local one if they didn't already have one. In 1951, in a further effort to appease the denomination's leaders, he gave $50,000 to Southwestern College in Oklahoma City.

Two years later, some of Oral's opponents in the denomination attempted to revoke his ministerial credentials, just as the Assemblies of God had done to Coe. The measure to bring Roberts before the church's executive committee was narrowly defeated by a 3-2 vote. A political brawl ensued at that year's General Conference, which Oral's supporters won. They successfully put him on the program to preach one evening, and Oscar Moore, Oral's old friend, was elected as one of the two bishops of the denomination.[55]

No matter his relationship with his denomination, Roberts was convinced more than ever that he had a message the world wanted to hear. In February 1953, Roberts met with nine of his closest advisors, including Lee Braxton, to discuss his plan to save one million souls by July 1, 1956. For the first six years of his healing ministry, Roberts was focused on North America. The million-soul campaign, the first of four, was part of Oral's global vision. In their talk, the ten men agreed that Roberts needed to grow the radio show and the subscription list for *Healing Waters*. But they also knew that these means of communication, however effective, weren't going to be enough. Oral told the men, "God is pressing me to take Bible Deliverance into the homes of the masses through television. The world has gone crazy over television. . . . If we can put this ministry on TV, I believe we can win souls faster than any other way. Also, I can pray for the sick on TV. When that is done you will see thousands healed and thousands saved who are not being reached any other way." Oral wanted to be on fifty TV stations by January 1954.[56] Television would help Roberts, the poor Oklahoma Pentecostal, enter the American religious and cultural mainstream.

4

A Million Front Seats

TELEVISION WAS AN EXCITING NEW MEDIUM when Oral debuted his first show in January 1954. Filmed on a Hollywood set in fall 1953, the program, *Your Faith Is Power*, comprised twenty-six thirty-minute episodes and cost $104,000 ($1 million in 2021 dollars) to produce. Roberts was optimistic about the show's potential. Just a few years earlier, few Americans owned a television. In 1948, only 1 percent owned a set. In 1953, 53 percent owned one. By the end of the decade, 90 percent of Americans owned a TV.[1] Television could do something that Roberts could only dream of. While his tent fit an impressive fifteen thousand people, TV could reach millions. As one of Roberts's wealthy supporters put it, the show had the potential to create "a million front seats" for people to see God's power.[2]

Each episode followed a similar format. It opened with a theme song, "Faith Is the Victory," which was followed by Evelyn reading one or two testimonies from people who had been healed. Oral delivered his sermon while sitting on a couch in a living room set. After the sermon, which usually lasted twenty-two minutes, he prayed for the unsaved and then the sick. The sick were commanded to "place their hands upon their chest over their heart" while Oral prayed for the "tormenting disease" to come out. The show premiered on sixteen stations.[3] *Your Faith Is Power* was canceled after six months. Roberts wasn't happy with the final product, believing there was a "woodenness about [the program] that was stifling." Evelyn agreed.[4]

Oral wasn't ready to give up on television, which he still believed had the greatest potential to reach the world for Christ. The pilot for the next television show was filmed in March 1954 in Akron, Ohio, the home base of Rex Humbard, who had begun broadcasting his church services in 1952. Oral initially asked NBC if they would be interested in picking up the show, but, after seeing a crusade in New York, they told him that it was impossible. The size of the crowds, the "complicated procedure of the services," and the limited mobility of the tent would have made filming a nightmare. But Oral wasn't the type of person to take no for an answer. Roberts and his team discovered Pathescope Productions, which had been experimenting with a new film that "is so high powered that fast action pictures can be taken with but very little auxiliary lighting," Oral beamed in 1971. Oral was happier with the results of this pilot. G. H. Montgomery remembered, "Every gesture, every expression of the face, and every word of the sermon were recorded on this new miracle film." The altar call, healing line, miracles, "the coming and going of the great crowds, the reaction of the congregations" were all beautifully caught on film.[5]

The pilot cost $42,000 to produce, money Oral didn't have. He came up with a simple plan to raise the money: the Blessing Pact. He first tested the idea during his tent crusade in Akron when he asked 420 people to each give $100 toward the project. Oral, of course, had asked for money before, but it was different this time. He remembered that he "dropped a bombshell into their thinking." He promised to use their money to win souls and earnestly pray that the Lord would return their gift in its entirety "from a totally unexpected source." If God didn't return their money, he would refund the "same amount immediately and no questions asked." But he told them they had to be doing it to save souls, not to make a profit. Despite the initial shock, 420 pledged to support the ministry. The Blessing Pact was supposed to be for a limited time. After its second year, he decided he didn't need it anymore. In less than a decade, though, over half the funds for winning souls came from the partners.[6]

This initial $42,000 was just to pay for the pilot. Oral needed to raise another $500,000 ($5.1 million) to buy the cameras, lighting, and sound and recording equipment. The cost may have seemed prohibitive, but purchasing it was cheaper than renting the equipment or paying a major studio to film, light, record, and edit the crusades. In June 1954, he asked 5,000 people to become partners with the ministry by giving $100 each toward the purchase of the TV equipment. He needed all the money by July 1, 1954. Money came quickly. By the end of June, Oral had raised $300,000 in cash—still about $200,000 short of the goal, but an impressive feat nonetheless.[7]

The Blessing Pact wasn't the only method Oral used to raise money. He also sold cheap trinkets like fourteen-carat yellow gold-filled "Jesus Heals" pins. The pins were available for one dollar a piece or six for five dollars and were reportedly "sweeping the nation."[8] In the mid-1950s, the ministry started to hold contests for supporters who could round up the most new subscribers. The winner would be rewarded with $2,500 in prizes, including a fifty-two-piece sterling silver service set.[9]

Fund-raising for television was a fairly new—and disreputable—phenomenon in the 1950s. With the passage of the Radio Act of 1927, networks donated time to religious organizations as a "public service." This policy, though admirable, tended to favor mainline Protestant churches with deep pockets and political capital. Airtime might have been free, but production wasn't. Even local stations skewed toward wealthy churches.

The other motivation was image. The four big radio networks (ABC, CBS, Mutual Broadcasting System [MBS], and NBC) wanted to present an image of respectability. And since mainline preachers, like Harry Emerson Fosdick, were assumed to be more polished and sophisticated than their conservative evangelical counterparts, like Aimee Semple McPherson or Paul Rader, the networks favored these urban pastors. The Federal Council of Churches of Christ (FCCC), a coalition of twenty-one liberal-leaning churches, controlled Protestant access to radio. Independent evangelists were upset with the FCCC's dominance. In the 1940s, they started to work through the National Association of Evangelicals and the National Religious Broadcasters to lobby for access to airtime.

With the advent of television, the National Council of Churches (NCC, formerly the FCCC) continued its dominance of the airwaves. Putting pressure on TV networks, the NCC successfully lobbied to continue its free access to television. Evangelists like Oral Roberts were left out in the cold. Shut off from the free airtime enjoyed by mainline churches, independent evangelists resorted to paying for airtime, but most stations had a policy against "commercial religion" and refused to sell time. Federal regulations regarding religious programming changed in 1960 when the Federal Communications Commission (FCC) decided that there was no "public interest basis" in providing free airtime to religious organizations, clearing the path for stations to fulfill their public service requirements and make money. In 1959, 47 percent of religious programming was free. In 1977, it was only 8 percent.[10]

In August 1954, about one hundred businessmen, among others, were the first to see the pilot episode of Oral's new show, also called *Your Faith Is Power*. What they saw would have looked familiar to any person who had attended a Roberts tent crusade. It started with Oral on the platform announcing, "My name is Oral Roberts. I am a minister of the gospel." A judge followed who affirmed that the recorded events actually happened, then Bob DeWeese, as he had done during the crusades, formally intro-duced Roberts, who gave a brief sermon. After the altar call came the main event: the healing line. The show ended with Roberts praying for those watching at home. He encouraged them to place their hands over their hearts or on their television sets while he prayed for them. The business-men were blown away with what they saw. One said it was more powerful than *Venture into Faith*. Another said it was more powerful than being at a revival because he "could see everything so much better."[11]

The show premiered on February 6, 1955, on a humble sixty-one sta-tions, which the ministry estimated had the potential to reach 19 million homes.[12] Oral remembered that the ministry's mail tripled overnight and that the subscription list for the monthly magazine increased to 1 mil-lion.[13] The show made national news when Anna Williams, a twenty-two-year-old from Wichita Falls, Texas, was healed while watching Roberts on television. Williams, who, over the previous four years, had suffered serious complications from a car accident, polio, and spondylitis, was watching Roberts's program on May 1, 1955, when she put her hand over her heart and prayed for healing. At that moment, she felt a tingling throughout her entire body and an urge to get out of her wheelchair and walk. Though her initial steps were weak, she was soon walking freely around the house and lifting her two-year-old-son in the air, much to the joy and amazement of her husband. Radio host Paul Harvey, creator and host of the popular radio show *The Rest of the Story*, interviewed Williams on his ABC show.[14]

The TV show expanded Roberts's national audience, but he still lacked a significant overseas outreach. Some of the other healing evangelists, most notably T. L. Osborn and Tommy Hicks, already had prominent interna-tional ministries. Hicks's sixty-two-day campaign in spring 1954 in Buenos Aires drew crowds as large as 100,000 to the city stadium.[15] Roberts had been talking vaguely about traveling overseas since 1949 but didn't make a serious effort until the end of 1954.

In December 1954, Roberts made a second visit to the Holy Land—he had previously visited in 1953—to film two television specials about the Easter and Christmas stories, respectively. From there, he flew to Johan-nesburg, South Africa, for a weeklong campaign at the beginning of Janu-ary. The crowds in South Africa were impressive. Nearly 25,000–30,000 people jammed into Wembley Stadium to watch Oral preach and heal the sick. According to the ministry's estimates, 20,400 people came forward for salvation and another 11,400 came for healing during the campaign.[16]

He left behind Lee Braxton to tour the world and help set the stage for his ministry "to reach all nations and other creature."[17]

Braxton's around-the-world trip took him to India, Hong Kong, Japan, the Philippines, and, finally, Australia. Though his time in Australia started with a slight hitch—Braxton was prohibited from showing the TV film of Roberts's Oakland campaign until government censors had viewed it—it ended on a high note: a group of Australian ministers invited Oral to visit Sydney and Melbourne the following year. Debriefing with Roberts in Tulsa, Braxton excitedly told him about the trip. When Oral asked, "Lee, do you really believe and feel that we can get the gospel around the world and to every creature?" Braxton responded, "Yes, Brother Roberts, we can do it. The door is open, and if we are given the tools, the partners and the prayers and backing of God's people, we can do it. I am confident we can."[18]

Even before Oral arrived in Sydney on January 14, 1956, there were signs that the campaign was going to be a disaster. A week before Oral's arrival, an opposition group, the Open Air Campaigners (OAC), distributed ten thousand copies of the anti-Pentecostal tract *The Modern Tongues and Healing Movement*, by American Presbyterian pastor Carroll Steagall Jr., in which Roberts is named frequently. The OAC included a label in the book: "It is vital that you read this expose of 'Pentecostalism' before the visit of Oral Roberts, the so-called 'faith-healer,' to Australia." Oral dodged reporters' questions about the tract, telling them that he didn't pay attention to his critics, and he refused to take a copy when reporters tried to hand one to him.[19] Despite this rocky start, Roberts had reason to be confident. En route to Australia, a hostile press in Manila greeted Roberts when he landed in the city, but, nonetheless, twenty thousand people converted to Christ.[20]

The Sydney campaign started on January 20. From the beginning, there was open hostility between Roberts's crew and the Sydney press. Press photographers refused to move away from the platform when ordered to do so. Some reporters snooped around the offering boxes to see how much money was in them. One reporter was allegedly caught trying to pour an alcoholic beverage into Oral's water cup; another admitted, "We are not writing what we want to write but what we are told to write," and a third said his orders were to "Get Roberts!"[21] One Sydney newspaper described Roberts as a "fraud and a liar masquerading as a man of God. At best he is a big blabbermouth."[22] Despite the media's hostility, the Roberts ministry believed that the Sydney campaign was a success. Nearly 75,000 people attended the services, and the ministry reported that 2,500 people were saved.[23]

The day before the Melbourne campaign was scheduled to begin on Sunday, February 5, a Melbourne newspaper published a scathing article about the Sydney campaign. The article savaged Roberts, calling him a "hot gospeler" and a "ringmaster," and accused him of inciting hysteria and bilking people out of money. The journalist told the Melbourne readers: "Anyway, as circus and theatre critics sum up these things: A good cast. Ideal setting. Plenty of laughs. And it's free—if you can dodge the Oral Roberts collectors."[24]

The first meeting instilled hope that, despite the negative press, the Melbourne campaign was also going to be successful. Ten thousand people filled the tent at Batman Park, and the meeting was described as "orderly."[25] Things started to fall apart the following evening. The local papers published articles, Roberts remembered, that were "anti-God, anti-Bible, and anti-American"; the crowd was smaller, with only about six thousand present; and hecklers yelled throughout the sermon and the prayer line.[26]

The hostility only intensified the following evenings. On Tuesday night, the hecklers increased in numbers and boldness. They kept quiet during the sermon this time but accosted the people who went forward for salvation. By Wednesday, Oral believed, there were signs that the disruptions were coordinated. "Well-known Communist agitators," he said, were seen in the audience directing the mob.[27] The mob seemed to have had its desired effect. The meeting that night was more subdued and quieter than usual. Roberts didn't talk about demons or hell, and the healing line moved "quietly and quickly." Even with this calmer atmosphere, the scene was so tense that Roberts had to be whisked away afterward in what one Melbourne paper called a "big, modern, American sedan." People shouted, "We aren't a mob of hill-billies." They told him, "Why don't you have a go at healing yourself?" After a fight broke out between a crowd member and one of Roberts's workers, someone intervened and said, "That bloke isn't worth fighting over."[28]

In response to questions about why the city allowed Roberts free use of a public park, a city council member interviewed Roberts on stage during the Thursday meeting. The city council had its own concerns. When it granted him the permit, it assumed that Oral was a missionary. It "never dreamt he would indulge in faith healing."[29] That evening, the mob frequently interrupted the service with cries of "Witchcraft!" "He couldn't cure a dog of distemper!" and "Why don't you look after your Negroes?" Halfway through the meeting, someone threw a stink bomb. After the healing line, the curious councilman asked questions about money, Oral's qualifications to be a pastor, and faith healing. At the end, he was satisfied that Roberts was operating legally.[30]

Chaos ensued anyway. The ministry estimated there were about two hundred hecklers and "probably one thousand irresponsible young people who were following the Communists to 'see the fun.'" At the end of the question-and-answer period, the mob stormed the stage to get Oral, but he had already been whisked off the grounds with a police escort. Oral wasn't the only Roberts to experience the mob's wrath. A crowd gathered around Evelyn's car and, believing Oral was in it, started to rock it back and forth. They stopped when they found out he wasn't in the vehicle.[31] An arsonist added to the chaos by setting fire to a semitruck trailer.

That evening, Roberts and his team, in consultation with his insurance company and the American consulate, decided to abandon the Melbourne campaign. The following day, February 10, the Oral Roberts Evangelistic Team released a statement to the press in which they thanked the Christians who welcomed them but decried how "sections of the public press" had denied them a "full and true report, and whose notices have had the effect of inciting opposition." They were closing the campaign to protect themselves but also as a "public protest" that they had not found "true religious freedom here."[32] A Melbourne newspaper had its own opinion about Roberts's departure. A headline read simply: "Good riddance!"[33] Eleven years later, Australian journalists were still having fun at Oral's expense. A Sydney-based paper noted that Roberts hadn't returned, "but his voice arrives in innocent little cans" over the radio.[34]

Oral and Evelyn left Australia on February 11. Even at the airport, Roberts couldn't escape the hostile Australian press. When photographers and reporters approached him, he said, "I don't want anything to do with you." In a final sign of indignity, a Sydney newspaper reported that Roberts gave a porter, who had to carry twenty heavy trunks and suitcases, a bad tip.[35] Oral and Evelyn arrived in San Francisco on February 13. The experience in Australia hampered Oral's overseas outreach. Apart from a second trip to South Africa in January 1957 and short campaigns in San Juan, Puerto Rico, and Canada in 1958, Roberts let his foreign crusading lapse. Oral's next major overseas campaign was in 1960 when he visited the Soviet Union.[36]

The Australian debacle followed the couple back to the States. Evelyn remembered, "We couldn't seem to leave that ugly experience behind us. The press in Australia had sensationalized our meetings, calling them a circus and Oral a clown." The stories, much to their embarrassment, were reprinted in the United States. She wrote in her diary, "What do you do when you've given your life to God's work, left your children, and done everything you know to do for the Lord, and then are misrepresented?" She believed that the "Lord had let [them] down."[37]

THE NATURE OF ROBERTS'S TELEVISION SHOW PLACED IT at the center of debates about the role of television in American culture. With 40 million television sets throughout the country, an audience of 133 million, a growing economic impact, and the fact that Americans spent an average of six hours a day watching it, few people could doubt TV's potential to shape American life. Its critics were afraid it would encourage mass conformity, political apathy, cultural decadence, and docility.

But not all were ready to entirely abandon television. Newton Minow, chairman of the FCC under President John F. Kennedy, voiced many people's opinions about TV in 1961. At a speech to the National Association of Broadcasters, he celebrated superb programming like *The Twilight Zone*, *CBS Reports*, *The Valiant Years*, and *The Fred Astaire Show* but also considered most of television to be a "vast wasteland." The majority of television shows and commercials were shrill, violent, and mindless, traits hardly conducive for developing character or a strong citizenry. Television, Minow and others agreed, can and should be harnessed for the public interest.[38] TV, in the wrong hands, could be a "one-eyed monster," according to Lee Braxton, but under the right hands (i.e., Christian hands), it could be the "one miraculous medium through which mankind can be brought to the knowledge of salvation and deliverance for soul, mind, and body."[39]

In February 1956, Jack Gould, cultural critic for the *New York Times*, published a scathing article about *Your Faith Is Power*. Gould's problem wasn't religious television, which he thought could be "beneficial and worthwhile," as long as it adhered to "purely religious objectives." His problem was faith healing. That the "enormously influential medium" was being used to show "undocumented 'miracles,' with all their aspersions on the competency of medicine," he wrote, was an affront to rationality and the public interest and called into question the "industry's code governing mature and responsible broadcasting."[40]

Oral generally avoided responding to critics because, like Jesus, he was "too busy doing good, too busy helping those who came to him for help," but the Australian campaign had deeply affected him. On February 21, he mailed a circular to his supporters asking them to write to the *New York Times*.[41] Roberts accused Gould of setting "himself up as a judge—not only of the standards of religious television but also of [his team's] religious faith." Roberts worried that articles like Gould's could jeopardize their "religious freedom in praying for the sick."[42]

By early March, the newspaper received 1,450 letters, most of which supported Roberts. The letters, a few of which the *Times* published, took issue with Gould's characterization of Oral's ministry and program, especially the charge that Oral claimed to be a "faith healer." Roberts never took credit for healing, but rather gave it to God. Letter writers also stated concern about the potential damage that could be done to religious freedom. One said that shows like Oral's should be encouraged because they instilled "a greater faith in God" instead of glamorizing violence and adultery.[43]

Similar arguments to Gould's were made in the mainline Protestant magazine *Christian Century*. One editorial described Roberts's show as a "travesty on Christian teaching." It also called on the "cooperative organization of the churches" to bring the dangers of Roberts's teachings to public attention.[44] Another admitted that Roberts's show had achieved one of its desired effects: it got "thoughtful Christians" to think about faith healing, something that "the church has not faced in this generation." There was little in Oral's tent that resembled Jesus's ministry, however, the *Century* claimed. Jesus never made healing the dominant part of his ministry; he never promised believers that they would not suffer; and he never resorted to the types of hysteria and drama seen under Oral's tent. Faith healing, as practiced by Roberts, amounted to heresy by "making use of God for human ends rather than making God an end and ourselves the mean."[45]

Fears that people would neglect medical care weren't necessarily unfounded. Starting in early September 1958, Florida newspapers followed the story of Terry Barker, an eleven-month-old boy who was suffering from a rare form of cancer. After multiple operations, Terry's mother took him to a Roberts crusade in Clearwater. She told reporters, "Oral Roberts is the only hope I have for Terry. If we can just see him—touch him—I feel he can save him." There was an outpouring of support for the Barker family. For Terry's first birthday in October, Clearwater locals sent gifts to the entire family, whose savings had been wiped out paying for Terry's medical treatment. Terry tragically died in May 1959.[46] That same month, a three-year-old died waiting to be healed at a Roberts crusade in Fayetteville, North Carolina.[47] In July 1959, a diabetic woman in Detroit, believing that she had been cured, threw away her insulin, only to die days later. Though doctors weren't convinced that insulin withdrawal killed the woman, the idea that she died because she threw away her medicine after attending a Roberts crusade raised questions about the efficacy of faith healing.[48]

While Oral reliably told people that prayer was a complement to medicine, not a replacement for it, he was less reliable on civil rights for Black people. Like many of his white contemporaries—Billy Graham, for instance—Roberts was slow to publicly support integration. In late 1956, when asked where he stood on the integration of the races, he responded, "I am a minister of the gospel, not a politician." When he prayed for the sick, it didn't "make one iota of difference amongst the people, whether they be Jew, Gentile, Protestant, Catholic, red, white, yellow, brown, or black." He called himself "a minister to all men."[49]

At his best, especially early in his career, Oral was paternalistic toward nonwhites. In his 1952 autobiography, he wrote, "The colored people have simple faith."[50] At his worst, he perpetuated white supremacy. When he returned from South Africa, he told Tulsa journalists that he "saw no serious trouble between the whites and blacks." The "natives," he further explained, were one thousand years behind and "cannot fit in this complex civilization. The South African government," he reported naively, "is doing a lot for them; building good brick houses for them, but they prefer their slums."[51]

In late November and early December 1956 in Raleigh, North Carolina, a reported seventy-five thousand people attended Oral's six-day crusade at the state's fairgrounds. Fairground officials told Oral he had broken all attendance records, and the state and sheriff's offices estimated attendance on the final day, Sunday December 2, 1956, at forty thousand. An article in *Abundant Life* reported law enforcement's numbers but editorialized that "an accurate estimate of the number of people who came to the meeting for the last service could not possibly be made" because people had to be turned away and hundreds of cars had to turn around without even entering the area. This winter revival was further evidence that North Carolina had "been the scene of some of Oral Roberts' greatest campaigns" and that he had "many friends and well-wishers in that state," the ministry said.[52]

One local paper, the Black-run *Carolinian*, had a different take on the revival. It described the first night as "so filled with curiosity that there was not time for segregation to raise its hoary head and as a result brothers in Christ, of all races, sat awe stricken to listen to what [Oral] had to say." Roberts's preaching that night was so powerful that Blacks and whites "gave vent to their feelings with a little hand clapping and foot patting." The next morning, Thursday, Roberts had breakfast with segregationist governor Luther Hodges. For many attendees, the meeting that night was noticeably different. Rather than a racially mixed Holy Roller meeting like the night before, a "pattern of segregation" was noticed. There were also rumors that the sheriff's department was attempting to "separate the lambs."

The newspaper had harsh words for Roberts. It was possible, it opined, that he didn't notice the bigotry occurring under his tent because it was hard to believe that the evangelist would support "segregation in any form." Ignorance, however, wasn't an excuse. If he really had the "milk of human kindness flowing in his heart, as all true Christians are supposed to have," he would have certainly noticed what was happening, and would have to "live with himself" as a consequence. The paper lamented that people had traveled from as far away as Mississippi to hear Roberts preach and, as was typical of the time, accused Roberts of financial chicanery, claiming that poor people were turned away. It saved its most scathing words for Oral's acquiescence to segregationist demands: "True Christianity is not strained, but rather plain. It knows no race or color. Oral Roberts, if a representative of the Risen Savior, cannot afford to practice anything but the true religion that works by faith and purifies the heart. He cannot dim his influence by practicing one thing in one section of the nation and another in another section. He must preach only Christ and Him crucified. Anything short of this makes him an imposter."[53]

Oral seems to have discussed this event in two of his autobiographies. The first night, without anyone's prompting, the meeting was integrated. It appeared to him that the people who came to his crusade felt the same way he did: "People are people, and all of us are created by God and are of one blood." Some of the ushers and campaign staff reported a different atmosphere. There had been integration, but it had mostly created tension. When Bob DeWeese asked what was wrong, one person shouted, "The niggers are trying to sit with the whites!" DeWeese, who was from the West Coast, had apparently never encountered this sort of blatant racism before, and while he stood there listening, a Black woman commented that they were "God's children just as much as any white folks." She added, "We've got a right to sit in the same place as the white man." As tensions continued to mount, another Black woman said they should wait until "Brother Roberts gets here. He won't treat us this way."

DeWeese tried to tell Oral about the smoldering conflict the following day but ended up irritating the evangelist instead. For years, Roberts had isolated himself in his hotel room for several hours leading up to a meeting so he could pray and prepare his sermon. DeWeese had actually recommended that Oral should have alone time, so he knew it was a major faux pas to interrupt his boss. But, at least for DeWeese, the potential problems that could be created by white racism were serious enough to seek Oral's advice. Roberts, annoyed that DeWeese interrupted him and that the crusade was being threatened, initially invited his associate evangelist inside to discuss the issue but changed his mind, instead telling him to plan a meeting for after the service to solve the problem.

But when he arrived at the meeting that night, the gravity of the situation finally occurred to him. Outside the tent, he saw people carrying signs protesting discrimination and crowds milling around the edge of the tent. This sight still wasn't enough for Roberts to confront the issue head-on. He had already decided on the car ride to the venue that he wasn't going to say anything during the meeting because "one-way dialogues seldom help any situation." Oral sensed that something was wrong during his sermon, but it wasn't until he made the altar call that it became clear. As people came forward to accept Christ as their Savior, most of them obeyed the local laws and remained segregated. Some Blacks, however, stood with the whites at the altar. Roberts admitted that segregation had occurred in many of the crusades in the South and that he generally brushed it off as "That's just the way things are." After the meeting, DeWeese told Oral that he could either obey local laws and keep the revival going or integrate and have the revival closed by the authorities. Roberts left the meeting unsure of what he was going to do.

The next night, when Oral took the microphone, he lamented the events of the previous evening. Rather than rejoicing that souls had been saved, he witnessed only hatred, as many of the crowd "were angry because blacks and whites were mixing here at the altar." He said that while seating would be segregated, the altar would be integrated. "Everyone," he said, "who steps forward comes to this altar as a sinner, not as a black or a white person." Oral claimed this was the last time he would compromise on integration. Every meeting from this point forward was going to be integrated, and if a city insisted on segregation, the ministry would turn down any requests to hold a revival there.[54]

A similar event happened in November 1958 in Nashville, Tennessee. One night, five Nashville ministers were reportedly threatened with forcible ejection if they didn't return to a balcony reserved for people of color. They refused to move, despite the threats and taunts from the audience, because "segregation and worship do not properly go together," the *Pitts-*

burgh Courier, a historic Black newspaper reported. One minister told an usher after being threatened to be thrown out, "It's all right; they crucified my Christ." Another said that a man sitting next to him turned his back when Oral told the eight-thousand-person audience to shake the hand of someone near, but gladly accepted the offering plate after he wrote a check. When Hart Armstrong, an official with the Roberts team, was told a recent Billy Graham crusade was integrated, he responded, "Brother Roberts is interested only in healing and salvation, not local customs." A minister further pressed, "But doesn't Mr. Roberts see any connection between salvation and the practice of segregation?" Armstrong was curt: "No."[55] A year later, the revivals were fully integrated.[56]

At about this time, Oral started to draw more attention to his Native ancestry. In early 1955, Roberts announced that he was launching a ministry project for American Indians as part of his Seven Outreaches for the World, which also included Jewish and children's ministries. The nation's indigenous people, he remarked, "are the most neglected people in this country." He went on, "I am of Indian descent myself, and God is stirring my heart to help win these first Americans to him."[57] In August of that year, during a crusade in Billings, Montana, Roberts organized an "all-Indian night." The night was a success. Not only was the tent crowded, but an Indian brave, on behalf of the twelve tribes in the area, presented Oral and Evelyn with a feather bonnet as a token of their appreciation. The bonnet, a Native spokesperson said while presenting it to Roberts, "is not worn by an Indian until he has proved himself on the battlefield." He added, "We Indians feel you have proved yourself on the battlefield for God." Oral was later a guest of honor at the Crow Indian Fair and a buffalo barbeque.[58] Roberts's reputation among Native Americans remained strong. He was named "Outstanding American Indian of 1963" at the American Indian Exposition in Anadarko, Oklahoma.[59]

Oral was also busy growing his relationships with businessmen. These relationships led to significant changes in Roberts's life and ministry in the 1950s. Lee Braxton introduced him to a world that would have been unimaginable to Oral when he was just a poor boy from southeastern Oklahoma. That world was one of wealthy, cosmopolitan, Christian corporate leaders. These men helped shape what Oral believed it meant to be a Christian and what he believed was possible for world evangelism. Thanks to Braxton, Oral met some of the most influential self-help writers of the day, including Dale Carnegie, Napoleon Hill, and Frank Bettger, whose book *How I Raised Myself from Failure to Success in Selling* Oral claimed to have read nearly fifty times. Napoleon Hill even spoke at the July 1955 World Outreach Conference in Tulsa and penned an article for Roberts's magazine in September of that year.[60]

In the mid-1950s, Oral began speaking in more positive-thinking idioms. Positive thinking, which pulled together various strands of transcendentalism, New Thought, mind cure, and Christian Science, worked hand in glove with post–World War II corporate culture.[61] Positive thinking's emphasis on the individual's power to shape one's own destiny and its defense of wealth made it a useful companion to the interests of business. Norman Vincent Peale, minister of the Collegiate Marble Church in Manhattan, New York, and author of the massively popular *The Power of Positive Thinking* (1952), was a staunchly conservative Republican. He worked with anti–New Deal organizations like the Committee for Constitutional Government and the Christian Freedom Foundation. Peale may have been politically conservative, but he was theologically liberal, belonging to religious foundations like the Protestant Council of New York and the National Council of Churches.[62] He also had a piece published in one of Oral's publications.[63]

Positive thinking allowed Roberts to expand the scope of his message. Belief could now be expected to produce not just healing from illness, but health, wealth, and happiness. Starting in July 1956, Oral called this message "abundant life." Controversial was Oral's growing attention to material prosperity. As a popular, globe-trotting minister, Roberts knew he had the potential to be wealthy, but he was also aware of what the slightest hint of financial abuse would do to his reputation and ministry. In October 1951, he promised the readers of *Healing Waters* that he "would touch neither the gold nor the glory."[64] This doesn't mean, however, that he shied away from enjoying the fruits of his labor. By 1956, not even a decade after he arrived in Tulsa with only $25, Healing Waters had a book value of $1.25 million ($12.8 million in 2021 dollars) and took in $3 million ($30.7 million) in cash in 1955. As chairman of Healing Waters, he made an annual salary of $25,000 ($256,000), an amount that didn't include the love offerings, which were about $40,000 in 1955, or the royalties from his books, about $80,000. He also had access to an Oldsmobile; a Cadillac; a twelve-passenger Aero Commander plane, which Oral said was "Jest like Mistah Eisenhower's"; and a 280-acre ranch called Robin Hood Farm outside of Tulsa, which was valued at $60,000 and where he raised sixty pure-bred Aberdeen Angus cattle. He also enjoyed playing golf, though at the time he was excluded from Tulsa's swankiest country clubs, a situation that would soon change. While in Atlanta, he liked to brag that he "played golf right out of Mistah Eisenhower's locker." How could Roberts not interpret his rapid success and wealth as a sign of God's favor? He had grown up dirt poor in the backwoods of Oklahoma, oftentimes barely clothed and fed, and was now wearing custom-made suits worth $90 each and eating a king's ransom of pinto beans, sorghum molasses, fried chicken, and rare steaks.[65]

Two years after meeting Braxton, Roberts met Demos Shakarian, a leading Pentecostal businessman and owner of the world's largest dairy farm. Their initial meeting was over Shakarian's interest in having Oral host a crusade in Los Angeles in late September 1951.[66] At the end of the sixteen-day campaign, which was attended by an estimated 200,000 people, Shakarian had nothing but positive things to say about the Oklahoma evangelist. He was especially impressed with Oral's "practical sense of business acumen" and financial integrity, which he wrote was the most ideal he had ever seen "for the operation of evangelistic meetings or meetings promoting the Gospel of our Lord Jesus Christ."[67]

Shakarian first floated the idea to start a ministry for lay businessmen in Pentecostal churches shortly after meeting Oral. One evening while sharing coffee and pie at an all-night diner, Shakarian shared his vision: "It's a group of men. Not exceptional men. Just average business people who know the Lord and Love Him, but haven't known how to show it." Roberts was intrigued but wanted to know more details about the group. Shakarian continued, "They tell other men, Oral. No theories. They tell what they've actually experienced of God to other men like themselves—men who might not believe what a preacher said—even someone like you—but who will listen to a plumber or a dentist or a salesman because they're plumbers and dentists and salesmen themselves." What was the name of this group? Roberts wondered. "The Full Gospel Business Men's Fellowship International," Shakarian replied, or FGBMFI.[68] Shakarian was the group's first president. Lee Braxton was named vice president. Oral was left off the board because these roles were reserved for businessmen.

The FGBMFI also gave credibility to Roberts's increasing emphasis on wealth. People were naturally drawn to the wealthy, according to Oral, because "rich men can often tell us things of great value."[69] The FGBMFI showed that there was no contradiction between being wealthy and being a Christian. Held in four- and five-star hotels, FGBMFI meetings had an air of dignity that was missing from open-air Pentecostal meetings.

Roberts increasingly relied on testimonials from wealthy supporters to demonstrate the effectiveness of the Blessing Pact. In 1955, Oral published a book that featured stories of successful Pentecostal businessmen, *God's Formula for Success and Prosperity*, but the most important place to read these stories was in his monthly magazines. These stories read like fairly straightforward rags-to-riches journeys with one important difference: they place giving at the center of success. There were tales of childhood poverty, addiction (usually alcohol, gambling, or tobacco), early success followed by failure, and, finally, prosperity. Universally, these men became successful only after discovering "Jesus' law of success."[70] Before long, these types of testimonies took up more space than healing or salvation testimonies, showing the growing significance of wealth to Roberts's message. There was a great deal of crossover between Roberts's magazine and the FGBMFI's magazine, *Voice*, which also highlighted the importance of giving and featured testimonials from many of the same people.

The prominence given to Shakarian and other Pentecostal businessmen revealed many Americans' celebration of wealth as an individual and national blessing. This acceptance of wealth, however, didn't come easily. There was always a danger in making consumption a cornerstone of American values because consumers were generally assumed to be selfish. After the deprivations of the Great Depression and the necessary sacrifices of wartime, postwar Americans were torn on consumption. On the one hand, they had endured two decades of economic and material shortage, years that taught them the fickleness of wealth and the value of sacrifice. On the other hand, the postwar economic boom and the fairly smooth transition from wartime production to consumer production fueled Americans' consumer desires. To encourage consumption, American business and political leaders worked together to convince Americans to think about purchasing not as a selfish desire but as a moral and civic duty. Consumption, they argued, was finally going to be the great equalizer. Americans could consume guilt-free, knowing that their purchases were helping to lift all boats.[71]

At about the same time that the nation's leaders were pushing consumption as a sign of American greatness and freedom, a cadre of Pentecostal evangelists, under the umbrella of what has come to be known as the "prosperity gospel," started promoting the spiritual benefits of prosperity and consumption.[72] These evangelists had their work cut out for them to convince Pentecostals, many of whom had grown up poor and had heard sermons about the dangers of wealth, that God guaranteed financial prosperity to believers. Oral made a number of arguments. The first was that everything they had heard about the relationship between poverty and piety was a lie. The Bible paints a very different picture. It "speaks with favor of the prosperity of God's people" while also sending "very stern warnings against all efforts to gain unrighteous wealth." How were God's people supposed to understand this apparent contradiction? Oral argued that the Bible's warnings about wealth focused on the *love* of money. That is, covetousness or money gained through extortion, fraud, dishonesty, and oppression of the poor and laborers.

One of the biggest lies Christians had been told was that Jesus was poor. Quoting 2 Corinthians 8:9, Oral argued that any poverty Jesus may have experienced on earth was relative to the riches he left behind in heaven. The stories about Jesus as a "borrower" were overblown, according to Roberts. Not even King Herod would have been able to find a room in Bethlehem the night Jesus was born. The other things Jesus borrowed—the boat in Galilee (Luke 5:3), the donkey in Jerusalem (Matt. 21:1-8), and the room for the last supper (Mark 14:15)—were things that "represented considerable value to their owners."

Oral also said that people needed to take into account the people that surrounded Jesus as evidence for his material wealth. For three and a half years, he traveled with twelve "rugged, healthy hearty men going over the country, some of them with families back home to support." Feeding this band of men couldn't have been cheap. Jesus also counted the wealthy as some of his closest friends and supporters and lavishly fed the multitudes in the miracle of the bread and fishes. These were hardly the activities of a pauper. And when Jesus said, "The foxes have holes, and the birds of the air have nests; but the Son of man hath not where to lay his head" (Matt. 8:20 KJV), he wasn't talking about his poverty but that he "had no church, no synagogue, no established religious system to offer as security to those who followed him."[73]

The emphasis on wealth didn't sit well with everyone. Writing in *Christian Century*, W. E. Mann worried that Roberts preached a "salvation largely divorced from any social ethic" and that the "danger of excessive commercialization is great." Moreover, Oral's belief that "God wants everyone to be prosperous undermines any tendency toward self-criticism with regard to his huge income."[74]

A series of articles in the Canadian newspaper *Flash* struck a similar tone, but in much harsher language. The articles called Oral various names: "Bible Beggar of the Airwaves," "holy howler," "oily hypocrite," "religion racketeer," "American gyp artist," and "shameless shyster." They suggested that Roberts's show appealed to people "with stomach strong enough to swallow his spiel," people who were stupid, or "aging spinsters and elderly wives" who were sexually attracted to Oral or were victims of mass hypnosis and hysteria. The paper took issue with Roberts's "fake cures" but saved most of its vitriol for his "slavering greed." Everything he did, from the healing line to altar calls, was only a mask "for the cunning mob manipulator who deftly slides in his pitch when he judges the time ripe." The paper called for authorities to intervene in the selling of airtime to Roberts. The disaster in Australia, which *Flash* reported with glee, was a sign that Oral's appeal was limited and that he could be stopped. If he wasn't stopped, "Roberts will go the limit, spouting pious malarkey and keeping a cold eye on the cash register as he goes."[75]

Oral made another significant change in early 1958 when he hired a New York public relations agency to schedule interviews with influential journalists. To this point, Roberts had shunned the press as if "it had dragon's teeth." In one interview with Associated Press religion writer George Cornell, Oral said, "I don't mind being opposed for what I am, but it bothers me to be opposed for what I'm not." Cornell was struck by Oral's magnetism. Calling him "oratorical lightning in the pulpit," Cornell went on to say, "in sitting room conversation he is a relaxed, unaffected sort of person with an engaging warmth and friendliness."[76]

And Oral started to make friends in high places. At the end of the 1950s, he counted several state governors, including Herman Talmadge of Georgia and Albert Gore of Tennessee, as acquaintances and supporters and Oklahoma senators Robert Kerr and Mike Montgomery and Governor Raymond Gary as close friends. Oral and Evelyn also found themselves becoming integrated in a circle of celebrity friends. Roy Rogers and Dale Evans introduced Oral to Henrietta Mears of Hollywood Presbyterian Church. In April 1958, General Mark Clark invited Oral to speak at the Citadel. In June, Oral and Evelyn were dinner guests of prominent television producers Mr. and Mrs. Oliver Presbrey, whose credits included *Meet the Press*.[77] In all his encounters with the nation's elite, Roberts discovered, "They are common, everyday people who feel the need of God's help and who appreciate the power of prayer."[78]

Minus a major scandal or his death, there was little that was going to stop Roberts's momentum at the end of the 1950s and into the 1960s. Starting in February 1957, Roberts wrote a weekly column for newspapers, usually small-town papers. By November, it was distributed to 500 newspapers in the United States, Mexico, and Canada. Two years later, it was carried in 674.[79]

Oral's maturing could also be seen in the scope of his ministry. Television was only one of his Seven Outreaches for the World plan. The other six were (1) tent crusades; (2) a world network of one thousand radio stations; (3) a special ministry for Jewish people; (4) a special ministry for Native Americans; (5) a special ministry for the world's children; and (6) a "missionary venture in reverse." Some of these outreaches were more successful than others. The "missionary in reverse" project didn't even get off the ground in the 1950s, but Oral's plan to educate young foreign nationals was never far from his mind. Others, like the mission to Native Americans, were a bit more successful.

While radio and television remained the greatest soul-winners, they were expensive and—perhaps one of the greatest obstacles—hard to translate. One of the major global transformations after World War II was an increase in the world's literacy rate. In 1820, only 12 percent of the people in the world could read and write; by 1950, 56 percent could read and write, and by 1970, the number was 60 percent. The world literacy rate has increased 4 percent every five years since the late 1940s.[80]

Oral wanted to take advantage of this improvement. In May 1956 he launched the Department of Literature Evangelism, which spearheaded the LIFE (*Literature of deliverance In all languages For Every creature*) crusade. Within a few months, the department sent out more than a million pieces of literature, including 462,395 copies of *Happiness and Healing for You*, a picture book about salvation and healing, and 204,000 copies of *Abundant Life* to missionaries throughout the world and to orphanages, federal prisons, and Native Americans in the United States.[81] After little more than a year, the department had distributed, free of charge, 22 million pieces of literature to 100 countries in 50 different languages.[82] Five years later, the ministry was distributing more than 50 million pieces of literature (about 1 million a week) in 187 languages.[83]

By 1956, it was once again clear that Roberts needed to find a new space to house his growing ministry. That year, he announced that he had bought 175 acres in Tulsa and that he was going to build a "City of Faith." The new headquarters would have movie and television studios. A year later, though, the plans for the City of Faith were abandoned. In May 1957, Vermont newspapers reported that Roberts, Evelyn, his brother Elmer, and Lee Braxton visited Rutland to buy two-inch white marble. The marble, which was quarried in France, was going to be used for a different headquarters in Tulsa, the Abundant Life Building.[84]

At the May groundbreaking, which was attended by about 750 people, Oklahoma governor Raymond Gary praised Roberts for his organizational skills, calling the growth of the decade-old ministry a "miracle." The governor commended Roberts for helping the United States spread the gospel. The United States had an obligation to meet the physical needs of the underprivileged, while Christians like Roberts "minister to the spiritual needs."[85]

When completed, the Abundant Life Building would measure 108,000 square feet, be seven stories high, and have enough room for three hundred employees. It would also house a 1,500-seat auditorium and have no windows. But getting there proved to be more difficult than Oral planned. The ministry had faced financial crises before, mostly when trying to raise money to keep the radio or TV show on the air on local stations, but none as severe as the one in the winter of 1957–1958. Oral wanted to fund the construction on a "pay-as-you-go basis," but by March 1958, in the midst of a nationwide recession and credit freeze, there was no money left. With only the skeleton complete, Oral, in a pattern that would become familiar throughout his life and ministry, went to his supporters with hat in hand asking for money. Every person, he told them, who gave ten dollars would have his or her name placed in the cornerstone of the building alongside his, his family's, and the ministry's staff.[86]

At the height of the crisis, Oral had a vision. Standing in front of the incomplete building, the devil whispered in his ear, "You are looking at 'Oral Roberts' folly.' As people pass by, *this* is all they will ever see." Then Jesus appeared to him and took Oral's hand in his. After Jesus disappeared, Oral witnessed the incomplete building change. He saw both the workers putting on the finishing touches and "our staff of faithful workers entering the building, going to their places to work for God." Next, he saw massive global evangelistic campaigns in China, Russia, Africa, Japan, Korea, Latin America, and Europe. He heard the people of the earth shouting for joy: "This is *abundant life*, life from above; and we are saved by Jesus of Nazareth." When he finally opened his eyes again, all he saw was the bare skeleton of the building, but he knew that things were about to change. Thanks to the generosity of his supporters and a $1.25 million loan from the First National Bank and Trust Company, the $3 million Abundant Life Building was finished in spring 1959.[87]

Oral's old restlessness started to bubble up in the late 1950s. He was proud of what he had accomplished in just one decade, but he knew that he needed to do more. For a number of years, he had been talking with family and close friends about starting a university. Lee Braxton remembered when Oral showed him a farm at Eighty-First Street and Lewis Avenue in south Tulsa. Roberts told Braxton that the grounds would make a perfect site for a university. Oral also took his family to the property several times to pray that "God would hold the property for building His university."[88] In December 1961, he announced plans to build a "university of evangelism" in Tulsa.[89] Four years later, he welcomed the first three hundred students to Oral Roberts University.

5

The Pearl of Great Price

ORAL'S SKYROCKETING POPULARITY MEANT he could provide for his family's basic needs in a way that his parents never could. While his parents may have been poor—and overbearing—they were at least a daily presence in his life. Oral was a distant husband and father. By 1958, he was home in Tulsa for about nine days a month, and when home he divided his time between his family and his office at the Abundant Life Building.[1] Evelyn admitted that it was often lonely being married to her husband. She especially noticed his absence when she was alone in bed. "Many times," she said, "I've been awakened by some sound and reached over to touch Oral—only to realize that he wasn't there." She had the further task of explaining to their four children—Richard was born in 1948, and Roberta in 1950—why their father was gone all the time. "He's serving the Lord. He'll be home soon," she'd tell them.[2]

Even in his absence, Evelyn still sometimes felt close to her husband. After being awakened by a noise one evening, she prayed that the Lord would let Oral, who was in Virginia, know that they were in trouble. About a week later, Evelyn told Oral about the attempted break-in, and all he could do was smile. He told her that a few nights earlier, he was suddenly awake at three in the morning and that a voice told him to get up; he eventually dropped to his knees to pray for his family's safety.[3]

Though Evelyn had to do twice the cooking and cleaning when Oral was home—he often left his personal things scattered around the house—things were more peaceful. Everyone slept better, and the odd noises in the night didn't bother anyone. Oral's playful side also came out when he was with his family. He liked to read Bible stories, ride horses, fish, and play ball. Evelyn said he was like a "bird out of a cage."[4]

Things, however, could be difficult. One time, Evelyn forgot to reset a clock radio after unplugging it while moving furniture, and then when it started playing in the background, Oral got angry. When she told him to turn it off, he told her that it was *her* clock, so he didn't know how to work it. She tried to fix his mood with coffee, but the coffee wasn't hot, which further ruined his morning. She told him that she'd pour it out and make a fresh pot, but Oral said that wouldn't resolve anything. The problem, Oral explained, was with the pot. It simply didn't keep the coffee hot. Evelyn replied that she didn't know what had happened to the pot. He then told her, "Well, you have all week to do something about it. . . . This is not the only kind of coffee pot made. Try a different kind." Another time, his oldest son, Ronald (Ronnie), got sick with diarrhea, and Oral didn't know what to do. He told Evelyn to never leave him alone with a sick baby again: "I can't manage that." His absence and aloofness didn't mean he was a bad husband, Evelyn often insisted. He was always faithful to her, never visited a female parishioner's house alone, and didn't smoke or drink.[5]

Oral's absence had a dramatic effect on all his children, but none so much as Ronnie, who was once described as having his "father's analytical mind and love for detail."[6] Evelyn believed that Ronnie, because he was so much like Oral, especially would have benefited from more contact with his father. He once told Oral, "I feel you weren't with me those years, and I *resent* it. I resent the fact that the people had you when I didn't."[7] By all accounts, Ronnie was brilliant. As a boy, he could repeat his father's sermons verbatim. In sixth grade, he was elected class president. He had an aptitude for language. In high school, he traveled to Germany for a semester, where in only three months he became fluent in German. At the end of his military service in 1967, when he was only twenty-four, he was fluent in five languages in addition to English and German: French, Spanish, Russian, Chinese, and Polish. He was an accomplished flutist. He was a great conversationalist. He was also a rebel.

His family believed his problems started in 1962, the year he started at Stanford University. He had wanted to attend the University of Kansas, but his parents pushed him to attend the more prestigious Stanford. Away from his parents for the first time, he dabbled in alcohol and tobacco, and, in addition to dealing with the questions and ridicule he received as Oral Roberts's son, Ronnie struggled internally. At the end of the first semester, he called his father in tears, because he was no longer secure in his beliefs. Oral immediately flew to be by his son's side. At Stanford, he met some of Ronnie's professors and classmates and was asked to speak on campus about his faith. According to Oral, the speech, which was actually at Ronnie's dormitory, was a success. Despite his father's attempts to help,

Ronnie's problems remained. A year later, Oral was back in California to check on his son. There, he was told to meet Ronnie's psychiatrist, under whose care he had been placed. Oral was shocked. He didn't think Ronnie needed to see a secular psychiatrist, because "Ronnie knows God." The psychiatrist reluctantly released Ronnie to Oral's care only after he promised to relieve her and the university of all responsibility for his son.

After two years at Stanford, Ronnie enlisted in the military. Evelyn and Oral's plans for their son definitely didn't involve the armed services, especially with the war in Vietnam ramping up. Oral hoped that Ronnie would one day earn his PhD and take over the ministry, specifically Oral Roberts University, but, Oral told some military officers at the time, "he was of a different bent in his nature."[8] The military's tendency to enforce stability and discipline made it seem like a good fit for Ronnie. There were also signs that Oral and Ronnie were healing their relationship. While he was stationed at Fort Ord in California, he came down with hepatitis. His parents were horrified to see their jaundiced son. After the doctor told them that Ronnie would need at least four months to heal, Evelyn asked Ronnie if he believed God could heal him. Ronnie said he did. His father then prayed for him, and, miraculously, four weeks later, Ronnie called home to tell his parents that he was completely healed.[9] At the time, his mother thought the military might have been the "best thing that ever happened to him."[10]

Things continued to look better at the end of his military service. In 1967, he married Carol Loy Croskery, a friend he had known since high school; finished his undergraduate studies in French at Virginia Commonwealth University; was awarded a Woodrow Wilson Fellowship, which promised to fund his education at the graduate school of his choice, for his expertise in French; and decided to pursue a PhD in linguistics at the University of Southern California.[11]

Oral Roberts University was founded as a school for young people like Ronnie: bright, curious, worldly, and Pentecostal. Oral lauded the first-generation Pentecostals' dedication to their churches and to the Holy Spirit but criticized their inattention to their children's education. Second- and third-generation Pentecostal youth believed in the faith of their parents "to some extent," according to Oral, but "felt that it was not relevant to the world they lived in or the challenges they faced in their minds." The biggest tragedy facing Pentecostals was the "possible loss of most of the second—and now much of the third—generation of their children from the Full Gospel experience."[12]

Oral had apparently known since the day he was healed of tuberculosis that he was going to establish a four-year university. Sitting in the backseat of his brother Elmer's car, he was told by God, "You are to build Me a university and build it on My authority and the Holy Spirit." Oral said that the "words sank deep" into his being, but he felt that the call to take God's healing power to his generation was more pressing than a university. Even when he was a full-time traveling evangelist, the university was never far from his mind. During his travels around the United States, he took time to visit some of the most prestigious universities in the nation, including Stanford, Harvard, Duke, Johns Hopkins, Vanderbilt, Wheaton, the University of Tennessee, and the University of California. He didn't just drive through campus. Whenever possible, he met with administrators, professors, and students, trying to gain as much knowledge as possible. He also wrote to universities for information and spent countless hours going over the materials.

The command to open ORU, though still somewhat vague, became louder in 1960. While conducting a crusade in Norfolk, Virginia, Oral was having dinner with Pat Robertson, future founder of the Christian Broadcasting Network and Regent University, who was chairman of the crusade, when God again spoke to him. The voice said, "Raise up your students to hear My voice, to go where My light is dim, where My voice is heard small and My healing power is not known. To go even to the uttermost bounds of the earth. Their work will exceed yours, and in this I am well pleased." He immediately wrote this command on a napkin.[13]

Roberts made his first move to buy the property at Eighty-First Street and Lewis Avenue in south Tulsa in the summer of 1961. He asked his lawyer, Saul Yager, to make an offer on the land. Yager told Roberts that he was wasting his time because the owner would never sell, but Oral insisted. Once Oral felt he had waited long enough, he told Yager to buy the property. Roberts purchased the 160-acre farm for $1,850 ($17,250 in 2021 dollars) per acre. Another 20 acres were quickly added.[14]

In an August 1961 telephone conversation with his staff, Oral laid out his plans for the property. He told them he wanted to build a series of "little cottages" to house visiting ministers. This initial plan, described as a "boot camp," resembled the "missionary in reverse" project Roberts first described as part of his Seven Outreaches for the World in 1955. Starting in fall 1962, Oral hoped to bring 40 students from overseas for two to three months of intense training. He hoped to have 100 students in 1963, and 1,000 within ten years. These plans soon changed. In December, he commissioned Cecil Stanfield, the architect who had designed the Abundant Life Building, to design three buildings for the Oral Roberts University of Evangelism. Oral wanted the buildings, which would include an administration and classroom building and two dormitories, to be "contemporary in design and built of native stone and large expanses of glass." Construction began in February 1962.[15]

The project was new and exciting for Roberts, but it was hardly innovative. Oral's description had all the telltale signs of a Pentecostal Bible college: it was tuition free, the only textbook was the Bible, and its focus was evangelism and missionary training. And though the focus would be on training ministers already in the United States, the school was going to invite a select few from overseas. The goal was not to "Americanize them or to spoil them so that they would not want to return to their own countries," Oral wrote in May 1962, but that they would "go back and have great revivals among their own people and thus help spark the coming great move of God in their nations." Oral hoped some of these foreign ministers would come from countries that had closed their borders to Christian missionaries. He would teach classes in between crusades.[16]

Roberts began to openly float the idea of a liberal arts university in July 1961. A year later, he fully committed himself to establishing ORU. Not everyone was pleased with Oral's plans. Some of his closest advisors and friends, including Bob DeWeese, Lee Braxton, and Manford Engel, among other leaders of the Oral Roberts Evangelistic Association (OREA), held a private meeting in which they discussed the university. They were already in agreement that the university was a bad idea, but they needed to prepare for the inevitable confrontation with Oral. One concern was the price tag. At the time, Roberts estimated that he needed $25 million ($233 million), which quickly rose to $50 million a year later and then eventually $100 million ($932 million). The other concern was that the university would distract from the healing ministry. Engel, who started as the Healing Waters office manager in 1949 and eventually became the executive vice president of the OREA in the 1960s, told Roberts that he and the other top twelve lieutenants were ready to walk if he went forward with the university.

Years of hostile press, opposition from religious leaders, and the debacle in Australia had forced Roberts to develop a fairly thick skin, but this rebellion from within hurt. Some of these men had known him for nearly twenty years and had stuck with him through thick and thin, so he probably expected them to jump behind his newest dream. In his final plea with the OREA's associates, Oral reminded them of the years they had been together and of the hundreds of thousands of souls saved and people healed. The fact of the matter, Roberts explained, was that he was obeying God by opening ORU. The venture may fail, but he had to do it. He ended by telling the twelve men that they could be easily replaced. Oral's plea worked.[17] The October 1962 issue of *Abundant Life* briefly mentioned that the University of Evangelism would open in 1963, and the academic phase would open in 1965.[18]

US HIGHER EDUCATION HAD GONE THROUGH significant changes by the 1960s. One change was a dramatic increase in the number of college students. Once the enclave for the wealthy, college became accessible to more Americans than ever after World War II. Thanks primarily to the 1944 Servicemen's Readjustment Act (GI Bill), by the end of the 1940s, about 15 percent of eighteen-to-twenty-four-year-olds were enrolled in college, besting the previous high of 9 percent in the late 1930s. The number only grew. At the end of the 1950s, 24 percent were enrolled, a number that increased in the 1960s when 35 percent of eighteen-to-twenty-four-year-olds were in college. About 74 percent of all students were enrolled in public institutions.[19]

Another change was cultural and religious. For much of American history, it was taken for granted that universities, even state schools, had a religious (i.e., Protestant) mission. In 1951, conservative icon William F. Buckley Jr. voiced the frustration of many conservatives when he published *God and Man at Yale*, an account of his undergraduate experience at the prominent Ivy League institution. In it, the Roman Catholic Buckley accused Yale faculty of indoctrinating students with ideas of collectivism and atheism. He argued that the university had abandoned its Christian heritage by allowing self-proclaimed atheists to undermine their students' beliefs. This irreligious atmosphere mattered because Christianity was one of the things that separated the United States from totalitarian countries. Yale's defenders fired back that any anti-Christian teaching could be chalked up to academic freedom and claimed that Buckley overstated the university's hostility toward religion. Students had ample opportunities to get involved with religious activities, whether they were Catholic, Jewish, evangelical, or mainline Protestant. Buckley rejected this response. He insisted that there needed to be limits on religious freedom and that if most Yale alumni were theologically and politically conservative, then it made sense that the faculty should reflect this outlook, especially since it was their dollars that kept the private university afloat.[20]

College life only grew worse in the 1960s. At a May 1966 campaign appearance at San Francisco's Cow Palace, gubernatorial candidate Ronald Reagan blasted college students at the University of California, Berkeley, for their role in the decline of national values. The university had become a "rallying point for communists and a center for sexual misconduct," the former actor bellowed. He then noted that a dance in the campus gymnasium sponsored by the Vietnam Day Committee was fueled by drugs— "The smell of marijuana was prevalent throughout all over the entire building." Three rock bands played simultaneously and borderline pornographic movies were the only sources of light for the three thousand attendees, which included some underage juveniles. The party stopped only when a custodian called an electrician at 2 a.m. to cut off power. This was just one of a number of shocking events. Many incidents "were so bad, so contrary to our standards of human behavior," that candidate Reagan refused to recite them for his stunned audience.[21]

Some Christians began to believe that their only hope was to open schools that were free from this moral rot. A major obstacle to many of these new institutions was financial. To stay afloat, universities like John Brown, Bob Jones, Harding, and Pepperdine adopted a philosophy called "Head, Heart, and Hand." The curriculum combined Bible study, liberal arts, and vocational training. Since these universities were private, they lacked access to government largesse, so to keep prices low for everyone, they required students to work in exchange for tuition. These universities usually had a politically conservative agenda. They specifically played upon the newly minted middle-class fears for their children's future. Now that they could afford to send their kids to college, opening a world significantly better than theirs, concerned Christians jumped at the opportunity, but they had also heard horror stories like Reagan's.[22]

With millions of eager supporters, Roberts had reason to be confident that he would raise the necessary funds, but a negative article in *Life* magazine threatened to derail his plans. The journalists were skeptical of Oral's ministry, referring to him as a "ringmaster." The pictures were even more offensive. There were photos of people speaking in tongues in various stages of hysteria. Equally problematic was a picture of Oral sitting in his office under a picture of Jesus. The caption noted that the chair cost $345 ($3,184 in 2021 dollars).[23] According to Wayne Robinson, an editor and writer at the OREA, over 400,000 regular contributors stopped giving, leading to a rare public statement directed at the press and a decline in the emphasis on speaking in tongues.[24]

This drop in income obviously came at an inopportune time. Oral still needed to raise tens of millions of dollars, design buildings, develop curriculum, recruit students, and find Holy Spirit–filled professors. One of the first people Roberts turned to for help was an old friend from the Oklahoma Pentecostal Holiness revival circuit. Raymond Othel (R. O.) Corvin was converted at one of Ellis Roberts's revival meetings in Center, Oklahoma, when he was seventeen years old. Oral was present at the meeting but didn't go forward to be saved; his healing and conversion were still a couple of years away. Within just a few weeks, Corvin gave his testimony at prayer meetings and received the baptism with the Holy Spirit. Corvin's mother and sister were also converted at one of Ellis's meetings, and the family soon became fixtures at his services, often traveling fifteen miles by horse and wagon to see the elder Roberts preach. Like Oral, Corvin grew up poor but ambitious. After a hard day of working in the cotton fields, Corvin's father, whom Oral described as a "pioneering farmer and a country philosopher," encouraged his son to pursue his education. He didn't want to see his son's efforts in school, only missing one day and walking through the heat and cold, go to waste. "It is hard to preach something you don't know," he told Raymond. From that point on, Corvin knew he had to earn a PhD to fulfill God's plan for his life. Roberts's and Corvin's paths crossed again in 1935 when they were seventeen and nineteen, respectively. At this meeting, the two made a pact before God. Oral said he was going to be an evangelist while Raymond said he was called to be an educator.[25]

By the time Oral reached out to his old friend about heading up Oral Roberts University, Corvin's reputation as an educator, man of God, and Pentecostal insider was impeccable. His academic credentials were less impressive. Though he had earned five degrees by 1962 and had been president of Southwestern Bible College since 1946, he had yet to earn a PhD, which he finally did in 1967, receiving a degree in education from the University of Oklahoma. In the meantime, he moved to Tulsa in June 1962 and was named the first chancellor of Oral Roberts University.[26]

For three days in late November 1962, Roberts and thirty of his most loyal supporters gathered in Tulsa to appoint a board of regents and install Oral as president. The first day, November 25, started with a buffet dinner and ended with some of the regents speaking in tongues, which was probably a first for a meeting intended to establish an academic university. The sound of the regents' glossolalia was the Holy Spirit's seal of approval for the venture.[27]

On the following day, the gathered businessmen got a taste of what it would be like to be a student at ORU. The thirty-member board toured the 160-acre site and inspected the administration building and two nearly complete dormitories. Roberts and Corvin laid out an ambitious plan for the university. By 1980, they wanted to have three thousand full-time students, who would win two million souls each year; they also wanted the university to comprise seven academic colleges, four graduate schools (theology, law, engineering, and education), a faculty of which 60 percent held doctorate degrees and 40 percent master's degrees, and full academic accreditation. Oral promised that ORU would have full academic freedom for faculty and students, but only if their views were consistent with Christian theism. Roberts and Corvin also detailed the price tag: $50 million. They needed $25 million for the physical expenditures and $25 million for the endowment. At the time, they had spent approximately $3 million.[28]

To get a fuller experience, the regents also sat in on classes. Roberts and Corvin spoke about the baptism of the Holy Spirit. Corvin, described as a "renowned Greek scholar," talked about the "background and meaning of many situations in the Bible." These talks, given by an evangelist and a scholar, represented what Oral envisioned for the university. He wanted to turn out not only "engineers, business administrators, lawyers, schoolteachers, musicians" but also "men and women of God—every one of them a soul winner."[29]

Oral Roberts University was formally established on November 27, 1962. Roberts was the unanimous choice to be president. And, once again, the meeting was sealed with speaking in tongues. One eyewitness concluded, "The spiritual foundation for the university has been laid. And it has been good to behold. Hallelujah!"[30] The university was chartered a year later.[31]

When it came to naming the university, it was clear from the beginning that it was going to bear Oral's name, though there was some grumbling among his aides that doing that was egotistical. Other names were considered, like Christian University and Pentecostal University, but because God had told Roberts that his name had "become synonymous with healing in the world. And this university is never to depart from healing," it was imperative to name it Oral Roberts University.[32] Oral was aware of the ridicule he would face naming the university after himself, but he was also aware that his supporters might not have his back if it didn't include his name.[33]

The Oral Roberts University of Evangelism opened in January 1963 with seminars intended to give more people an ORU-like experience. For one week, 350 ministers and their wives from eleven denominations and several foreign countries met in Tulsa. They stayed in campus dorms, attended sessions in the administration building, and listened to Oral deliver lessons on the Holy Spirit. Corvin gave a series of lectures titled "Christology of the Epistle to the Hebrews" and one entitled "Agape Love."[34]

These seminars continued throughout 1963. A second ministers' seminar was held in April, a youth seminar in June, an international seminar in November, and, finally, a laymen's seminar in December.[35] After one year, two thousand ministers, laypeople, and youth from across the United States and fifty-six foreign countries had attended seminars in Tulsa.[36] In 1970, Roberts, reflecting on seven years of university-sponsored seminars, said they constituted their largest outreach, with over twenty thousand people attending seminars.[37]

The seminars also revealed the ongoing tensions between Roberts and Pentecostals. A number of issues arose between the two groups. The most pressing obstacle was limited resources. The university posed a serious threat to the small Pentecostal Bible colleges that dotted the United States, several of which yearned for accreditation as junior colleges. Some of the fiercest opposition came from the Assemblies of God, whose own liberal arts university, Evangel College in Springfield, Missouri, opened in 1955, was struggling for accreditation. Despite Oral's promise at the April 1963 ministers' seminar that ORU wouldn't interfere with the already existent "excellent full gospel schools," the AG's leadership was skeptical. Some leaders reportedly told Lee Braxton that they had forbidden Oral to build a university, and AG general superintendent Thomas Zimmerman told Al Bush, another Oral lieutenant, that he would suspend the ministerial license of any AG preacher who associated with the university.[38]

In 1963, there was a subtle changing of the guard within the hierarchy of ORU. One of the people the *Tulsa Tribune* described as a "consultant" in November 1962 was John D. Messick.[39] By January 1963, Messick was named dean and Corvin's role was changed to dean of the Graduate School of Theology. When Messick met Roberts in the summer of 1962, he was at the end of a distinguished career. After completing a PhD in education at New York University in 1934, he taught at Asheville University and then returned to Elon College, where he had completed his undergraduate studies in 1922, to lead its education department and serve as dean of administration. His next post was as dean of Montclair State Teachers College in

New Jersey, where he served for three years before going to East Carolina College, a small teacher's institution, in 1947, where he served as president until his retirement in 1959. He continued to work as a research specialist for the House of Representatives Committee on Education and Labor and then served as dean of instruction at Lyndon State College in Vermont.

Messick's religious credentials were less clear. Described as a "Methodist educator" in the press, Messick, like many of his generation, had turned against his strict Pentecostal Holiness upbringing. Messick was never fully onboard Roberts's religious vision for the university, but he was intrigued by the idea of Spirit-led people in positions of leadership and believed he was following God's call by moving to Tulsa.[40]

Messick had his work cut out for him when he arrived in Tulsa in July 1963. Almost immediately, Frank Wallace, Oral's architect, and Bill Roberts, Oral's nephew and head of construction, approached Messick about getting the university off the ground—basically no work had been done yet. He told them that he needed an hour to collect his thoughts. After an hour, Messick was ready to go. Though he would often clash with Oral over the future of the university—he favored its academic development while Oral favored its spiritual development—Messick spent the next five years working closely with Roberts to create the university that the evangelist envisioned.

With the administration taking shape, Roberts also had to find suitable faculty. The task of finding Spirit-filled PhDs wasn't going to be easy. With limited options, Roberts, Messick, and Corvin recruited mostly within the Pentecostal world, primarily the Pentecostal Holiness Church. Much of the early faculty came from Emmanuel College and Southwestern Bible College. Oral also encouraged some of his most promising young lieutenants to pursue graduate degrees, offering $50,000 a year in grants to graduate students. One of the most promising was Carl Hamilton, who had taken time away from his work in the evangelistic association to pursue a PhD in English at the University of Arkansas. Of the twenty-six original faculty, twelve held some sort of doctorate.[41]

More than anything, though, Oral needed money. The first significant call for money came in May 1963. In *Abundant Life*, he encouraged readers to become Blessing Pact partners for $10 or more a month. In return, they would receive a copy of Oral's most recent book, *Expect a New Miracle Every Day*. He reminded them that God wanted them to prosper. Most donations likely remained small, but every now and then, Oral reached out to his supporters with deeper pockets. In a spring 1964 catalogue, he asked three hundred readers to each send $10,000 to complete construction on the Learning Resource Center (LRC). Based on the Old Testament story of Gideon, in which three hundred Israelites lit torches and defeated the Midianite army, the LRC would be surrounded by three hundred eternal flames. The modern-day Gideons marched on October 31, 1965.[42]

These fund-raising efforts were just for the physical buildings on campus. Roberts also needed to find $50 million for the endowment. For this, Oral looked for more long-term solutions. In December 1964, he told the Tulsa Chamber of Commerce that the most promising sources were wills, trusts, life income, life insurance policies, and "special gifts of money, stock, and properties."[43] A few years earlier, in an interview with Lee Braxton, Clinton Davidson, described as one of the "foremost authorities on Estate Planning," explained the importance of a Christian will. Persons who didn't leave a will left their money in the hands of a government administrator who wouldn't make any provision for the "Lord's work" when distributing the money.[44] At a January 1969 partners meeting in Los Angeles, Oral explained that the government also took its cut in the form of taxes, which sometimes amounted to half of what a person left behind. A Christian will meant the deceased could rest assured that his or her money was being used according to God's wishes. One person, who purchased an ORU annuity, said it was attractive because not only was her money going toward a good cause, but an ORU annuity was also a safer bet than the secular stock market.[45] By 1962, the OREA had its own department for handling wills, the aptly named Oral Roberts Christian Wills Committee.[46]

This money was going to be put to good use. One striking aspect about the university is how modern it was from the beginning. In December 1964, Oral wondered whether Tulsa, after the founding of ORU, could become a "modern Athens of the southwest."[47] The centerpiece of ORU's innovation was the LRC, a 192,000-square-foot six-story hexagonal structure that has continued to be the center of campus since construction started in March 1964. In early promotional literature, Messick described the building as one under whose roof the entire academic life of the university would unfold. The first and second floors would house art studios, science labs, auditoriums, classrooms, offices, lounges, a television and radio studio, and the speech and drama departments. Floors three through five would house the library, which Oral hoped would eventually have 500,000 volumes. One floor, the fourth, was going to contain a center for research into the Holy Spirit, which Oral bragged would eventually have the "largest number of books and periodicals on the Holy Spirit ever assembled." The sixth floor would contain offices for the president and his staff, conference and reception rooms, terraces, and lounges for students and faculty. The structure's projected cost was $3 million, but its price tag would reach close to $4.7 million by July 1965.[48]

The LRC was most daring in its use of electronic media. Its innovation was recognized by both the Ford Foundation and the federal government. In 1964, the Ford Foundation described the LRC as one of the "most creative facilities on the American campus today." The *Tulsa Tribune* celebrated it by saying that with the "explosion of knowledge," an electronic retrieval system that could make vast amounts of data available with the push of a button was becoming a necessity.[49] A year later, the US Office of Education, under the Higher Education Facilities Act of 1963, a law that provided $230 million a year for college facilities, gave Roberts $5 million—a $2.9 million loan, a $500,000 grant for the LRC, and a $1.4 million loan for a women's dorm. The only strings attached were that the money couldn't be used for athletic events to which admission was charged or for sectarian worship services. However, the federal money raised concerns about the separation of church and state. An anonymous editorial printed in several newspapers throughout the nation questioned the validity of federal dollars going to a religious institution.[50]

The most exciting piece of the LRC was the Dial Access Information Retrieval System (DAIRS). DAIRS wasn't the first time Roberts experimented with computers in his ministry. Since 1959, the OREA had been using computers to help efficiently answer the hundreds of thousands of letters that streamed through its offices.[51] DAIRS was a bit more ambitious. Housed on the first floor, DAIRS was a $500,000 push-button computer system that allowed students to watch or listen to lessons previously recorded on motion picture film and slides, and on video- and audiotape. The plan was to have 130 individual study carrels—100 equipped for both audio and video and 30 for audio only—from which students could access lessons. Each booth had a nine-inch television screen, a telephone dial, headphones, and a guide with the available materials.

The retrieval system had lots of potential. For one, it would allow students to watch film of missed classes, but it would also benefit students who wanted to see a lecture more than once. And since the lecture rooms were synced in, professors could also utilize the system. Messick described one possibility: "The professor could press a button and through closed-circuit tv show how an English company would do the play, then switch to a Broadway production, and possibly listen to a philharmonic orchestra doing accompanying music." There was also a performance analysis studio that would allow theater majors to rewatch their own performances. Paul McClendon, the first director of the LRC, said that DAIRS would give ORU students the opportunity to view material before it was available in "conventional textbooks." The hope was to eventually expand this system to dorm rooms.

If the retrieval system had one major weakness—besides complaints of too few carrels and that lectures did not automatically return to their beginning after use—it was its potential for abuse. With the opportunity to watch or listen to classroom lectures in the LRC, students had little motivation to actually go to class. DAIRS was meant to be a supplement to classroom learning, not a substitute for it, school leaders explained. Only abridged lectures were going to be made available. Professors could record their lectures live, but it was predicted that most would likely record portions of them in a studio or condense five lectures onto one tape.[52]

Over the next several years, ORU continued to invest in new educational technologies. In 1971, the LRC added a language cassette lab. The lab had thirty "cassette audio-comparators" that allowed students to record their own voice and simultaneously listen to a prerecorded master tape. That same year, the university's education students gained access to a Curriculum Media Center. The center, also housed in the LRC, gave education students access to materials they could use to design future course material.[53]

The classrooms were also going to be high tech. The Space Age technology wasn't just for show; there seemed to have been a genuine attempt to encourage creativity in the classroom. Every classroom had a podium equipped with a tape recorder and wall projectors that allowed the professor to write on the walls with felt pencils, eliminating the need for chalkboards.[54]

With the LRC attending to the mind, another building, the Health Resources Center (HRC), attended to another part of the whole person: the body. Three years before he broke ground for the HRC, Oral instituted weight-loss requirements for OREA employees. After losing some weight of his own, he decided that some of his employees could afford to slim down themselves. Starting in fall 1961, employees who needed to lose weight, about two hundred of the four hundred, were required to report monthly on their progress. By the beginning of the next year, however, it was obvious that many of the employees weren't taking the project seriously, so, in January 1962, an ultimatum was set: lose weight by March 1 or face a three-month leave of absence without pay. If they lost weight within those three months, they could go back to OREA, but only if there were open positions. Though three people failed to meet the March deadline, several employees had lost an astonishing amount of weight, including one woman who lost more than one hundred pounds. Though the ministry tried to put a positive spin on the weight-loss program by saying it was popular, at least one employee was irritated enough to write to the local paper. In her letter, she cited inadequate access to doctors, bad communication, and high costs coming out of the employees' pockets. Another writer, who didn't appear to have had any association with the Roberts ministry, had a bit less tact, comparing the weight-loss project to Hitler's plans for a master race and pondering if such weight requirements were why "our forefathers (short, tall, fat and thin) fought and died."[55]

Students at ORU would also be required to participate in a wellness program, which included physical education classes and intramural sports. Under the direction of Dr. James Spalding, the HRC was the main hub of the university's physical education program. At the center, students would learn about the mental, physical, and spiritual benefits of proper exercise and diet. The building would have two floors. The first thing visitors would notice was that they were entering an "atmosphere of health." In the foyer would be paintings that illustrated the "magnificence of God's creation," anatomical reproductions "showing man in motion—stressing the physical harmony and coordination of the parts of the body," and a $10,000 "glass man" whose body parts lit up and bore the inscription "Your body is the temple of the Holy Spirit" (1 Cor. 6:19). The first floor would also house a double basketball court, a 25-meter swimming pool, men's and women's showers and lockers, therapy rooms, and a gymnastics area. This would also be the first arena for the ORU basketball team. There would be rollaway bleachers with seating for 1,300 people. The second floor contained two large classrooms and rollaway bleachers for 700.[56]

The most visible building on campus was the 200-foot Prayer Tower at its center. The tower was, in part, the result of promises Oral made to the rebellious associates back in July 1961 that he wouldn't neglect healing after he was a university president. In a May 1966 fund-raising article, Lee Braxton pitched the Prayer Tower to Oral's supporters. He told them that no matter how modern and excellent ORU's study facilities were, they could never take the place of prayer. The tower, the tallest building on campus, would be a reminder of this truth.[57] The exterior went through significant changes between its earliest sketches in 1964 and its completion in 1967. In early promotional literature, the Prayer Tower looked like a crown, but that design was modified to its current shape as a combination of a cross and a crown of thorns with an eternal flame on top. A university publication described it as a "20th century cross."[58]

Inside, the Abundant Life Prayer Group would take up shop twenty-four hours a day, seven days a week, answering phone calls for prayer and healing. The Prayer Tower stuck out. Roberts told DeWeese, "It will symbolize that healing prayer on this campus permeates everything we are and do." Its proximity to the LRC was intended to show that faith healing could exist in an academic atmosphere.[59] The $1.5 million glass and steel structure was immediately popular with the public, becoming one of Oklahoma's most-visited tourist attractions.

Some of the first students, however, were skeptical of the utility of such an expensive structure that was partially pitched as a tourist site. For most people, the Prayer Tower would be nothing more than a "passing curiosity" that students would see little benefit from. At the end of the day, though, the students would delay judgment, because, it was asked, "who is able to foretell the influence of an unbroken chain of prayer going on for the students and the world until there has been an experience of it?"[60]

The design of the buildings had symbolic meaning that was obvious to Oral and his supporters. The three-sided buildings represented the Trinity, and "the school colors of blue and gold symbolize divinity, while the white color of some of the buildings stands for purity."[61] Wayne Robinson speculated that there were psychological motivations behind the design as well. The gleaming gold symbolized that Oral had made it. He was no longer the poor Oklahoma farm kid, but the president of a university.[62]

To further distinguish it from other evangelical and Bible colleges, Oral said he wanted ORU to embrace intellectual openness. Students would not be required to sign a statement of faith, but other aspects of their behavior would be tightly monitored. Upon registering at the university, all incoming students signed a contract pledging that they would adhere to the strict rules laid out in the code of honor. Students were expected to exemplify the Christian life as Roberts envisioned it by attending class, chapel services, and Sunday worship services at a local church; by training their mind and body to the fullest through exercise and intramural sports; by dressing modestly; and by abstaining from immoral activities: premarital sex, tobacco, alcohol, drugs, and excessive public displays of affection. At a time when Roberts and other conservatives believed that the United States was coming apart at the seams as a result of rampant drug use and sexual promiscuity, the "God is dead" movement, and youthful rebellion against authority, ORU's strict moral code was a beacon of hope for many conservative evangelicals.[63]

ORU's code of honor made the university something of an oddity. One of the most effective parts of the student movement of the 1960s was challenging *in loco parentis*, Latin for "in the place of a parent." This legal doctrine grants schools the responsibilities and powers of a parent. While usually understood in relation to minors, it has also been used to frame the relationship between colleges and what are now considered legal adults. Though *in loco parentis* can be traced all the way back to the Code of Hammurabi, its application in the United States, of course, is more recent. There were a number of reasons universities in the United States monitored their students' behavior. One was the age of students. Most college students early in the nation's history were teenage boys, aged thirteen to fifteen, meaning they were basically children. Other reasons included creating well-mannered gentlemen, religious instruction, and, quite simply, because it's what parents wanted. After all, they were entrusting their children to the care of potential strangers. Parents could rest assured that the rules enforced at home would also be applied at school. These rules weren't only popular, they also had the backing of American courts. In several cases, state supreme courts deferred to colleges and universities in determining proper student conduct.

The idea that universities had the authority to regulate students' lives came under fire in the 1960s when students started to challenge the constitutionality of *in loco parentis*. Students argued that many of the rules that regulated their lives, everything from restrictions to due process to restrictions to their speech to dress codes, violated their rights as citizens of the United States. Federal courts agreed with them. In 1961, for instance, the Fifth Circuit Court of Appeals defended a group of college students who had been expelled without notice from Alabama State College for participating in a civil rights demonstration, which violated their right to due process. Other cases soon followed that established students' rights, at least at public institutions.[64]

One of the benefits of a private university was that ORU would be able, according to Lee Braxton, "to establish and to perpetuate a religious concept, doctrine or purpose."[65] A sure way to get under Oral's skin was to question the legitimacy of the honor code. He often harangued students and faculty who showed signs of rebellion, telling them that its existence had salvific significance and that he'd rather close the school than compromise on it.[66] In 1971, he told the student newspaper that he didn't believe one "can follow Christ and have individual freedom." Oral usually spun the code in positive rather than negative terms. The honor code existed to protect the wholeness of the group, *not* to infringe on the rights of the individual.[67]

For the most part, except for the occasional kerfuffle over student dress, ORU's students heartily accepted the honor code. An article in the first issue of the student newspaper talked about the code of honor not as a "rigid system set up to restrict and control the students, but as a guide toward individual[s] working for a common goal."[68] A year later, students reportedly wanted to upgrade the honor code, but not in an attempt to change it. Rather, they wanted their fellow students to understand that it was based on "love." And the thing about love is that it isn't always easy. Sometimes the "love of a friend is love that says what it thinks is best, not what one wants to hear."[69] Some students' argument in support of the honor code reflected the logic of *in loco parentis*. When one student had allegedly complained about ORU enforcing its dress code off campus, the student newspaper reminded its readers that, as undergraduates, "we have placed ourselves under 'their' jurisdiction and that 'they' are responsible for us." If a student didn't like the rules, the solution was simple: leave.[70]

Local papers also praised the code, celebrating ORU as a "school for squares" that offered an exciting opportunity to combine academic and personal excellence. Church-related schools tend to be "academically narrow" or "timid of demonstrated truth," while elite universities, however academically excellent, "seem perfectly happy to be pouring information into ethical imbeciles."[71] The *Tulsa Tribune*, long one of Oral's most vocal cheerleaders, contrasted ORU's possibilities with the contemporary state of universities like the University of California, whose students were carrying placards with obscene words "in behalf of 'freedom.'" ORU had the potential to help a "disgusted nation" rediscover the "necessity of some moral leadership at the university level."[72] After returning from his commencement address to the graduating class of 1969, Senator Jennings Randolph of West Virginia was so impressed with ORU's students that he inserted a description of a campus prayer into the Congressional Record.[73] Secretary of Housing and Urban Development and father of a future Republican presidential nominee, George Romney was also struck by ORU's students when he visited Tulsa in June 1969. Romney contrasted the upbeat ORU students with militants on other campuses whose primary goal was destruction.[74]

All of these things—the curriculum, the construction, the honor code, and the faculty—fell under the umbrella of "wholeness." Ever since Oral discovered 3 John 2 in 1945, the idea that God's promise of salvation was threefold—mind, body, and spirit—had been the cornerstone of his message, but with the founding of ORU in 1965, he was trying something different. At ORU, the idea of wholeness would be institutionalized. Whereas Oral had emphasized the whole person in articles, books, and crusades, ORU was physical. Its buildings, faculty, and students were living, breathing models of wholeness. At ORU, Oral told the university's first incoming class in September 1965, wholeness was a "way of life." He boldly predicted that ORU's emphasis on the whole person would make its students the "most wanted college graduates."[75]

6

Tulsa's Greatest Natural Resource

ORU'S IMPACT WAS IMMEDIATE. In 1964, the year construction started to pick up, the *Tulsa Tribune* included ORU in an article noting that Tulsa would witness $100 million ($899 million in 2021 dollars) in new construction the following year, a record for the city. Two years later, ORU was contributing $8 million ($72 million) annually to the city's economy. By 1969, it was believed, this number would climb to $12 million, and then $24 million in 1980. In 1967, at the beginning of fund-raising for new building projects, Tulsa papers and businessmen voiced support for the university. The president of the Tulsa Chamber of Commerce remarked that ORU, with its 150 employees and $1.2 million payroll, was the equivalent to six new retail establishments and that it represented a "brain gain" rather than the "brain drain" of the past. In 1971, a Tulsa banker estimated that Roberts was attracting $15 million a year to the city and that, since his arrival to Tulsa in 1947, he had invested from $200 to $250 million in the local economy. A little more than a decade after its founding, ORU was being praised by local newspapers for helping to make Tulsa a "university city."[1]

The university changed Oral's life for the positive as well. For the next decade, Oral, the dirt-poor, stuttering, TB-stricken Oklahoma youth, finally found what he had been looking for his entire life: acceptance. For most of his life, Oral was insecure. His charisma and stage presence gave off an air of confidence, even cockiness, but, like so many people in his position, Oral was lonely. Wayne Robinson, who worked closely with Oral in the late 1960s and early 1970s, believed that Bob DeWeese, Oral's longtime associate evangelist, was the closest thing Roberts had to a real friend. And even then, it wasn't a relationship of equals. Patti Roberts, Oral's first daughter-in-law, commented, "*Nothing* comes before his ministry—not his wife, his children, or anyone or anything else.... He will sacrifice anything for it." Oral's first biographer, David Edwin Harrell, agreed that he had few close friends. The most important thing in Oral's life was "the call," according to Harrell, which meant, "Everyone he came into contact with became an actor in that larger drama."[2]

One person in this drama was Billy Graham. Oral and Graham first met in September 1950 in Portland, Oregon. At the time, Graham, just one year removed from his 1949 "Christ for Greater Los Angeles" crusade, was conducting a revival where crowds of nearly sixteen thousand were gathering nightly to hear him preach the good news. Oral's tent had just been destroyed in Amarillo, Texas. Roberts was in Tacoma, Washington, visiting friends and convalescing from the trauma of the Texas storm when he heard that Graham was in Portland. Like many in the United States, Oral was watching Graham's ascendancy with curiosity and wanted to see his counterpart in action.

The emerging giants in their respective worlds, Pentecostal and fundamentalist, met outside their hotel and rode to the crusade together in Graham's cab. On the way, Graham asked Roberts to pray at the meeting. Oral was certainly flattered, but he was worried about how Graham's constituents would react to a Pentecostal praying at one of his crusades. Graham assured him that he had nothing to worry about. He had been personally blessed by watching him preach in Florida, and one of his aunts had been healed through his ministry. He told Oral, "God has not given me that kind of ministry, but He has given it to you."[3]

Graham and Oral met again in 1959 while both were in Washington, DC. When Graham heard that Roberts was staying in the same hotel, he invited him to his room to visit. Oral rejected the invitation. Earlier that year, Graham had held a four-week-long revival in Australia, where an estimated one million people attended. In February 1959, the *Age*, the Melbourne-based paper that attacked Oral as a fraud, celebrated Graham as handsome, energetic, and, most painfully for Roberts, sincere.[4] Roberts was jealous and, quite simply, didn't want to talk to his rival. The two eventually met in Oral's room. During their conversation, Oral told Graham that he was upset that the media had "built [Graham] up as an honest man and [Oral] as a dishonest man." The wounded evangelist was blunt. He told Graham, "You've never seen the day when you were more honest than I am." Graham responded that he knew and went on to explain that he also experienced his fair share of persecution and told Oral how much he appreciated his ministry.[5]

Six years later, Carl F. H. Henry, editor of *Christianity Today*, wrote Oral to congratulate him on the opening of ORU and to invite him to the World

Congress on Evangelism, which was scheduled for Berlin from October 26 to November 4, 1966. The aim of the congress, attended by over 1,200 delegates from 106 countries and 120 journalists in addition to five Roman Catholic observers and one Jewish observer, was to revitalize global evangelistic activity. The need for such a discussion was becoming increasingly urgent. Many observers had noticed that evangelical Christianity was rapidly changing not only in the United States but also across the globe. It was becoming clear that the so-called Global South—Africa, Southeast Asia, and South and Central America—would soon be the center of global Christianity. The question the congress wanted to answer was how evangelicalism, which *Christianity Today* called the "lifeline of Christianity," should respond. In the lead-up to the congress, *Christianity Today* asked a wide variety of church leaders their opinion. The list included the infamous "God is dead" theologian Thomas J. J. Altizer, Billy Graham, Norman Vincent Peale, Reinhold Niebuhr, Oral Roberts, and Archbishop Iakovos, the primate of the Greek Orthodox Archdiocese of North and South America. The responses were, not surprisingly, varied. Altizer said Protestants must be willing to embrace the radicalism of early Christianity or "submit to Rome." Niebuhr, who was too sick to attend the congress, said that his problem wasn't with "apostolic evangelism" but with "American evangelicalism." The archbishop commented that evangelism was the "truest and most valid basis of Christianity." Oral argued that the main problem with evangelism was its focus on correct doctrine. Christians, he said, needed to adopt a person-centered approach.[6]

Nothing summed up the congress's purpose more than the large digital clock in the main lobby of the Kongresshalle. The clock issued a loud beat for each of the 150 children born every minute, reminding the delegates of the urgency for evangelism. One attendee, the emperor of Ethiopia and protector of the Ethiopian Orthodox Church, Hailie Selassie, even got the German government to intervene. That a gathering of conservative evangelicals would invite an official head of state to its meetings annoyed the Germans; such gatherings were almost exclusively handled by government officials. The German government got back by not inviting Billy Graham to a reception for Selassie. Other controversial guests included two Auca Ecuadorean Indians who had participated in the murder of five American Christian missionaries in 1956.[7]

Oral was initially reluctant to accept the invitation to attend the congress. His skepticism proved correct, at least early on. Oral and R. O. Corvin, who traveled with Roberts, spent most of their time in their hotel room.

Roberts was only coaxed out after Calvin Thielman, Ruth Graham's personal pastor, arranged a luncheon for the Oklahoman and several world ecclesiastical leaders, including the bishop of London. Oral disarmed the lunch crowd with his candidness in the face of difficult questions. When word got to Billy Graham that Oral was finally being incorporated into the congress's activities, he was overjoyed and told Thielman that he wanted Roberts to come to dinner with a group of conference leaders. At the end of the supper, Graham spoke personally with each of the attendees. When it came time to talk to Roberts, he asked when he was going to be invited to speak at ORU. Oral asked him if he would be interested in dedicating the university. Graham said he was.[8]

Oral got more chances to shine. Over the course of the congress, some delegates expressed concern about how to make the gospel relevant for young people, who, no matter where they lived in the world, were being, as one person put it, "deluged on all sides with the assertions that the old standards of their parents are worn out."[9] According to Corvin, ORU was a major topic of conversation. One afternoon, while sitting in on a panel about Christian education, Oral stood and told the crowd that they needed to create at least "12 evangelical universities with their own doctoral programs" if they wanted to revitalize Christian education. And when someone responded that the cost to build just one university was $90 million, Roberts responded that he knew and that ORU was actually going to cost $100 million. Christians simply needed to have faith that God would help them cover the costs.

Toward the end of the congress, Oral and Corvin were approached by a man who introduced himself as an American living in South America. After explaining to them that the amazing growth of evangelical churches had already altered the political balance in his country, he told them that Communists threatened this newfound power. Some evangelical pastors had even been won over to the Communist side. What his country needed was an institution like ORU. One that could counter the Communist forces and train young Pentecostal Christians.[10]

On the final Wednesday of the congress, Oral chaired a panel on "twentieth-century evangelism." The session, scheduled in the largest room in the building, attracted an overflow crowd. Oral was rightfully nervous. Some of the most prominent Protestant intellectuals were in the room. Dr. Harold Ockenga, a member of Billy Graham's brain trust and former president of Fuller Theological Seminary, sat on the stage with Roberts. The questions were often pointed and direct. But as Roberts would do for the next decade, he easily disarmed his audience with his vulnerability. He admitted that some people weren't healed and that he had made some mistakes early in his career. Oral got a major boost when Ockenga testified that he had been healed by faith.[11]

Oral's next big moment came when Graham asked him to pray and share his observations the night before the congress was set to close. Roberts told the gathered delegates that he had been humbled by the treatment he received. If there was one phrase that summed up his experience, it was "We have been conquered by love." The congress showed him that real Christian unity was possible, and it forced him to confront his own ego. He drew laughs from the audience when he said that he found "men here that can preach better" than he could and that he had been "out-preached, out prayed, and out-organized." He thanked the organizers "for helping to open [his] eyes to the main stream of Christianity."[12] A United Press International story reported that Oral's performance in Berlin "unveiled a sophisticated new image with a candid 'confession' of previous faults."[13] Roberts didn't waste any time telling people that Graham had agreed to speak at ORU's dedication. Tulsa papers started reporting in early November that Graham was coming to Tulsa in the near future.[14]

THINGS WERE LOOKING GOOD FOR ORU AT THE END of its first year. Provost John Messick told local newspapers in April 1966 that he was impressed with the university's students, who had to deal with the "normal freshmen problems" but had zero upper classmen to help them. The students formed their own campus government, began a newspaper, wrote a student handbook, participated in intramural and intercollegiate sports, and formed a history club. He anticipated that the university would add another 250 to 300 students the following year. The university was also in good financial shape. Its estimated income for its first year of operation was a little over $2 million, with expenditures at about $1.5 million. Most of the income, about $1.5 million, came from gifts and grants. Other sources included student fees; endowment income; "auxiliary enterprises," which included dining halls, bookstores, student union, and athletics; and student aid. The university spent the most money, about $292,000, on instruction, departmental research, and specialized educational activities. It spent another $255,000 on the library and $273,750 on general expenses. Other expenditures included general administration, student aid, student services (record maintenance, guiding, testing, and advising), operation of the power plant, and public services and information. It listed its debts as $2.9 million for the Learning Resource Center and $1.4 million for a new dormitory. All the debt was owed to the federal government. The only major complaint among faculty and students was the cost of living in Tulsa. At the time, there were no plans to add more buildings.[15]

Perhaps the most pressing task was to get ready for accreditation. ORU would have to wait at least four years before even being considered— accreditation agencies liked to wait until a school graduated its first class— but it had reason to be optimistic. Its finances were on solid footing, its buildings were state of the art (one Oklahoma publication said Buck Rogers would probably attend ORU), it had a strong faculty and curriculum, its average salaries were second in the state behind only the University of Oklahoma, and its library was adding about 1,500 volumes per month. The most likely obstacle was a concern about academic freedom. University officials said it existed at ORU but that the school didn't accept "doctrines which are contrary to the accepted way of life in American society" nor "doctrines opposing principles which are considered fundamental in Biblical theism."[16] In January 1967, the Oklahoma State Board of Regents for Higher Education accredited ORU.[17]

In December 1966, Oral launched a $15.3 million fund-raising drive to finance four new buildings on ORU's campus, increase endowment, and add to the university's scholarship program. Of the funds, $2 million was for a seven-story men's dormitory, $1.5 million was for a student union and dining commons, $3 million was for a performing arts center with seating for 2,500 and space for fine arts classrooms, and $750,000 was for an administration building. Money was also needed for the library— about $600,000 for acquisitions of books and publications. Other costs included $500,000 for faculty support, $600,000 for student financial aid, $150,000 for outdoor athletic facilities, $250,000 for plant operation, $350,000 for computer facilities, $350,000 for the infirmary, $500,000 for additions to the power plant, $48,000 for a student radio station, $1.5 million for other upgrades to the student union and facilities, and $3 million for the endowment fund. Roberts hoped to raise $3.3 million locally in Tulsa and $1 million from the rest of the state, with the remaining $11 million coming from his national and international supporters. The $15 million price tag would nearly double ORU's investments at the time. At the end of 1966, the *Tulsa Tribune* reported that the university had already invested $16.2 million ($129 million in 2021 dollars) in land, buildings, books, equipment, dorms, and endowment funds.[18]

A *Tulsa World* editorial voiced its support by encouraging Tulsans to give to the drive. So far, the relationship had been one-sided, the paper commented. In his announcement, Oral gave credence to this view. He explained that ORU annually spent $2 million in the local economy, that for every $1 given, the university brought in $9 in expenditures, and that, as a result of the three-year construction plan, it would add $10 million in jobs and material purchases to Tulsa's economy. In summer 1967, a group of Tulsa businessmen, calling themselves the Tulsa Development Council for ORU, banded together to help raise $2.5 million. The leader of the group, C. C. Ingram, president of Oklahoma Natural Gas Co., echoed the newspaper. Few cities had a multimillion-dollar university fall into their lap with little to no investment on their part. It made good sense, Ingram said, for businessmen and philanthropists to support a private university because its educational standards were generally higher than its tax-supported counterparts. In less than a month, the Tulsa ORU fund raised $750,000. By January 1968, the group announced that $1.5 million had been pledged, most of it from corporations.[19]

Oral Roberts University was dedicated on Sunday April 2, 1967. More than eighteen thousand people from all over the world, and representatives of 128 colleges and universities, converged on Tulsa to witness the ceremony. The crowd heard from speakers representing the student body, the faculty, the Oklahoma board of regents, the city of Tulsa, and from the governor of Oklahoma, before finally hearing the two most important speakers. Oral Roberts, the first of the two, was understandably emotional during his address. Talking through tears, he spoke about the "communistic and atheistic force" that was threatening the world and the fact that one-third of the world's population was illiterate, and he encouraged the audience "to think of the desperate problems man has that are based on his lost faith, or in having no faith at all." The world needed an answer to these problems. ORU was evidence that God wasn't "done with man."[20]

Graham struck a similar tone. Some of the United States' most important educational institutions were founded on explicitly Christian beliefs. One of the founding principles of Harvard, he told the crowd, was that every student had to be instructed "to know God and Jesus Christ" and "to lay Christ at the bottom as the only foundation of knowledge and learning." Yale, Columbia, and Dartmouth had similar objectives. Even a cursory glance at the contemporary spiritual state of these universities revealed how far "they have gotten away from the concepts of their founders." ORU, with its focus on biblical theism and the whole man, was in a perfect position to resurrect the once-great Christian heritage of American education.[21] One day after attending the dedication, Ed Edmondson, a Democratic representative from Oklahoma, reported to the US House of Representatives his excitement about ORU. The university was "destined for greatness," and its presence would be "felt in our State and in the Nation, and its influence will be for good."[22]

Oral wasn't content with just saving the United States. One month after the dedication, the student newspaper, *Oracle*, announced that a group of twelve ORU students were going to accompany Oral on his upcoming revival in Brazil.[23] The two-week trip, July 21–August 7, 1966, showed the early promise of ORU's students. Patti Holcombe, a member of the inaugural freshmen class, remarked that "Oral knew that we were his best advertisement," and with the university still in its infant stage, the "appearance of a group of ORU students singing the praises of the university was a sure-fire money raiser." He recognized that conservative Pentecostals, many of whom were already wary of higher education and radicalized college students, would more likely give money to a university full of clean-cut young believers.[24]

The trip also gave the students a firsthand look at some of Oral's questionable methods. Holcombe remembered that ORU students were happy to promote Oral's dream because they believed in it and were almost zealous in their desire to maintain it, but the Brazil trip showed kinks in the armor. She recalled that the "services had been exciting, with many people saved and healed" and that she "had never seen such an awesome display of God's power." The problem came when *Abundant Life* printed what Patti and some of her friends believed to be misleading articles about the trip. The magazine apparently inflated the numbers of people saved and "recounted miracle stories" that the students weren't sure had occurred. The whole situation was silly. The success of the trip spoke for itself. There was no reason for the paper, what some students started calling *Abundant Lie*, to misrepresent what had happened. The students made their frustration known to the paper and around campus. Oral quickly quashed their modest rebellion when a rumor was spread that they were going to burn copies of *Abundant Life* in the parking lot and call local papers to witness it. He was furious. He told the students that he should expel them. However, he understood that they had been vocal out of their search for the truth and desire to hold ORU accountable to its own stated principles. He told them that he would have *Abundant Life* print a more accurate story. The whole experience reinforced their belief in ORU's mission at the same time that it alerted them to some of its potential weaknesses. Patti and her friends developed what she later called a "love/hate relationship" with the university.[25]

The next overseas trip, this time to Vietnam, brought more risks. In January 1966, the editors of *Christianity Today* expressed many evangelicals' feelings toward the war in Asia when they wrote, "we are caught in a predicament." The United States, unfortunately, found itself in a land and air war in Vietnam, one that left few, if any, good options. Americans, who had "no tradition of cruelty," would be shocked to learn about the ways in which the Vietcong treated the living and the dead. Their animist religion even led them to believe that, "by devouring the organs of an enemy," they could achieve universal bliss. No Christian wanted the war to continue, but, the editors concluded, the United States needed to increase its land and air presence in the country.[26] A year later, any nuance that may have been found in *Christianity Today*'s editorial was disappearing as the United States became increasingly polarized over the nation's presence in Vietnam. In February, nearly two thousand clergymen and four hundred seminary students rallied in Washington, DC, to voice their opposition to the war. In April, Martin Luther King Jr. delivered his most fiery antiwar sermon to date. A month later, the *New York Times* reported the words of a Reform Jewish rabbi, just returned from Vietnam, who accused antiwar clergy of aiding the enemy. Their calls for peace were doing the work for the Communist propagandists in Hanoi. That same month, the paper of record published a story about how the Episcopal Diocese of New York called for the inclusion of the Vietcong in any peace negotiations, though it stopped short of demanding that these talks be "immediate and unconditional."[27]

Billy Graham beat Oral to Vietnam by several months, visiting the troops at Christmastime 1966. The trip was an eye-opener for him. He told reporters that he didn't think the war would be over anytime soon and pondered even whether peace were possible. Few Americans truly understood the gravity of the situation, but he assured them that they could be proud of the nation's soldiers. Part of the deal Graham had made with President Lyndon Johnson before he left was that he would give a full report upon his return. Graham, along with Cardinal Francis Spellman, met Johnson in the White House, where, though he was far less hawkish than the Catholic leader, he recommended that the nation had an obligation to stick it out through the end.[28]

Oral followed Graham that summer. On the morning of June 17, 1967, Oral was optimistic about the trip. He had just helped lead an ORU professor's family to Christ and was getting ready, along with twelve ORU students and several lieutenants, to leave for an overseas trip to Indonesia and Vietnam. The twelve students and the campus pastor, Tommy Tyson, would lead a revival in Jakarta while Oral, Bob DeWeese, and a photographer stayed in Vietnam. Roberts proudly reported that the college troupe attracted attention at every airport they stopped in not only because they broke out in gospel songs but also because "they were neatly dressed, well-behaved, with not a beatnik among them."[29]

Oral, who received press credentials for his trip, said he was sobered by his visit to Vietnam. Roberts never shied away from talking about the evils of Communism, but he remained mostly silent on the ongoing war in Vietnam. Like Graham, Roberts returned from the warzone with a sense of dread and lack of optimism about the American war effort. He was shocked when he visited a morgue that had three hundred to four hundred bodies of dead soldiers, many of whom were unrecognizable or whose dog tags had been lost. At the end of the rows of dead bodies, the mortician, guiding Roberts by the arm, picked up a single hand: "This is all that's left," he told the evangelist.[30]

His visit to the front also led him to conclude that the United States wasn't fighting a traditional enemy. Instead, a Vietcong soldier was "elusive" and a "brutal, almost senseless being, killing, maiming, dismembering as part of his Communistic training. He recognizes no God, he puts no value on human life." The average Vietcong also wasn't a soldier in the traditional sense. Flying one thousand feet over rice fields, Oral was told that it was common for a farmer to work in the rice fields all day and then join a Vietcong gang at night. The United States couldn't allow such a godless enemy to win because it would mean the "end of the Gospel" and "freedom" and the beginning of totalitarian rule. His initial experiences in Saigon didn't instill much confidence. He had been told that US soldiers often spent "as much on pleasure in one night at a bar, as a Vietnamese will earn in six months." It was admirable that the United States was attempting to keep the country open for the preaching of the gospel, but the "American soldier, generally speaking, is not much of an example of Christianity."[31]

It wasn't all bad in Vietnam. For one thing, the trip certainly boosted Oral's ego. He was delighted that no matter where he went, people recognized him. Many had heard him on the radio, had seen him on television, or had gone to his tent services when they were young. A missionary suggested that he should title his account of his journey in South Vietnam

"Aren't You Oral Roberts?" Despite the horrors he witnessed, Oral was surprised by the high morale and faith of the average American soldier and officer. At a marine base, where twelve marines were responsible for protecting 2,200 people, the battle-hardened soldiers were softened by a reading of Psalm 91. When the sergeant said they had been "lucky" that none of the marines had been killed, Roberts asked, "Or has it been something else?" The sergeant replied, "Mr. Roberts, I know why and all the men do too." Oral further learned that the sergeant and his men all grew closer to God during their deployment. There was a valuable lesson here, Roberts told supporters. While "riots, hatred, bitterness are breaking out in cities everywhere" and the "population explosion has now overtaken the growth of the churches," American servicemen were, according to a number of officers, adopting a "higher moral standard and a deeper spiritual commitment in Vietnam than they had at home." He continued, "We believe they will go back to America better men."[32]

Roberts was also struck by the racial harmony of the soldiers. Everywhere he went, he noticed that white and Black soldiers were openly integrated and worshiping together. Just like in their spiritual and moral lives, American troops were setting an example for the people back home about racial equality. With each one depending on the other, "something hopeful for the future may arise. God has made all men of one blood. . . . I pray that when these men return home, they will carry the same dependence upon each other."[33]

There was even hope for the enemy. When a Vietnamese military officer heard about Oral's presence, he requested that the evangelist speak to seven hundred Vietnamese prisoners. The officer wasn't a Christian himself, but, Oral reported, he "was interested in seeing" the prisoners' "lives touched by Christ." Despite the language, religious, and cultural barriers, Oral had an in with the Vietnamese soldiers. Tuberculosis had ravaged the Vietnamese, giving him a "point of reference," for he had once shared in their suffering. Even though only 10 percent of the "little men" at the POW camp had heard of the Christian faith, nearly one hundred took a stand for Christ after hearing Oral speak.

Before leaving for the next leg of the trip, to Indonesia, Oral spoke to over five hundred Vietcong and other "hard-core Communists" who had accepted the American government's offer for amnesty. The post commander told Roberts that he could preach but that he wouldn't have time for an altar call. After sharing the story of "Jesus' life and death and resurrection and the purpose He had for each human life," Oral said, "We are not political men. Our Government did not send us to you. Neither has the Vietnamese government sent us." He said his team had traveled thousands of miles because they wanted to share Christ's love with them. At the end, Oral and Bob DeWeese lined up to hand out kits containing a towel, soap, food—Roberts specifically mentioned Pop-Tarts—and a copy of the Gospel of John. The purpose of these gifts, the missionaries explained, was to show that they cared about the Communists' physical needs as much as their spiritual ones. When he saw their faces light up, Oral said to DeWeese, "Imagine the Communists giving gifts like these." DeWeese replied, "They would never do it."[34]

When Oral met Tyson and the students in Jakarta, he was pleased to hear that the students had laid the groundwork for a successful revival. For a week before Oral's arrival, they visited businesses, schools, churches, and universities distributing literature, sharing the gospel, and singing to thousands of people in the largely Muslim country. The students excitedly told Roberts about everything they had witnessed. The results were so spectacular that they told Oral that his upcoming four-day revival in Jakarta was going to be his "greatest crusade." They predicted that the "auditorium will be filled the first night." For four days, Oral and the students spoke to over twelve thousand people in the Di Istora Auditorium about God's saving and healing power. The sight of ORU students leading thousands of people to the Lord and praying for healing was a revelation to Roberts. When he opened the university, he "knew it was God-ordained to increase this ministry and to help us reach the masses for Christ. Now I was seeing it with my own eyes."[35]

The overseas successes convinced Oral that it was time to renew the Abundant Life Youth Teams, a briefly lived evangelistic program from the late 1950s.[36] This time, they would be known as World Action Teams (WAT). Their first trip was to Chile. A month before Oral left for Vietnam, Chilean minister of education Juan Gomez Millas was in Tulsa to talk with ORU administrators about the possibility of starting a university in his home country. Corvin explained that the goal was to establish a university on five thousand acres, which, over a twenty-five-year time span, would eventually be worth $150 million and have ten thousand students, making it significantly more expensive and larger than the school in Tulsa. Corvin expected the university to open in three years, and to "grow into full fruition" in five to seven. He hoped to establish a study commission in July or August 1967, preparing the way for Oral's planned trip to Chile in December.[37]

Chile had great potential as a landing place for an ORU satellite campus. It, along with many other countries in Latin America and the rest of the Global South, was becoming increasingly Protestant in the twentieth century.[38] John Nichols, a consultant for the Evangelical Church Council of Chile and a somewhat mysterious figure, said that Oral's success was almost guaranteed, because he was even more popular than Billy Graham in Latin America. Especially important was the WAT's potential for reaching Chilean college students, most of whom were apparently indifferent to the gospel. The average age for a Chilean Pentecostal pastor was fifty-one, meaning there was going to be a need for a new generation of preachers.[39]

The political situation in Chile was also friendly. Declassified documents reveal that the CIA spent $2.6 million ($23.3 million in 2021 dollars) directly funding the 1964 presidential campaign of Eduardo Frei, the leader of the Christian Democratic Party, a political party friendly to the United States, and another $3 million attacking his chief opponent, Salvador Allende, an avowed leftist.[40] Frei "won" the election. The new president was apparently impressed enough with Corvin, whom he met for forty-five minutes in the buildup to Oral's trip in December 1967, that he offered him a building worth $2 million and a $3 million sports stadium. All the Tulsans had to provide was ten teachers.[41]

The trip was a disaster. The ministry spent $50,000 in precrusade publicity, money that the ministry's Chilean point man told them was well spent. Wayne Robinson, who was in Chile and would soon take over as editor of *Abundant Life*, doesn't mention the man's name, but it might be safe to assume that John Nichols was that person. In his reports, the contact said that banners, billboards, and posters were plastered throughout the country and that he could guarantee crowds as large as 100,000 for the trip's final rally in Santiago. From the time Oral's plane landed at Santiago's airport on December 7, 1967, to his early departure on December 14, the promised crowds never materialized. Over the next several days, Oral and his crew learned the truth. The contact in Chile was apparently a CIA operative who not only fled the country but was also writing bad checks to the advertising agency that was handling the crusade.

Oral also had a run-in with his old nemesis, the press. When a news reporter asked him about opening a university, Roberts abruptly said, "There will be no university" and that the people who promised such a thing did so without his consent. This is hard to believe, considering the Chilean delegation approached him a year earlier in Berlin and that, right before he left Tulsa for Chile, he said the trip had "educational" purposes.[42] In response, President Frei withdrew Oral's invitation to meet him, and, to add insult to injury, newspapers began running anti-Roberts headlines.

The disastrous trip culminated in what was supposed to be record crowds in Chile's capital city, Santiago. The crusade, which was scheduled for the capitol plaza and was supposed to last from December 14 to December 17, started poorly. The grounds were inadequate, with crudely constructed stands, a "monstrous cross," and "four strings of light bulbs," according to Robinson. Even if the conditions had been adequate, there was nobody to fill the seats. Robinson estimated that barely three thousand people showed up. Almost as soon as Oral took the stage, the power went out. When the lights finally came back on, Roberts was gone. Tommy Tyson, the ORU chaplain, was standing there instead. Oral, who regularly suffered stomach problems on overseas trips, went back to the hotel complaining of diarrhea, but when Bob DeWeese, Wayne Robinson, and the rest of the crew returned to the hotel after the service, they learned that Oral was already on an airplane back to the United States. There were still a few days left of the crusade. DeWeese and Tyson took over the preaching responsibilities as if nothing had happened. It wasn't until the final night of the crusade that they admitted that Oral had returned to the United States.[43]

THE FIRST FEW MONTHS OF 1968 WERE MOMENTOUS FOR ROBERTS. In January, he announced that John Messick was retiring. The plan was for Messick, who was going to move to Greenville, North Carolina, to continue on ORU's staff as a consultant for the construction of a new science building. Messick described the building, which had secured support from the Ford Foundation, as "tomorrow's science building built today." Messick described his time in Tulsa as the "happiest and most beneficial years" of his life. He hoped to spend his retirement years hunting, fishing, and spending time with his family.[44]

Behind closed doors, the relationship between Messick and Oral had been souring for some time. The relationship was a weird one from the beginning. Messick was never fully onboard with Roberts's hope for ORU to be a platform for his healing message. According to Corvin, Messick didn't think the academic and evangelistic goals belonged together.[45] The longtime college administrator feared, probably rightfully, that too explicit an association between faith healing and the university would be a liability in the accreditation process. Oral had hired Messick to get accreditation. He didn't hire him to evangelize.

When one of the accreditation teams visited ORU, it mainly criticized Messick's handling of the process. He had apparently done most of the self-study and paperwork himself, never fully involving the faculty and staff. Messick blamed Oral. It was faith healing, not his botching of the process, that was stalling accreditation. In the end, Messick probably wasn't lying, but that he shifted the blame to Oral rankled the university president. Messick had also apparently started openly defying and making fun of his boss. At the meeting in which Oral first revealed his idea for the World Action Singers, he used a split infinitive. Messick corrected Oral, who played it off as a joke, but then Messick wouldn't let it go. It was quickly obvious to everyone in the room that Oral didn't know what a split infinitive was. As it became clear that accreditation wasn't going to happen as quickly as Oral had hoped, he wanted Messick gone and replaced with a more pliable dean, in this case, a thirty-three-year-old assistant dean named Carl Hamilton.[46]

Though some were skeptical of the hire because of Hamilton's age, most people seemed to agree that it was a smart move. Hamilton was the exact type of person Roberts envisioned as an ideal ORU graduate. Like so many other early leaders, Hamilton was raised in the Pentecostal Holiness Church. He attended Southwestern College in Oklahoma City and taught English there from 1957 to 1960, where he said he "was disappointed with the academic quality," before joining the Oral Roberts Evangelistic Association as an editor. He eventually climbed to assistant professor of English in January 1966. Hamilton finished his academic training a year later, earning his PhD in English at the University of Arkansas. Dr. Hamilton exhibited Messick's strengths without any of his weaknesses. He was academically trained, he was a Pentecostal, and, perhaps most importantly, he was young.[47]

A similar struggle played out between Oral and R. O. Corvin. Oral talks about the decay of their relationship in his 1972 autobiography, *The Call*, though he never mentions his old friend by name. In the beginning, Roberts was skeptical that the United States needed another seminary, but he became persuaded that a seminary offered "one way to train young men in the concepts of this ministry." Much to his frustration, this training never happened. Then, adding to his irritation, what he referred to as "representatives from the seminary" botched the trip to Chile. He also came to believe that the seminary faculty was sowing discord by teaching material hostile to his ministry. Whenever he lectured on evangelism at the seminary, he remembered, he "found little response to the concerns that had given birth to this ministry." His biggest fear, it seems, was that, under Corvin's influence, the seminary would become a Pentecostal Holiness school. He had done too much work to bridge the divide between Pentecostals and evangelical and mainline Christians to let his seminary become a mill for the Pentecostal Holiness Church.[48]

Even if Corvin wanted to turn the ORU theological seminary into a Pentecostal Holiness institution, the real problem was that Oral felt his authority was being undermined. From the beginning, there was only one vision for ORU that mattered: Oral's. He had little patience for dissent, which he interpreted as disloyalty, and, according to Carl Hamilton, he used to describe himself as a "benevolent despot—sometimes benevolent, always despotic."[49] This single-minded vision, mixed with all of Oral's insecurities, could be toxic. The seminary faculty were the most distinguished at ORU, Wayne Robinson remembered. Several had earned their PhDs from prestigious schools like Harvard and Princeton. They also tended to be older and were less likely to be intimidated by Roberts's strong-arm tactics. The students at the seminary also appeared to be unafraid of Roberts. Whenever he lectured at the seminary, they freely questioned and disagreed with him, which Oral believed was a sign that they were learning material that was antagonistic to his ministry.[50]

In the end, despite Oral's insecurities, he was clearly in charge. In conversations with the Tulsa press, Corvin and several faculty members, who remained anonymous, painted a picture of a bitter power struggle between Roberts and the embattled seminary head. On March 12, Oral reportedly gave Corvin an ultimatum: resign or he would close the seminary. The faculty didn't seem particularly enthused about Oral's decision to join the Methodist Church. They told newspapers that they weren't consulted about Corvin's forced resignation and feared that academic freedom was being violated, a serious accusation during the accreditation process. While Corvin didn't elaborate, he said that he submitted a five-point letter protesting his ouster from the school he helped start. There was one point he was willing to share, however. He had grown increasingly concerned with the type of reading his boss was doing. Most shockingly, Roberts read the great Christian existentialists, like Søren Kierkegaard, Paul Tillich, and Karl Barth, along with some atheistic existentialists, including Jean-Paul Sartre and Albert Camus. Roberts admitted that he had read these thinkers and that he was intrigued by the questions they posed, but that he ultimately rejected their conclusions. Though Corvin said he remained friends with Oral, he thought his friend's "dominating influence" over the university was detrimental to the institution and to the democratic processes there. Neither Corvin nor the seminary faculty had a solution for dealing with Roberts's absolute control. Howard Ervin was selected to replace Corvin.[51]

The conflict between Oral and the faculty came to a head in April 1968 when Oral joined the Boston Avenue Methodist Church in Tulsa. Oral's decision to join the much larger and more prestigious denomination, the *Tulsa Tribune* commented, was as surprising as if the pope had decided to become a Methodist.[52] For some of those who knew him, however, the decision wasn't that surprising. Oral's ties to the Methodist Church went back decades. His grandfather was a steward in the denomination. When he was twelve years old, the local Methodist church in Pontotoc County held a revival, and, in order to attract children, the revivalist gave out candy. For the poor Pentecostal preacher's son, such treats were rare, so he attended the revival and, along with some of his friends, joined the Methodist Church.[53]

Wayne Robinson, who had also grown up in the Pentecostal Holiness Church but became a Methodist as an adult, said his first inkling that Oral was interested in joining the Methodist Church came in September 1966 while the two were playing a round of golf. Roberts asked Robinson his opinion of the Methodist Church. Robinson told him that he was happy in the denomination.[54] Some of Oral's friends believed that his experience in Berlin pushed him to seriously consider rejoining the Methodist Church.

The tensions between Oral and the hierarchy in the Pentecostal Holiness Church can be traced all the way back to when he was a young evangelist, but the relationship declined as Roberts became more popular and independent. Robinson suggested that the Pentecostal Holiness Church took issue with Oral's methods and success, believing instead that poverty and social unacceptability were requisites for salvation. An attempt in 1952 to terminate his membership failed. There were enough votes, however, to reject a $50,000 gift from Oral and Lee Braxton to help fund a new headquarters in Memphis, Tennessee. The relationship improved a bit in 1962 when Oral began to emphasize speaking in tongues at his revivals, which then led to unfavorable coverage in *Life*.[55]

It was during the construction of ORU that Oral realized the importance of denominational affiliation. There were some positive things about hiring people who came from a Pentecostal Holiness background. As the university began to take form, though, Oral began to fear that many of them were taking ORU "down the denominational trail." It made sense for early Pentecostals to form their own denominations centered around the experience of speaking in tongues, Roberts argued, because the hostility coming from the more established denominations, like the Methodist Church, made cooperation impossible. The need for separate denominations based on speaking in tongues, healing, and the other gifts of the Holy Spirit stopped making sense in the 1950s as people in the mainline churches began not just practicing the gifts of the Holy Spirit but staying in their denominations as well, marking the beginning of charismatic Christianity.[56] Oral told a laymen's seminar in November 1969 that one of his motivations to become a Methodist was to show people that they didn't have to belong to a particular denomination to enjoy the baptism with the Holy Spirit.[57]

The first time Oral met Dr. Finis (rhymes with "highness") Crutchfield was at a Christmas party in 1967. Crutchfield, who was then pastor of the Boston Avenue Methodist Church, was an up-and-comer in the denomination's hierarchy. Robinson described him as a "near bishop"—someone whose career trajectory was pointing toward the episcopacy. After graduating from Duke Divinity School in 1940, Crutchfield quickly climbed the ranks of the Methodist Church, eventually making his way to Boston Avenue in 1960. If he was going to become bishop, the Tulsa church was the place to go; five of its ministers had already earned the title, it was the fifth-largest Methodist church in the United States, and its buildings were designed by Frank Lloyd Wright. Crutchfield would have never had his remarkable career if it became public that he was gay, a secret he carried with him until his death in May 1987 of complications with AIDS.[58]

During his conversation with Oral, Crutchfield jokingly told him to consider becoming a Methodist. Much to his surprise, Roberts took the invitation seriously. Crutchfield was still a rising star in the denomination, and his invitation to Oral risked upsetting powerful people in the Methodist fold. The other problem was theological. Crutchfield apparently respected Oral as a man of integrity and influence but chafed at the idea of speaking in tongues. In fact, when people at Boston Avenue started speaking in tongues, he quickly squashed it.[59]

Oral said he became a Methodist because "it was the will of God." There were also other, more earthly reasons for Oral's switch. A number of people who knew Roberts personally believed that much of his life was driven by the insecurities of growing up poor and the "fear," as Robinson put it, "of personal unacceptance." Joining the Methodist Church, especially one as wealthy as Boston Avenue, was one way that Oral could tell the world, "I ain't poor no more."[60] There was the hope of freedom as well. In an interview at the time, he explained that part of the attraction to the Methodist Church was that it didn't attempt to impose conformity on its members and that it was the type of denomination that had room for "men to make a difference." He had also been assured that he would maintain control of ORU.[61]

Evelyn had a feeling they would change their church membership for at least two years before Oral formally announced it. For a number of years, she had been attending Boston Avenue with some regularity and, in 1966, became a member of the Women's Society of Christian Service at the church. She remembered these early relationships as fulfilling. Not only were the women "hungry for more of the Lord," but they were also friendly. When one of the women asked her to join their small group, Evelyn replied that she couldn't because she wasn't a member of the church. "Oh, you don't have to belong to the Methodist Church to join our Circle," she answered. "Just be a part of us." Evelyn was shocked that "they would accept an outsider as they accepted [her]."

Evelyn knew the decision to join the Methodist Church was a good one after a dream. In the days before they were received as members of Boston Avenue, Evelyn had been fretting over how friends and supporters would respond. One night she dreamed she was in a car driving through a small country town with houses on both sides and children playing in the yards when suddenly she became paralyzed. Unable to control her arms, legs, or feet, her foot pressed hard against the accelerator and her hand knocked the gear shifter into reverse, sending her barreling backward toward the children. She pleaded with God to stop the car before she killed anybody. He then comforted her, saying that she didn't have to worry about anything because he was in control and that he could take her backward as easily as he could take her forward. Not only did the dream ease her fears about joining the Methodist Church, but it also gave her the confidence to finally tell Oral that she supported him. She told him that she had been thinking about becoming a Methodist for a couple of years but waited to tell him because she didn't want to influence his choice.[62]

It didn't take long for Oral's supporters to voice their opinion of his decision. Some of his closest friends, including Lee Braxton and Oscar Moore, opposed the move, believing it would damage his ministry. Almost immediately, rumors started swirling that he was giving up control of ORU to the

Methodist Church, and he was accused of "having gone liberal, turning communist, and being a backslider" by many of his Pentecostal supporters. One of the most common accusations, from both Pentecostals and Methodists, was that he joined the more respectable denomination because he was going to be named a bishop. Oral firmly denied this accusation, of course. The OREA's revenue dropped by half within a month, and by one-third for the entire year. The decline in income forced ORU to delay construction on the student activities center, and the ministry was forced to borrow money twice to meet its payroll. Five years later, Ron Smith, who was executive vice president and chief operating officer of the OREA, called it the "Dark Summer of '68."[63]

The change to the Methodist Church signaled the end of the tent crusades, which had been the bread and butter of Oral's ministry for twenty years. In response to his new allegiance, Pentecostal Holiness churches throughout the United States stopped sponsoring Oral's revivals. The end of the traveling revivals wasn't inevitable, but there were signs that they had been in decline for much of the 1960s. In July 1967, a Detroit newspaper noted that Oral's crowds had shrunk significantly. It estimated that only three thousand to four thousand people attended the evening meetings. Eight years earlier, Oral had attracted not just ten thousand people but British royalty as well.[64] Wayne Robinson, who recalled being dazzled by Oral's preaching brilliance in 1949, remembered that, by 1968, Oral's ability to captivate an audience had declined. Part of the problem was that Oral was simply exhausted. The incessant traveling would test the mettle of any human being. There were also the nightly sermons of forty-five minutes to an hour; the constant presence of television cameras, reporters, and photographers; and praying individually for thousands of people. At the end of a six-day revival, according to Robinson, Oral was a "zombie."

Two weeks after joining the Boston Avenue Methodist Church, Roberts was in Florida conducting a crusade when a weight seemed to have been lifted from his shoulders. At the revival, an angry sponsoring committee confronted the evangelist about his switch, and, despite his best efforts, Oral failed to successfully explain his position. The crusade was also a failure. While walking on a golf course late at night, Oral opened up to Robinson about the recent failures. He told the young confidant that he believed they had seen the end of the crusades, adding, "I'm not married to any method, and this one has outlived its usefulness."[65]

The decline in interest in the crusades happened alongside a dip in television ratings. By the late 1960s, Christian television had left Roberts behind. The most exciting work in television was being done at an upstart station in Portsmouth, Virginia. The station, Christian Broadcasting Network (CBN), which went on the air in October 1961, struggled to draw an audience until its founder, Pat Robertson, heard about a young pair of traveling Pentecostal evangelists whose puppet show was a hit on the revival circuit. The couple's first show, the *Jim and Tammy Show*, named after its hosts, Jim and Tammy Faye Bakker, premiered on CBN in September 1965 and was quickly popular with local children, but the real innovation came a year later with the premiere of the *700 Club*, a Christian talk show. The show, modeled after Johnny Carson's *Tonight Show*, demonstrated that Christian television didn't just have to be a sermon, lecture, or healing line. Instead, it could be entertaining as well as spiritually enriching.[66]

After nearly fifteen years on television, Oral admitted, the format had grown stale. It was time to leave television and try something new. Talks with producers and directors were fruitless because, Oral believed, "there was too strong a pattern already set in their minds." In 1965, despite the howls of protest from his staff, Roberts decided to phase out his TV ministry. Over the next two years, as ratings dropped, airtime became too expensive, or favorable time slots were lost, Oral's first television show came to an end. Half of the stations were dropped in 1966, and the remainder were dropped one year later. The decision wasn't an easy one, but, Roberts later claimed, it was meant to be temporary. He knew that it would be only a matter of time before he was back on television.[67]

7

Contact

ORAL HAD BEEN THINKING ABOUT GOING BACK on television shortly after he canceled *Your Faith Is Power*. In August 1968, Rex Humbard invited Oral to his television studio in Akron to view his color cameras and tape-reproduction equipment. Roberts immediately recognized the possibilities of color television. Though they were unlikely to stand in Oral's way, many of the ORU and OREA executives weren't particularly excited about a return to television because the ministry was still reeling from the financial trauma of Oral's switch to the Methodist Church.

At a chapel service in March 1969, Oral remembered his own thoughts on the projected costs. His plan was to begin production on two different shows. One show, initially called *Something Good Is Going to Happen to You* but changed to *Oral Roberts and You* in 1975, was to be a weekly half-hour revival service. Oral described a brutal yet cost-saving shooting schedule. If they filmed eight half-hour episodes at once, each would cost $2,500 ($18,000 in 2021 dollars) to produce. That was just the price to bring in the mobile filming unit—ORU still didn't have its own filming equipment or production studios. Similar to his radio and first TV show, Oral had to pay for airtime in individual markets. The bigger the market, the more expensive. To get *Something Good Is Going to Happen to You* in a large city like Los Angeles or New York, which potentially had nine million viewers, Oral would have to pay $2,000 a week. There were four of these markets, adding up to roughly $416,000 ($3.1 million) a year. The next tier, $1,000 a week, had moderately sized cities like Kansas City, St. Louis, and Dallas. There were twelve of these markets, which would cost $624,000 ($4.7 million) a year. Then there were thirty-four $600 markets, or $1 million ($7.5 million) a year. He was confident that the costs were worth it. In New York, for instance, even if only one out of nine people tuned in, that was one million viewers. There was another cost the ministry had to consider: tape duplication. To duplicate in color, each tape—Oral wanted to make about 150—cost $60.[1]

Oral's other show, *Contact*, was more ambitious. This show was set to be aired quarterly. To just film the one-hour pilot at NBC's Burbank studio, which would take about twelve hours, Oral would have to pay $75,000 ($527,000), or about $7,500 per hour. When he complained to NBC executives about the price, they told him he was getting a deal. They charged Dean Martin $180,000 for the same studio, cameramen, and equipment. Airtime for the specials was projected to cost even more than *Something Good* because Oral wanted them to be shown in prime time. The cost to show the one-hour specials in the four largest markets, like New York and Los Angeles, was $5,000. The next tier, ten cities, including Washington, DC, Houston, Atlanta, and Detroit, cost $2,000 a week. The third tier, thirty-six cities similar to Tulsa, cost $1,000 per airing. The cost to duplicate a tape, of which Oral wanted to make 190, was $120. Oral knew many people found these costs outrageous, but it was the best money could buy.[2]

With about 190 million Americans, or 94 percent of the population, watching TV daily, it was as large an audience as Oral could have ever imagined. From their first appearance in early 1969 to their end in 1978, the quarterly specials were a hit. The first one had 10 million viewers, and the ratings only increased from there. The spring 1973 special had an estimated 37 million viewers, placing it third in ratings the week it aired. The only shows that season with better ratings were *All in the Family* and *The Flip Wilson Show*. The Christmas 1974 special drew 50 million viewers. Incoming mail exploded to new heights. After the 1970 Expo Special, which was filmed at the World's Fair in Osaka, Japan, and was seen by an estimated 30 million people, the ministry received 125,000 letters in one day. The ministry started to print 1.25 million copies of *Abundant Life* each month, and requests for ORU promotional material doubled. After one special, nearly 50,000 teenagers mailed letters. The 1971 Valentine's Day special was nominated for three Emmy Awards for art direction and lighting direction. The specials attracted an impressive number of stars, both religious and secular, including Billy Graham, Roy Rogers and Dale Evans, Florence Henderson, Charley Pride, Roy Clark, Anita Bryant, Robert Goulet, Pat Boone, Jimmy Durante, Lynn Anderson, Lou Rawls, Johnny and June Carter Cash, H. R. Pufnstuf, Jerry Lewis, Johnny Mathis, Burl Ives, Della Reese, Tennessee Ernie Ford, Peter Graves, and Jimmie Rodgers. He also drew popular athletes like 1969 Heisman Trophy winner Steve Owens and UCLA basketball legend John Wooden and politicians like Oregon Republican Mark Hatfield. Specials were filmed in Hawaii, Alaska, England, and at the Grand Ole Opry in Nashville.[3]

While *Your Faith Is Power* focused on Roberts and the healing line, the quarterly specials showcased the ORU students. With the university still in its infancy stage, Oral needed to find a way to sell it to the American public. At a time when televised images of student protests were filling living rooms each night, the sight of students—white and Black—radiating wholesomeness and decency was welcomed by many middle-class Christians. Talking at a faculty orientation in 1971, Oral said the World Action Singers helped to make him a more respectable household name. When parents watched the specials, they could say, "'My son, my daughter can be like this.' They are giving me a floor where I can preach the gospel and people will say, 'Well this man that so many have said is a phony and a racketeer' and all that kind of stuff in my healing ministry, 'he can't be so bad if he builds a university, if he turns out young people like this.'"[4]

The *Contact* specials also gave Oral the chance to groom his son Richard to take over the evangelistic side of his growing empire. Much like his older brother, Ronnie, he had wanted to make a name for himself separate from his famous father. The biggest difference between Ronnie and Richard, Evelyn remembered, was that Richard was more openly rebellious. Whenever Oral broached the subject of God, Richard generally fired back, "Dad, get off my back." In high school, he showed little to no interest in his studies, spending his time singing at dances for a local rock band instead, despite his parents' prohibitions against dancing. One day while he was sick at home, his parents prayed for him and believed that "God was dealing with him." Nothing changed. After barely graduating from high school in 1966, he further distanced himself from his family by attending the University of Kansas in Lawrence with the hopes of majoring in music and becoming a famous singer. Even if he had wanted to attend ORU, he wasn't exactly the type of student who would thrive in the university's restrictive environment. He had picked up the nasty habits of smoking cigarettes and drinking alcohol on the nightclub scene.

At first it looked like Richard might thrive away from his parents. He sang at coffeehouses and nightclubs in the Lawrence area and at the Starlight Theater in nearby Kansas City. He even started to earn a reputation outside of the Midwest. While still a freshman, he was apparently offered a contract to sing in Las Vegas. Ralph Carmichael, who later worked with him on television, commented that Richard had one of the best singing voices he had ever heard. A final confrontation between Richard and Oral came at the end of Richard's first semester. One day while they were playing golf, Oral, who was usually a decent golfer, struggled to hit the ball because his mind was occupied with everything he wanted to say to Richard. Their day on the golf course ended early when Oral finally got the nerve to say something about his concerns. Richard was having none of it. He told his dad to leave him alone. Oral partially blamed himself for his son's behavior. His own teenage rebellion, he believed, was coming back to haunt him.

There were signs, however, that all wasn't well in Lawrence. Richard's letters home revealed that he was deeply unhappy. In one letter, he said that he was made to feel like a number instead of a person at the state university, which had an enrollment of seventeen thousand. His mother believed that his discontent was a sign that God was pushing him in the right direction to come back home. God began speaking directly to Richard shortly after he told off his father on the golf course. When he returned to Lawrence, he suddenly became ill with a colon problem that required surgery. Lying in the hospital bed, he began to pray and bargain with God. He told God that if he healed him, he would serve him. The next day, his doctors canceled the surgery. Back in his dorm room, he heard a voice tell him that he was in the wrong place. Richard was confused: Where was he supposed to be? The voice told him, "You're supposed to be at Oral Roberts University." He immediately called his mother about transferring. She told him that he would have to make significant changes in his life. He promised he would and began his studies in the fall of 1967 at ORU, where he could start being groomed to take over for his father.[5]

While Richard continued to be a lackluster student, preferring to spend his time working as a disc jockey for ORU's student radio station, he was central to Oral's vision for the future of his ministry. Richard's greatest assets were his age and his singing voice. When Patti Holcombe first started dating Richard during his first year at ORU, he often confided to her that he felt torn between his desire to be a famous singer and God's will for his life, or, less cryptically, working for his father. To her later regret, Patti pushed Richard to become involved with Oral's ministry because, at the time, that seemed "to be the most spiritual thing to do."

Patti was a talented and outspoken woman, traits that attracted Richard to her in the first place. Just one year removed from nearly being expelled for allegedly threatening to burn copies of *Abundant Life* for its coverage of the crusade in Brazil, she was initially skeptical of Richard, whose reputation as a playboy had preceded him. Richard, however, was attractive and charming. In summer 1968, while Patti was on a tour of

Europe and Israel with the Collegians, the forerunner to the World Action Singers, Richard, who stayed in Tulsa to work for the ORU radio station, sent a can of Dr Pepper as a gift. Referencing Jesus's words at the Last Supper, he wrote, "As often as you drink of this, think of me." Later that summer, he sent her a short telegram: "I have decided that we will get married this Christmas."[6]

Six weeks before they were supposed to get married, Patti called it off. The relationship reached a breaking point one day when they were supposed to go shopping. Richard, like his father, was prone to bouts of intense anger. While they were dating, Richard apparently got irritated because Patti never wore blue jeans, not out of any sort of holiness, but simply because she didn't own a pair and was too embarrassed to tell him. On this day, he was especially angry with her. When they reached his car, she recalled, he grabbed her shoulders and shook her, yelling, "What's the matter with you anyway? You think you're too good to wear blue jeans? Why can't you ever relax and act like a normal person?" Patti, who was justifiably upset, decided that she no longer wanted to marry Richard. Between his temper, his bad language, and his drinking, this incident in the parking lot confirmed that "he was still playing games with God."[7]

At the time she broke off the engagement, Oral was in California and Evelyn was home alone in Tulsa. In her own way, Evelyn seemed to sympathize with Patti. When Richard told his mother that Patti had called off the wedding because she wasn't convinced he truly loved her or was actually saved, Evelyn understood where she was coming from. She pressed her son on the depth of his commitment to the Lord. Had he made a "one-sided commitment"? That is, did he pray, "Lord, I'll do anything for You if You'll just give me Patti"? It became clear that this is exactly what he had prayed. In a dramatic moment, Richard fell crying to his knees and put his head in his mother's lap and promised to give his life to the Lord whether Patti married him or not. The next day, Richard told Patti what happened, and she told him that she had also prayed and that God had given her "a green light." Then he called his father in California to tell him the good news: "Dad, everything is okay now. I want to do what I can to help you in your ministry."[8] Oral was ecstatic. In September 1968, Richard, for the first time as an adult, appeared alongside his father at a crusade in Dayton, Ohio.[9] Two months later, on November 27, 1968, Patti and Richard were married.

Now that she was a Roberts, Patti learned very quickly how much control Oral had over his son's life. Before the newlyweds were set to leave for their honeymoon, Oral called them into his study, where he immediately broke into tears. Nobody said anything for several minutes. The only sounds came from the hissing and crackling of the fireplace and the ticktock of the clock on the mantel. When he was finally ready to speak, Patti's new father-in-law had a chilling message. The night before, it had been revealed to him in a dream that if either of them left the Roberts ministry or turned their backs on God, they would die in a plane crash. He then told them that he loved them and expressed hope that they would have a nice honeymoon. Their first night as a married couple was another sign of things to come. The first time Richard saw Patti naked, he said, "You know, you look fatter with your clothes off." After a disappointing consummation of their marriage, Richard and Patti attempted to fall asleep, but Patti couldn't because the vibrating bed wouldn't stop shaking; she eventually drifted to sleep after unplugging the bed. In just a few months they became, in Patti's words, "professional newlyweds."[10]

WHEN ORAL'S FIRST QUARTERLY SPECIAL PREMIERED in March 1969, viewers expecting a fiery sermon or a long healing line may have been surprised—and maybe disappointed—to see neither of these things. What they saw, instead, was a Christian variety show. Rooted in the American vaudeville tradition, variety TV programs were fast-paced entertainment that featured comedy, song, dance, and sketch performances. The advent of television brought a number of possibilities—and problems, namely, talent and money. With many skeptical of TV's utility, early TV pioneers in the late 1940s and early 1950s turned to variety-style entertainment because they could easily recruit stage and radio vaudeville entertainers and, most importantly, they could afford it. Since videotape didn't come into wide use until the 1960s, variety shows could be filmed live at a minimum cost. All that was needed was a cheap, movable set. Another advantage of variety TV was its malleability. For nearly three decades, variety programs like *The Ed Sullivan Show* (1948–1971), *The Carol Burnett Show* (1967–1978), *Hee Haw* (1969–1992), and *The Dean Martin Show* (1965–1974) appealed to broad audiences in the United States.[11]

With Oral acting as emcee and musical numbers performed by the World Action Singers, the quarterly specials were unlike anything on television. Contemporary critics praised their unique blending of entertainment and religion. One recommended that parents arrange an "at home" party for their children so they could enjoy the show together. The music was fast paced, but it came "with a message that speaks to today's searching young people." Another critic pointed out that while most people would recognize Roberts as a Christian leader, they would probably be surprised to see guests like the Jewish comedian Jerry Lewis. When asked if Roberts convinced him to convert to Christianity, Lewis said no, but that he had "come nearer making a Jew out of Oral." He said he appeared on the show because Oral promised $5,000 to his charity for children with muscular dystrophy. He said he'd have done the show for Adolf Hitler if he offered $5,000. The *New York Times* journalist Edward Fiske wrote that one of the main reasons the program worked was that one could watch it for a half hour before realizing it was a religious program. Oral had discovered how, Fiske wrote, "to use the mass media as a way of communicating the same earthly pastoral concern that marked the old prayer lines."[12]

The presence of non-Christian guests meant *Contact* often had a secular feel, especially in its musical numbers. The first person, besides Richard, Oral recruited was Ralph Carmichael to produce the show's music; Carmichael was a Grammy-nominated songwriter and composer who had written songs for Nat King Cole, Roger Williams, Bing Crosby, and Ella Fitzgerald. In a 1967 interview with ORU's student newspaper, he said his seventeen-year-old daughter's taste in music gave him a feel for the "pulse of a new generation." Music could reach its full potential only if it was made listenable to modern ears. To stifle music's creativity, he argued, was like "taking a jet aeroplane, cutting off its wings and saying, 'you stay on the freeway.' Our music needs to soar."[13] When Oral first pitched the idea for his new show to Carmichael in the fall of 1968, the composer was reportedly excited. He told people that helping with the show was a dream come true for him, and if Roberts was successful, he would be a pioneer in religious music. In the past, people had apparently scoffed at him when he talked about his desire to create a more youthful Christian music scene.[14]

For help with production, Carmichael introduced Oral to his friend Dick Ross, a Hollywood-based producer and director. Ross was well prepared to work with Oral on his vision for the new show. He had directed twenty-six hour-long variety shows for *George Jessel's Here Come the Stars*. The episodes that featured Bob Hope and Bing Crosby were nominated for Emmy Awards.[15]

Ross was better known in evangelical circles for his work with Billy Graham's film ministry, World Wide Pictures. After working with Graham for fourteen years, 1952–1966, Ross started his own production company; after that he worked with Kathryn Kuhlman on her second TV show, *I Believe in Miracles*. Debuting in 1966, *I Believe in Miracles* helped change what a Christian television show could be during its nearly ten-year and five-hundred-episode run. Ross took credit for talking Kuhlman out of televising her miracle services and adopting a talk-show format instead. Kuhlman was wise to take his advice. Her first show, *Your Faith and Mine*, filmed in the 1950s, was recorded in large auditoriums and featured Kuhlman interviewing people who had been healed. This show, however important for the development of religious television, had an impersonal feel to it. By the mid-1960s, television audiences expected more. *I Believe in Miracles* replaced the auditorium with a more intimate setting where Kuhlman interviewed her guests about their lives, oftentimes getting them to share deeply personal stories. Kuhlman's show was important, according to one of her biographers, because it helped to normalize charismatic Christianity in the United States.[16]

When preparations for the specials began in September 1968, Oral tasked the creative team—Carmichael, Ross, and son Richard—with designing a program that could be shown in prime time and "would have the look and musical sound of top-flight productions" in order to appeal to a non-Christian audience.[17] Luckily for Oral, they took his instructions seriously. At a November 1969 Laymen's Seminar, Richard said it was often hard for a nonbeliever to relate to Christian music because "most gospel music is just gospel"; he wanted to "present a program to them of their kind of music." That meant rock music but "with our kind of words, and our kind of message."[18]

The specials were at their strongest when Richard and the World Action Singers were allowed to shine. The musical medleys included not just original sacred compositions by Carmichael but secular hits as well. In the summer 1970 special, for example, they sang "Raindrops Keep Falling on My Head," "Monday, Monday," "Leaving on a Jet Plane," and "Put a Little Love in Your Heart." On that same special, singers Lou Rawls, who had just been voted the number one vocalist in the world by *Downbeat* magazine, and Jeannie C. Riley, whose single "Harper Valley PTA" sold 6 million copies and earned her a Grammy in 1969, and comedian Stu Gilliam added to the diversity of the show. Two years later, the World Action Singers belted out the John Denver hit and West Virginia University football stadium favorite "Country Roads" and James Taylor's "Fire and Rain," a song that Oral said he liked.[19] After a year of quarterly specials and complaints from "old-timers," Richard defended the music: "You can't reach young people by coming out and singing 'The Old Rugged Cross.' You've got to do something they like." Richard and other evangelicals in their late teens and early twenties were the target audience of the burgeoning Christian rock-and-roll scene. Christian rockers like Larry Norman and Randy Stonehill, along with Broadway hits like *Godspell* and *Jesus Christ Superstar*, revolutionized the use of rock music to present a biblical message.[20]

The music wasn't the only thing that needed to be updated. Oral recognized that the way he delivered his healing message needed to change as well. A weakness of his first show, Oral reflected in 1970, was that the only thing people remembered were his hands. Instead of a long healing line, Oral ended each episode of the new show with a universal prayer for healing. At the end of the first special, Oral and his guest, gospel singer Mahalia Jackson, grasped hands, placed them on a model globe, and prayed for worldwide revival and healing.[21] Oral's sermons also had broader appeal. The specials saw him talk more in depth about contemporary issues, including the Black Freedom Movement, indigenous history, sports, patriotism, war, and student unrest, than he had in the past. Part of this decision was pragmatic. A narrow focus on faith healing was a surefire way to alienate people. More importantly, though, the sermons were Roberts's opportunity to show off his new image as a sophisticated thinker, rather than simply a fire-and-brimstone Pentecostal faith healer and college dropout.

The show brought him more mainstream recognition than he had ever had before, but in the months following the first special, the amount and vitriol of hate mail were unprecedented. He admitted that he was surprised to receive so much angry mail from Christians upset that he was trying to reach young people with the gospel. Most of the angry letters lashed out at Oral for allowing dancing on the specials. Much to his regret, Oral confessed that he didn't always handle this mail in a Christian manner.[22]

The frustration wasn't just external. Like most of his projects, Oral started to grow restless. His irritation boiled down to a desire for more creative control. The presence of secular entertainers was simply a means to an end, he told ORU students in December 1972. The networks wouldn't have allowed him on prime time if the specials were too religious. Yes, he said, he had been allowed to preach, but the sermons were short—the average was about eleven minutes—and he'd "never really let out like" he wanted to. The early specials may not have been everything he wanted, but he'd rather have a "half loaf than no loaf at all."[23]

With his new television show humming along, Oral made moves to expand ORU. In April 1969, he announced a $4.5 million ($34 million in

2021 dollars), 262-room retirement village in south Tulsa. Plans to build a retirement center had been in the works for four years, but the rapid pace of construction at ORU and the decline in contributions in 1968 put the idea on hold. The housing project, called University Village, would have everything its elderly population needed from medical care, exercise facilities, and business services. Where University Village would distinguish itself was in its relationship to ORU. At the time, only one other university, Emory University in Atlanta, was attached to a retirement community, but its focus was on medical care. People who came to University Village, where monthly rates were predicted to average from $140 for a one-bedroom cottage to $505 for a four-room, two-bath apartment, would be able to take courses at ORU. They could take the classes in person or watch them on television in the comfort of their living room, via DAIRS. And the elderly residents wouldn't have to sign the university's honor code. By November 1969, eight months before it was set to open, University Village received 3,000 applications. A year later, 19,000 inquiries about the retirement complex had been sent. When it was completed, Claudius Roberts was the first person to move in. She was going in alone. Ellis had died in November 1967 at the age of eighty-six. In April 1972, University Village experienced a $450,000 ($3 million) upgrade to include sixty additional cottages.[24]

First announced in July 1970, the 10,500-seat Mabee Center would comprise studios to film the TV specials and a state-of-the-art basketball arena to host the ORU Titans men's basketball team. Originally projected to cost $5.5 million ($39.5 million) in 1970, its cost had climbed to $11 million ($73.3 million) by the time of completion in 1972. Filming Contact at the Burbank studios had been beneficial, Oral told ORU students in December 1972, but the experience had also taught him the importance of being surrounded by like-minded people. If any NBC crew members were in the audience to hear these remarks, they may have been offended. He bragged that in the beginning, most were reluctant to work with him, but now they requested months in advance to work on the quarterly specials. And Roberts bought the camera equipment from RCA at a discount. He claimed to have talked the electronics company into selling him a $130,000 camera for $72,000.[25] Moving production to ORU would also save the stress and cost of travel, which was especially important for the World Action Singers, who were full-time students as well as entertainers.

Oral and Richard hoped that moving the specials to ORU's campus, which they did after the completion of the Mabee Center in 1972, would give them a greater spiritual emphasis. Now that the specials could be seen on over four hundred stations, Oral was confident that viewers were ready for a more Holy Spirit–filled program. Richard told the ORU student newspaper that the "American public is beginning to accept us for what we are, and we're becoming bolder in our witness for Christ. America is more ready now for fewer guests and entertainment and more of the basics of what we believe."[26] Oral also hoped the Mabee Center, named after John Mabee of Tulsa, whose foundation donated $1 million for its construction, would serve as a meeting place for the city. As a sign of its openness for widespread use, smoking was allowed inside the arena. Tulsa itself recognized the benefit of the arena by allocating $1 million toward road construction. The investment was a smart one. In summer 1972, Tulsa was experiencing $97 million worth of local construction, much of it driven by ORU.[27]

In March 1971, Oral laid out plans that would make money, pay back loans, lower tuition costs, and provide employment for work-study students and future graduates. Tulsa papers described the plan as an "industrial research center," but this was a bit misleading, ORU vice president Bob Eskridge explained. More accurately, the building complex, called University Park, was going to be "multipurpose." At the time, he reported that the university was in negotiations with "financial institutions, educational services, research corporations, laboratories—enterprises of these type." One of the most exciting was a data-processing company. Tulsa had the most data processing capacity in the region, bigger than larger cities like Houston, St. Louis, Denver, and Kansas City. Many of these businesses were likely to provide part-time employment for university students. Oral hoped that the money generated by leasing the buildings would go into the university's endowment and would help lower tuition costs, which were rapidly going up in the 1970s. The investment might take fifteen to twenty years to turn a profit, but it was believed that it would be worth it.[28]

With most of his focus on expanding ORU, Oral made sure that the partners who had been the university's original students in 1962 weren't forgotten. He wanted to build a complex on campus for his annual seminars. By the early 1970s, Oral started to face a good problem. ORU had grown so quickly that there weren't adequate resources for the students and yearly visitors, whether tourists or seminar attendees. He needed to find a way to accommodate everybody. The adult education complex was going to resemble the university but at a much smaller scale. It would have two residence halls and an auditorium and dining commons. It was estimated to cost $1.4 million ($8.9 million).[29]

A third part of the March 1971 plans would be more directly suited for ORU students' spiritual life: a $2.5 million ($17.2 million), 70,000-square-foot chapel with a capacity of three thousand people. Designed by Oral's longtime architect, Frank Wallace, the chapel, like the rest of campus, would have a modern look. As visitors approached the entrance, they would see the Prayer Tower in the background. The idea was that the Prayer Tower would serve as the spire for the chapel. The chapel's hard angles were meant to look like the flying buttresses of Gothic Catholic churches.[30]

At the time, Oral's public pleas for money were subdued. The costs of his organization were real, but none of the episodic crises were likely to be catastrophic. Oral, then, didn't have to beg on TV. On the specials, Oral never made any direct appeals for money. Instead, he offered his viewers something. It was usually a book, but sometimes it was a long-playing record or a cheap knickknack like a paperweight or Prayer Tower lunch tray. By this time, Roberts was so well known that envelopes addressed simply to Oral Roberts, Tulsa, Oklahoma 74102, would arrive safely. It was only after mailing a request for the free item or more information on ORU or the ministry that appeals for money began.

The ministry's finances had mostly recovered from the decline in revenue after Oral's switch to the Methodist Church. By the end of 1969, income had doubled to $12 million ($91.1 million).[31] In November 1970, the ministry's assets were valued at $40 million ($303.8 million), and revenues were around $20 million ($151.9 million). The ministry had about $7 million ($53 million) in debt, most of which was in long-term, low-interest loans.[32] The mostly healthy finances, however, didn't mean Oral had the money to begin construction on new projects. He would have to start fund-raising again.

Wayne Robinson credited himself with eliminating any mention of the Blessing Pact when he took over as editor in chief of all ORU and OREA productions in August 1967. Much to his frustration, Oral returned to the Blessing Pact in 1969. Gene Ewing, a onetime traveling evangelist who made a career out of helping evangelists get out of financial binds, was responsible for pushing Roberts to bring back this fund-raising scheme. Oral and Ewing's working relationship began when Oral needed to sell his ministry's plane during the financial crunch of the late 1960s. According to Robinson, Ewing and his team, whom he portrayed as uneducated bumpkins, fell in love with the plane when they first saw it, so someone proposed selling it to them. Instead of selling it, Roberts exchanged it for Ewing's advice for raising funds.

At a January 1969 meeting, Ewing told Oral that earlier missteps had led longtime supporters to abandon him. These mistakes included opening a university, becoming a Methodist, and ending the crusades and television program. Ewing suggested that Oral return to the basics of mail and prayer. He said that he should drop all talk of ORU and the Methodist Church because people on his mailing list didn't care about these things. He needed to tell them that he wanted to pray for them and that he could help them as long as they wrote to him.

Ewing laid out a fairly simple plan. First, Oral needed to spend three days alone in the Prayer Tower, with no visitors, not even family. His meals would be brought to him and dropped off at the door. Second, he should write a letter telling his supporters that he was locked up in the Prayer Tower praying for them. Finally, he needed to tell his supporters that he was taking their letters into the Tower with him so he could pray over them. There were no requests for money. Ewing also suggested a catchy saying: "Something good is going to happen to you."

After hearing this plan, reading the proposed letter, and reviewing the upcoming issue of *Abundant Life*, Robinson took his concerns to Oral. In the meeting, Robinson grew increasingly frustrated as his boss sided with Ewing. Once he had heard enough, Robinson said, "Oral, if you want to be editor, then you do it, but my name's not going out on that kind of crap." He then threw all the papers in the air, stormed out, and slammed the door behind him. Robinson's name didn't appear in the March 1969 issue of *Abundant Life*.[33] He left the Roberts ministry to work for the Oklahoma Conference of the Methodist Church but returned in 1971 as vice president for public affairs, only to leave again a year later after a spat with Richard over the TV show. He never returned.[34]

The June 1969 issue of *Abundant Life* was dedicated to the Blessing Pact. The next month's issue featured a story about Oral spending time alone with letters in the Prayer Tower. Looking over the range of human problems—depression, cancer, addiction, family strife, and trauma—he concluded that persons suffering such maladies shared something in common: "They had not thought of the necessity of entering into a Blessing Pact covenant with Him as a continuing spiritual relationship with God for their needs to be met."[35] The Blessing Pact soon became a regular feature in Roberts's publications. Nearly every issue of *Abundant Life* had articles about how the Blessing Pact worked and testimonies from people who had experienced God's returns. While these blessings weren't always financial, material blessings were the most frequent.

In 1970, with the publication of *Miracle of Seed Faith*, which quickly exceeded 1 million copies in circulation, Oral entered into an era of breathtaking and aggressive fund-raising. With "seed faith"—Oral used the terms "Blessing Pact" and "seed faith" interchangeably—he stumbled upon innovative and ultimately self-destructive language to raise money. The most controversial aspect of seed faith was its main thrust that there was a direct causal relationship between the amount of money one gave to Christian evangelism and personal income. The formula was straightforward: the more one gave, the wealthier one could expect to be. The less one gave, the poorer one could expect to be.[36]

The Bible was clear that "everything starts with a seed." In Genesis 8:22, God talked about "seedtime and harvest." The apostle Paul, in Galatians 6:7, warned, "A man reaps what he sows." In Matthew 17:20, Jesus said, "Truly I tell you, if you have faith as small as a mustard seed, you can say to this mountain, 'Move from here to there,' and it will move. Nothing will be impossible for you" (NIV). A seed didn't have to be money. It could be a "seed-smile," "seed-time," "seed-love," or "seed-compassion." Jesus himself was the seed that God planted so that humanity could have everlasting life.[37]

Though a seed could be just about anything, there were three key principles of seed faith. Citing Philippians 4:19, "My God shall supply all your need according to his riches in glory by Jesus Christ" (KJV), Roberts explained that the first key principle of seed faith was to trust God as one's "source." The idea that God provided for people's needs would have been uncontroversial for most Christians. Oral made this verse controversial by making it about prosperity, not just basic needs. God promised to supply needs out of *his* riches, which were boundless. If believers turned to God, rather than humanity, for their needs, they could expect great riches. The second key was that giving was central to receiving God's abundance. In Luke 6:38, Jesus said, "Give, and it shall be given to you; good measure, pressed down, and shaken together, and running over, shall men give into your bosom. For with the same measure that ye mete withal it shall be measured to you again" (KJV). The third key principle was "expect a miracle." This final principle may have been his most innovative. Christians had always been taught to give but had never been taught to expect something in return. The return may not be immediate, but it would eventually come.[38]

Oral didn't create the idea of a relationship between wealth and salvation. Everyone from Puritan divines to Gilded Age robber barons talked about riches from heaven. After World War II, the belief that God materially blessed the faithful found its fullest expression in the prosperity gospel. Prosperity had been a part of the healing revival since its beginning in the late 1940s, but it was a minor theme. It didn't become a full-fledged movement until the mid-1970s. Its leaders, people like Jim and Tammy Faye Bakker, Frederick Price, Kenneth Copeland, Charles and Frances Hunter, and Jan and Paul Crouch, according to historian Kate Bowler, "proclaimed a palpable gospel, one that could be clearly seen and measured in the financial well-being of its participants."[39]

Oral's financial crisis in 1968 and the volatility of the American economy showed that these blessings came and went. Seed faith, then, wasn't just a fund-raising ploy. It gave a name to some of the anxieties surrounding wealth in the post–World War II United States. Television shows, Hollywood movies, advertisements, fully stocked supermarkets, suburban homes, and automobiles all touted the promises of capitalism. The hard truth, though, was that the United States was still deeply unequal. Popular exposés like Edward R. Murrow's television documentary *Harvest of Shame* (1960) and Michael Harrington's *The Other America* (1962) showed that the material benefits of the economic boom were limited to white suburbanites and that fixing this problem would require a massive overhaul of the status quo at nearly every level of society and politics. The American economy looked especially bleak in the 1970s. With stagflation—a deadly combination of inflation and stagnated wages—unemployment, rising energy costs, and deindustrialization, the "golden age of capitalism" seemed to be coming to an end.[40]

Oral's belief in the objective weights and measures of seed faith was meant to be positive. He reportedly had little patience for people whom he deemed overly negative. Being too pessimistic in his presence was a firable offense. At the same time, seed faith could often—and would increasingly—sound sinister and cynical. In the midst of the Great Stagflation of the 1970s, Oral refused to accept the economic downturn as an excuse for Christians to not prosper. The American economy might be susceptible to the ups and downs of the marketplace, but God's prosperity was immune from the same ups and downs. In the March 1974 issue of *Abundant Life*, he confronted Christians' concerns with the state of the American economy head-on. He explained that he had grown tired of answering endless questions about the energy crisis, the oil embargo, and the looming economic depression. Christians, he scolded, should not allow periodic economic downturns to control their thoughts. If they truly trusted God, they had no reason to worry and would continue to prosper in spite of adverse economic conditions. He felt sorry for people "who get up and down about conditions and think these conditions are going to affect them very drastically." "Conditions," he added, "are only going to affect you if you let them. But if you let God affect your life, He's going to take care of you. God is bigger than the whole thing—all the shortages and problems in the nation and the world—put together!" Christians who practiced seed faith were especially immune from economic cycles because they demonstrated that they were not dependent on the fickle marketplace.[41]

Evelyn added her voice to Christians' relationship with economic turmoil. Writing from the point of view of a housewife, she said she was shocked that the price of something as simple as bacon had increased. One day, after returning from the grocery store, Evelyn wrote, she told her husband that food prices were becoming prohibitive even to just feed the two of them, so she could not imagine the burden put upon women who had children to feed. Oral rebuked her negativity, telling her that he did not want to hear such doom and gloom language in their home and that the "source" had not changed, just the circumstances.[42]

In his public statements, Oral was measured when it came to raising money. In more intimate settings like partner seminars and even ORU chapel services, he started to sound like a hardened salesman. When raising money for prime-time slots, Oral used a selling tactic he had almost certainly picked up from his friends in banking and sales. He told an audience at a June 1969 World Action Conference to write two numbers on a piece of paper. He wanted them to write 10 and $7,500. That $7,500 was the mechanical cost per hour for NBC studios to make an hour-long special for Christmas that year. He then asked them to write 4 and $5,000. That $5,000 was the cost of airing the prime-time special on the four largest networks. He asked them to write down the number of stations and the price of each station. This was likely a wise tactic. Rather than just hearing the costs, the audience was forced to look at them too.[43]

Seed faith and Oral's increasing use of its metaphors to raise money naturally raised questions regarding his personal wealth. In interviews, the one topic he refused to discuss was money. Wayne Robinson told of an incident on a Canadian news program, *Face the Newsmen*, in 1968. When one of the panelists asked Oral how much he made, he responded, "Not nearly as much as you think." The moderator kept pressing. Did he make $100,000? $50,000? $25,000? $20,000? Oral answered no to all these figures. His salary at the time was $19,000 ($140,000 in 2021 dollars).

Oral soon turned the tables, asking the newsman how much he made. The newsman, clearly embarrassed, apparently answered $6,000 ($44,000). After this revelation, Oral told the moderator that he was finished discussing money.[44]

Starting in 1962, ORU was Oral's only source of income. That year, he and Evelyn divested themselves of all their personal income and created a trust fund for their children out of his book royalties. His salary steadily grew to $25,000 ($154,000) by 1972. One journalist reported, "No longer a millionaire, he merely lives like one."[45] Out of all the things said about Oral's finances, this statement was perhaps the most accurate. Oral and his supporters were right that he earned a modest income when compared to other celebrity figures, but over the years he had developed expensive tastes. He wore tailor-made suits; drove Mercedes and Cadillacs; had a membership at the exclusive Southern Hills Country Club in Tulsa, which one former insider claimed had an $18,000 membership fee along with $130 in monthly dues; and lived in numerous homes, including one in Palm Springs and another in Beverly Hills. It's fair to say, as Oral frequently did, that few of his active partners cared about how much money he made.[46]

When ORU opened in 1965, Oral set the ambitious goal of receiving national accreditation by 1974. Accreditation moved rather quickly. In January 1967, the Oklahoma State Regents for Higher Education granted ORU provisional accreditation at the state level, which meant that ORU credits carried the same weight as credits earned at other institutions in the state. Three years later, the state board of regents granted permanent accreditation. On March 31, 1971, ORU won the crown jewel. The North Central Association of Colleges and Secondary Schools granted the university full accreditation. The approval was good for ten years, at which point ORU would need to be reexamined. Oral was deservedly excited. Perhaps most thrilling for him was what it meant for ORU athletics. The academic recognition was certainly nice, but it also meant the university could apply for entry in the National Collegiate Athletic Association (NCAA). Roberts could finally achieve his next dream: a basketball national title.

8

Titan

ONE OF ORAL'S MOST ENDEARING TRAITS, according to Patti Roberts, was
his playfulness.[1] This childlike excitement is on full display on the summer
1970 *Contact* special. The guests included Jeannie C. Riley; comedian Stu
Gilliam; and Oklahoma University Heisman Trophy–winner Steve Owens,
but the most exciting guest was UCLA legend John Wooden, who had already won six national championships and been voted coach of the year
five times. Oral spends part of the interview recounting that year's national
championship game between UCLA and Jacksonville University. The two
then talk about how their faith shaped their relationships with young people. "My belief in them," Wooden said, "is part of my belief in Christ himself." The conversation quickly returns to basketball. Oral bragged that
even though ORU was relatively young, the basketball team, the Titans,
had been quite successful. Next, he challenged Wooden's powerful squad
to a game, but Coach Wooden had a better idea, "Maybe we could play for
a national championship." A beaming Roberts exclaimed, "That would
be better."[2]

Few things brought Oral more national recognition than ORU's men's
basketball team, the Titans. In the early 1970s, several positive articles
noted that the squad was part of Oral's new, more sophisticated image.
In November 1970, *Sports Illustrated* celebrated ORU as a "cross between
the Houston Space Center and a Bible Belt Xanadu" whose "hard-driving
small-college basketball team" was on its way to major competition. Jeff
Prugh, writing for the *Los Angeles Times*, noted that when the ORU team
first began making national headlines, people had to ask, "What's an Oral
Roberts?" That "question is rarely asked nowadays," Prugh explained.
Roberts's ministry brought him fame, Edward Fiske wrote for the *New York
Times*, but it was limited to Pentecostal circles, and he was often mistakenly
associated with Tulsa's other conservative son, Billy James Hargis. "Now

all this has changed," Fiske said. "Roberts has, as it were, gone straight—and made it in the big time." A writer for *Christianity Today* suggested that other evangelical colleges should follow ORU's example by investing in big-time sports programs.[3]

Besides the obvious talent, the Titan squad was notable for its friendliness and racial diversity. At a time when players and fans were sometimes violently hostile toward referees and opponents, yelling expletives or throwing dangerous objects like liquor bottles and ball bearings onto the court, the ORU players and student section didn't argue with bad calls and even cheered for opponents. One visiting coach said that the ORU crowd was so friendly that his players may have been fooled into thinking they had won the game. Prugh said ORU's friendly confines was a "miracle in itself these days, when college basketball is tormented by hate-laced rivalries, flying fists and unprintable banners."[4] *Sports Illustrated* noted that Tulsa had a "touch of Dixie"—a 1974 study discovered that Tulsa was one of the most segregated cities in the United States—so it was surprising that four of the five starters were Black. "We're treated with a Christian attitude," Haywood Hill, one of the Black players, told the magazine. Hill said elsewhere that even though race relations at ORU were good, it was awkward when white students called him "brother." Black players also complained about the excessive "evangelistic zeal of some students."[5]

Few things would have been more satisfying to Oral than this positive press, not only because it boosted his ego, but also because it communicated the raison d'être of the basketball team. In 1972, he confidently told the *Los Angeles Times* that his goal was to win a national championship by 1975. "When you have a modern campus and a strong athletic program that is Christ-oriented, you have a strong voice in the country. What we try to do is put Christ in 'the Now.' We may never achieve our goals 100%, but we're striving," he explained to the newspaper.[6] When talking about the Titans' star Richard Fuqua in 1972, Oral described the 6'3" guard as a "natural leader of the highest Christian standards, a churchgoing young man and a gentleman of the finest order. He also is the purest shooter I've ever seen."[7] Basketball, he told the *Los Angeles Times* three years later, was the "perfect pulpit" because it matched his ministry's "idealism." "'We don't say,' he further explained, 'Go ye unto all the world and preach the gospel,' but we say, '*Go ye unto every man's world.*'" And with 40 million men reading the sports page every day, "basketball is certainly one way to get our message across to them." He told *Sports Illustrated*, "Our black students are a part of us. They are not an adjunct. We are all treated as human beings."[8]

While Oral was never as interested in electoral politics as some of his contemporaries, he still believed it was his obligation to help save the United States. ORU as a whole, along with the basketball team, were Oral's key contributions to the nascent culture wars. The problem with the country, he told the *Los Angeles Times* in 1972, was "permissiveness." The night before the Titans beat Louisville in the 1974 NCAA tournament, Oral, talking courtside, said, "This country is losing discipline in government, in politics, in our family lives. Athletics is the last arena where discipline reigns. I want discipline in my school, not permissiveness. If we lose the discipline of athletics, I see chaos in the country."[9] Like the World Action Singers, the ORU Titans, with their wholesome look, behavior, and winning ways, were proof that not all young people were drug-addled hippies or militant Black radicals and that a cleaner, more racially equitable society was possible with the right behavior and mind-set. Indeed, as Oral once said, young people liked rules "even though they don't say it."[10]

THE TITANS, WHOSE FIRST SEASON ENDED WITH AN 18–10 RECORD, created their first national buzz in April 1967 when 6'10" Dana Lewis signed a letter of intent. Lewis, an all-American center from New Jersey, was one of the most-recruited athletes in the country, reportedly receiving offers from nearly three hundred universities. Sportswriters hailed Lewis as the next Wilt Chamberlain or Lewis Alcindor (later Kareem Abdul-Jabbar). College basketball experts were shocked when Lewis signed with ORU. One anonymous scout said that a California university saw "quite a few bills go down the drain in their bid to recruit 6-foot-10 Dana Lewis of Newark." He continued to explain that this was "trans-continental recruiting: California to New Jersey. And what do they have to show for it with Lewis having decided to enroll at Oral Roberts University in Tulsa?"[11] On why Lewis chose ORU over more established programs, including the University of Southern California and Kentucky, ORU head coach Bill White said, "He's not out for individual glory."[12]

His mother, though, was the most important influence. Lewis later told the *Washington Post* that as a child he attended one of Roberts's rallies and that the first person ORU flew out for a visit was his mother. Then they flew him out for a visit. Though Lewis played reasonably well at ORU, he was unhappy. It is likely that, in addition to wooing his mother, Oral may have made some promises of his own. At the time he signed with ORU, Lewis recounts Oral saying, "It was going big time right then and that I'd have a big name." But after arriving to Tulsa, Lewis believed Oral had lied to him. The university was still several years away from having the type of dominant program Roberts promised. Lewis initially wanted to transfer to Southern California, but neither the "scout, [n]or businessman" who was supposed to get in touch with him ever did.

To keep the young star at ORU, one of the school's vice presidents called Lewis's mother. Lewis told a reporter that the administrator told her that "he'd just talked with the Lord and that He'd said it was His will that [Lewis] stay at Oral Roberts." He then decided to transfer to the University of Tulsa, but because Oral refused to release him from his scholarship, Lewis had to pay his own way the first year. The evangelist still wouldn't give up. That season, Tulsa made it to the National Invitation Tournament (NIT), but due to NCAA regulations, Lewis couldn't travel with the team, so he stayed behind. Oral called Lewis and told him he wanted him to have lunch with some businessmen and that his "room was back there anytime" he wanted it. Oral eventually gave a handwritten note to Tulsa coach Ken Hayes releasing Lewis from his obligations. Lewis said that Oral had the resources to reach big-time status, but that he needed to stay "nearer the pulpit and away from the gym."[13]

Lewis's exit was certainly disappointing, but it wasn't all bad. If nothing else, his signing demonstrated that ORU could recruit top-tier talent. The university's ability to recruit got a major boost when it lured head coach Ken Trickey from the Middle Tennessee State University (MTSU) Blue Raiders. Oral first became aware of Trickey in December 1968 when the Blue Raiders beat the Titans by fifteen points, the team's worst defeat, and only its third home loss, up to that point. Roberts remembered that during the second half he "just sort of cried inside" and said to himself, "Well, this is the kind of man I want."[14] Trickey, a thirty-five-year-old alumnus of MTSU, where he once held several records for scoring and passing, was known for his innovative, fast-moving offense, which he dubbed WRAG ("We Run and Gun"). He was also known for his attempts to modernize the game, including signing MTSU's first Black scholarship athlete and purchasing a camera that produced instant videotape so players could get immediate feedback from their play. When a Murfreesboro, Tennessee, paper announced Trickey's move to ORU as head basketball coach and head of its athletic department, it celebrated his four-year tenure at hometown MTSU for bringing the "Blue Raiders from a lowly basketball ebb, to one of the area's most respected basketball programs." MTSU's president noted that Trickey had "breathed life into the MTSU basketball program," that Trickey's recruiting ability and knack for "showmanship" had drawn record crowds to home games, and that the student body "supported Trickey's teams consistently with tremendous enthusiasm."[15]

When Trickey arrived in Tulsa in spring 1969, Oral gave him what must have seemed like an impossible task, to win a national championship by 1975. However herculean, Trickey quickly appeared that he might be able to pull it off. That year's recruiting class was considered the best yet. Three of its players, junior transfers Milton Vaughn and Haywood Hill and freshman Richard Fuqua, had been all-Americans. *Sports Illustrated* described Fuqua as an "All-Everything."[16]

The Titans continued their winning ways under Trickey. They posted a 27–4 record in the 1970–1971 season, and a 21–5 record the following season. Despite this success, the team's visibility and options were limited. This changed when ORU gained accreditation. Besides the obvious academic benefits, the university could now apply for membership in the NCAA, which would allow its athletic teams to participate in national tournaments and schedule major college competition. Trickey believed, probably correctly, that even though the Titan squad was good, ORU's unaccredited status had kept away larger programs.[17]

The team didn't disappoint in its first year of major college play. It went 25–1, made the top twenty in national polls, and led the nation in scoring with an average of 106.6 points per game. Fuqua, dubbed the "Mad Bomber," was the second-highest scorer in the nation, and the team played at the NIT at Madison Square Garden, where it made it to the quarterfinals. The following season, ORU opened the 10,500-seat, $11 million Mabee Center. The squad reached its peak in the 1973–1974 season when it played in the NCAA tournament, upsetting Louisville in the second round before losing in overtime to Kansas in the quarterfinals.[18]

The loss to Kansas marked the end of Trickey's career at ORU. As early as February, newspapers had reported that Trickey was planning on leaving at the end of the season, but his departure was sped up the night his team beat Louisville when he was arrested on suspicion of drunk driving. Though he denied that he was intoxicated—one friend commented that Trickey could nurse a single beer filled with ice for hours—Trickey knew that by drinking alcohol he had violated the university's honor code, so he turned in his resignation. Oral accepted it but allowed Trickey to coach the team in its loss to Kansas.[19]

The Titans' rapid rise raised some suspicions that they were an "outlaw school," with some people finding it hard to believe that a Pentecostal university in Tulsa could field high-caliber teams in just a few short years. Publicly, Trickey never admitted to any recruiting violations, but in private he apparently admitted that he had "sent kids home for Christmas, helped them buy their cars, and got them coats in the winter." Dwayne Roe, one of Trickey's assistant coaches, expressed skepticism that any of the players, most of whom were Black, would ever graduate, and said his main job wasn't to coach but "to teach those kids how to use a bar of Dial soap and a tube of Ipana toothpaste. I'm the guy who has to get them to turn down their goddamn stereos at three A. M. so my family can get some sleep. Then I have to drag their asses out of bed at eight so they'll go to class."[20]

Any serious inquiry into ORU's recruiting tactics started at the top with President Roberts, who never shied away from using his name to draw top talent. One of the more embarrassing recruiting attempts came in 1974 when Roberts reportedly tried to sign Moses Malone by promising to pray for the young star's mother's ulcer.[21] Negative stories continued to plague the university throughout the 1970s. In 1977, Jimmy "The Greek" Snyder said the NCAA was investigating ORU for "proselytizing." Although Snyder said he wasn't joking, ORU officials, who initially thought he was poking fun at Roberts, were put in the uncomfortable position of saying there was no investigation. At least for the moment. Speaking by phone from the Bahamas, Snyder told reporters that complaints "have been or will be" made against the school's athletic program.[22] Two years later, the university received more negative attention after Jerry Sholes, a former OREA employee, published his supposed tell-all book, *Give Me That Prime-Time Religion*, in which he claimed that one reason the university built a separate athletics dormitory in 1974 was to hide the athletes' "Christian shortcomings," that coaches were pressured to recruit more white players to offset the number of Black players on the team, and that the school had offered University of Arkansas basketball coach Eddie Sutton a multimillion dollar contract to move to Tulsa. Sholes's revelations were serious enough that the NCAA launched an investigation into ORU's recruiting tactics.[23]

ROBERTS WASN'T THE ONLY CAMPUS LEADER TO BELIEVE there was a direct relationship between athletics and proper order. Readers of *Sports Illustrated* may have been shocked to read the stories in John Underwood's 1969 "desperate coach" series. One story was about F. Melvin Cratsley, who was fired after seventeen successful years at Carnegie Tech in Pittsburgh before moving to Point Park College, also in Pittsburgh, where he was fired before his third season even started. He was told that he was too "inflexible" and that he "didn't listen to the players." Cratsley said he was fired for being "disciplined": "I wanted my players to wear blazers, get haircuts, wear a tie, take a bath once in a while, be on time. They didn't want to do these things. I object to players telling me they want beards, long hair and all the rest, because the next thing they want to do is run the team. More important than the beard is what it represents—rebellion. If you can't tell them what to do, they don't need a coach." And in case there was any doubt about who was to blame, the former coach said, "It probably started as a black problem, but today it's not race. It's kids of all types." Underwood also took the opportunity to blame Black players for the problems. Black athletes "read race into almost everything a coach says or does," the journalist wrote.[24] Even John Wooden had trouble controlling his players. In May 1972, Bill Walton was arrested at an anti-Vietnam rally where, while being loaded into a paddy wagon, he yelled, "Fuck you, Chuck," to UCLA's chancellor, Charles Young. When asked how he would deal with Walton, all Wooden said was, "That's not in my bailiwick. It's out of season and a student's conduct is out of my hand." Walton was placed on probation, but the school didn't suspend him from classes or the basketball team.[25]

While Wooden may have allowed his star athletes a little wiggle room, ORU apparently didn't. Oral said he had no interest in a player who couldn't meet the university's strict standards because "he might be playing somewhere one night and do something that will destroy my effectiveness as a creature of the gospel of Jesus Christ."[26] In December 1971, when the team got its first real national exposure in a game against Hofstra at Madison Square Garden, Roberts told the *New York Times* that it was true he was seeking a national championship, "but it must be done without violating any rules. Our Lord must be lifted up." The players, he added, were expected to abide by the same rules as other students on campus. That meant no smoking, drinking, swearing, or dancing on campus, and they "must wear shirts and ties to classes."[27] After the team beat Hofstra, Oral remarked that it "was a victory for God, not basketball."[28] Coach Trickey said he had to change his behavior. Instead of yelling at referees for a bad call, something he did in the past, he learned to "quiet down." The players were also expected to show respect toward the officials: "When we get a bad call," the coach said, "the players smile and raise their hands. They've got to represent the university, and a lot of people look at us all around the country."[29]

Sportswriters at the time expressed surprise that ORU was able to recruit top-ranked talent to a school that put so many demands on their behavior. When Oral said that one of the basketball team's top players, David Vaughn, went to ORU "specifically for this way of life," one sports journalist quipped, "To me, statements like these seem slightly incredulous considering the general attitude of today's youth, and in light of the incredible success Oral Roberts' team has enjoyed on the basketball floor the last two years."[30] Trickey seemed to have had a little more realistic view of players' decisions to go to ORU. "Most of the time," he said, "the parents have a say, and, if they do, ORU usually has an advantage."[31] Some ORU players, at least according to their public statements, were fine with the rules. Six foot eight forward Greg McDougal said that the restrictions were "not so bad. All these dudes here are just like anyone else—no angels, no religious freaks. They just came to play basketball and maybe get an education, but you know what? They learn about themselves and about God, things that help them grow into good men." He may not have been particularly religious himself, but "this place works on your attitude."[32]

The behavior of the ORU players had apparently rubbed off on the rest of campus. The athletes had set such a good example that Oral claimed that he basically "licked campus problems."[33] In a 1974 fund-raising brochure for a new athletics dormitory, Oral wrote that the $750,000 ($4.2 million in 2021 dollars) building was a worthy investment because "Discipline through athletics at ORU helps all the students."[34]

Oral's passion for the basketball team meant he had little patience for people who questioned its utility. At an August 1971 faculty meeting about the honor code, Roberts reminded the faculty that it was the World Action Singers and the basketball team that made ORU a national news story, not the English or Sociology Departments. He also scolded them for how they graded members of the singing group and athletic squads, accusing them of narrowly focusing on the accumulation of knowledge rather than the "whole person." Faculty needed to get excited if the university recruited a superior athlete and go out of their way to make sure the student succeeded in their classroom. This wasn't a small matter. Not only did their unrealistic expectations jeopardize the team's ability to win, but the professors' salvation was also at risk. How, he asked, would they stand before God if they didn't help every student succeed? To be sure, he wasn't asking them to cheat, but he wanted them to think about the pressure student-athletes faced: "How would you like to give your final examination before 3,000 people?"

Part of the professors' problem, Oral continued, was that they didn't consider individual students' backgrounds when issuing grades. To make his point, he brought up the experience of ORU's Black students, many of whom, due to years of discrimination, had gone to inferior schools. He had one athlete in mind, whose vocabulary consisted of "less than 200 words." This student had been raised by a single mother, had over ten siblings, and was the first person in his family to graduate from high school and attend college. "No black family," Oral said, "had been lower economically than his family." Oral also wanted the highly educated and mostly white faculty to consider the experience of many of ORU's white students, whose skin color and relative wealth meant they came to ORU prepared for the demands of college. In case anyone accused him of caring only about athletics, he said they "could never be more wrong." He went on, "I am concerned about the minority people in this country. The Bible says the strong should support the weak."[35]

Though far from a radical crusader, Oral became more vocal about racism in the 1960s. By this time, his earlier noncommitment to civil rights became increasingly untenable as images of state-sponsored violence, the Black Freedom Movement's moral clarity, the passage of the Civil Rights Act of 1964 and Voting Rights Act of 1965, and his interactions with Black students forced him to take a position. Some scholars point to these same years as the beginning of the new Religious Right, emphasizing its origins in the battles over school integration rather than abortion or sexuality. In the twenty years since the Supreme Court ruled that racially segregated schools were unconstitutional, conservative Protestants had tried to find ways around the law by founding so-called segregation academies. In 1954, there were 123 non-Catholic private schools. Sixteen years later, there were 20,000. A 1976 study, aptly titled *The Schools That Fear Built*, concluded that "Christian schools and segregation academies were 'indistinguishable.'"[36] Reflecting the growing division in American society at large, white evangelicals began choosing sides.

Some evangelicals adopted what one scholar has described as a "theology of racial colorblindness." Now that open white supremacy was becoming taboo, many white evangelicals "emphasized the spiritual unity of all true believers in Jesus Christ, the power of the gospel to solve racial problems, and the importance of interpersonal relationships to heal the wounds of racism." Any person—white or Black—who centered race was both unfaithful to the gospel and divisive. This theology, no matter how sincerely held, tended to uphold white supremacy because its individualistic message failed to challenge structural problems and, despite its "colorblind" label, because of its bent toward centering the white experience as the norm.[37]

Oral often echoed the colorblind theology. On the first *Contact* special in March 1969, speaking about the "untamed violence in men," he told a story about an encounter he had with a "Black militant pastor" in Harlem. This preacher, who was radicalized while in prison and had done "outstanding work for Christ," gave a sermon that Roberts praised for addressing the suffering Black people had endured at the hands of whites. And though the Harlem pastor knew that Oral disagreed with his militancy, he was still able to hug him and call him "brother." The reason that he and the militant preacher were able to embrace was, Oral told the integrated audience, because "Christ is colorblind. . . . He just loves people."[38]

There was one other thing that Oral promoted as the great equalizer: seed faith. Though the university administration and board of regents remained mostly white, Oral began to promote Black alumni to important positions. Clifton ("Cliff") Taulbert, a US Air Force veteran and ORU graduate, who had been denied housing because of his race, was named administrator of University Village, the university's retirement home. He and his mother appeared on television with Oral in 1974. She may have had a high school degree and some college, but she was still limited to work as a domestic servant "earning $12.00 a week which had to feed, clothe, and school my six children," Mary Taulbert told Oral during a segment that, unfortunately, wasn't aired due to time limits. "Suppression, hopelessness, and despair was a way of life," she recalled. She had never been taught to believe that God cared for her daily needs until she saw Roberts on television. His sermon "kindled a spark" in her soul, she said. "It gave me hope that leaped over the barriers of suppression, hopelessness, and despair." She began to see herself "as a person that God loved, and that He really cared about our everyday needs." She planted a seed that night. Her life immediately changed. She found work as a far more respectable "educational supervisor with the preschool program in the state of Mississippi," was spared heart surgery after a serious car accident, and moved out of their rickety shack that swayed in the wind into a brick house, which she was able to buy through a bank loan. Oral responded, "Bankers are nice people, Cliff." "They are," Cliff said back, "especially when the Lord goes before you." Oral and Mary also talked about Philippians 4:19, "But my God shall supply all your need according to his riches in glory by Christ Jesus" (KJV). They both agreed that the verse, in Oral's words, showed that "His economy, not our economy, regardless of circumstances, will meet our needs."[39]

There were also times when seed faith was necessary as an antidote to a sense of entitlement. During a February 1971 chapel observing Black

Heritage Week at ORU, Oral related a story about some Black Tulsa businessmen whose attempts to open a savings and loan were stalled by the "white business structure," whose cooperation was essential. When the leader of the Black interests went to New York for help, the New York bankers turned him away and said Oral was "the one man in Tulsa" who could help them. The problem they faced was collecting enough deposits to qualify for federal insurance. Oral agreed to help. He gave them some ideas, explained some deposits the university's endowment could make, and agreed to have his picture taken and published in the *Oklahoma Eagle*, Tulsa's Black newspaper, "and let people know how we felt about it and what we were personally doing."

This help, though, "was only a drop in the bucket." Oral then asked the men if he could speak freely even if it meant they would be offended. They agreed. "There's no way you can win with your present attitude," he told them. When they asked what he meant, he said, "All this evening you've been telling me what the white men owes you and every word of it is true." They still weren't convinced. "Well then why isn't it right, if they owe it," they asked Roberts. "Look what we have been for 300 years, we've been forced to do this and forced to do that." Instead of worrying about what they were owed, they needed to start focusing on giving. When they pushed back that they had been giving for hundreds of years, Oral responded, "No, you haven't given. It's been taken from you. You hated every moment of it and the people who did it hated you. It's been hate on both sides. And God can never do anything for anybody through hate and bitterness." Rather than being preoccupied with what they thought they were owed or looking to the government for help, he told the gathered businessmen, they needed to turn to God as their source. They were apparently convinced. The leader of the group, according to Oral's account, turned to the other Black Tulsans and said, "Brothers, we've got to change. It's true what's been done to us, but the question is, what are we doing? What are we doing back? Are we loving and are we giving?"[40]

Oral's colorblind theology led to some other potentially uncomfortable situations. On September 13, 1972, just months after an assassin's bullets left him paraplegic, Alabama governor George Wallace phoned in to the ORU campus to speak to the chapel audience. Just a few days earlier, Oral met Wallace at the governor's mansion where he said "the air was fraught with the gloom and with the suffering" of a man who was nearly shot to death and that it was obvious to him that the racist governor was a changed man. Once the governor was introduced, Oral asked four students from Alabama—two white and two Black—to pray for healing.[41]

Oral was sometimes sympathetic to civil rights radicals. He expressed dismay that most American clergy weren't as brave as "the militants and the students on campus" who were willing to die for their beliefs.[42] Elsewhere, he said, "The black man must be treated as a human being before he's treated as an athlete." And if a Black person is not treated fairly, "he's justified in his rebellion."[43] At other times, he acknowledged that white people were the biggest hindrance to racial progress. In an early 1968 issue of *Abundant Life*, whose circulation was well over one million, he told readers, "Our ancestors brought the Negro from Africa against his will. They made him a piece of property and denied him the meaning of his existence. They built separate schools and made him live apart." And now that "we have been ordered to grant him first-class citizenship," white people "are resisting accepting him as an equal."[44]

Far more interesting were the discussions happening on ORU's campus. From its founding, Oral wanted ORU to be multiracial. Right before the university opened, a federal regulator called Roberts to ask about their admittance policy. Would they admit Black students? Due to a provision in the 1964 Civil Rights Act that prohibited segregation in private schools that accepted federal funds, ORU would have to be integrated. Oral told the person that the federal government could keep its money for all he cared, because with or without the money, his namesake was going to be multiracial.[45]

Black students at ORU were open with their hopes for the university and their frustration with it. At times, these students fairly pointed out, it seemed to be a university at cross-purposes with its purported racial openness. In a 1968 straw poll involving a little over 50 percent of the student body, 76.7 percent of ORU students supported Richard Nixon. George Wallace was a distant second. Four years later, 81.3 percent of ORU students supported Nixon in his reelection campaign.[46] One of the vocal Black students, Henry Smith, wrote a scathing commentary for the student newspaper, the *Oracle*, in December 1970. When Black students came to ORU, they knew that because most of its students were white, it would be "white oriented." What they didn't expect was how pervasive this whiteness would be. The chapel and vesper services were white, making the spiritual atmosphere "irrelevant to the blacks," Smith wrote. It was true that ORU had invited talented Black singers like Lou Rawls to campus and had promoted talented Black students, but Blacks had more to offer than entertainment for whites. Smith wanted to know why ORU had never invited prominent Black intellectuals. He also appealed to ORU's foundation in the "whole man." The undergraduate curriculum needed to start offering "courses that will provide a liberal education identifiable with all students." Smith hoped that ORU could move beyond "token integration" to a place where Black students were integrated into the "social, spiritual, and academic life that relates to them."[47]

During a Black Awareness Week chapel in February 1972, a transfer student named Joyce said there was probably less prejudice at ORU compared to other universities but felt that "as Christian young people we've really got to fight hard." She had heard that the university was looking to hire two new sociology professors and hoped that at least one of them would be Black. "We need a lot more black things that we don't have," she told the largely white student body, and expressed hope that that week's activities would draw them "closer together as a student body." The next student, Mack Holland, spoke in Black Power idioms, pointed out the irony of a supposed Christian nation enslaving its own people, and said that a time was coming when "white religious liberals and middle class blacks sitting in churches discussing the racial issues" would have to make a choice between the radical demands of Black theology and their staid ways.[48]

The university seemed to have listened to some of the Black students' demands because, throughout the 1970s, more and more Black voices were heard. On September 27, 1972, ORU held a "Charles Evers Day." Evers was the older brother of slain civil rights leader Medgar Evers and had at one time made money in drugs and prostitution and had then become a violent Black radical after his brother's assassination, and, at the time of his visit to ORU, was mayor of Fayette, Mississippi. At his chapel talk, he spoke out against the evils of racism and told the ORU students that they should be proud to be affiliated with a university that believed in actively promoting racial equality rather than simply talking about it.[49] In December, the student newspaper announced that the university was going to start offering a Black studies course.[50]

Six years later, ORU invited the Reverend Jesse Jackson to deliver the commencement address and granted the civil rights leader an honorary doctorate for his, in Oral's words, "untiring endeavors for the understanding and cooperation among all people, and for being God's servant in the now." Jackson commended Oral for his commitment to racial equality. As a boy in South Carolina, Jackson said he remembered watching Oral on TV and that his family was impressed with the evangelist because his meetings were integrated, which convinced them that Oral was authentic. He was also healed of pneumonia while watching Oral's program. ORU's emphasis on personal discipline and racial unity showed that it was the wave of the future.[51]

In the mid-1970s, Oral started to bring Carlton Pearson, one of the most talented and charming World Action Singers, into his orbit. In 1973, Roberts told Pearson, who had grown up in a poor neighborhood in San Diego, that "the last human being to help Jesus Christ on this earth before he died was a Black man." He then prophetically said, "The next great move of the Holy Spirit would be among Black people and the next great revival would be initiated by Black people and that he [Pearson] was going to have a leading part in it."[52] A year later, Oral referred to Pearson as his "black son." As a student, Pearson was a regular fixture on campus and the prime-time specials, and when he graduated, he was named "associate evangelist" and chaplain for Oral Roberts Ministries, before launching out on his own in 1977.[53]

Of Oral's two white sons, Ronald was clearly the one better equipped to run the university. In 1973, after finishing coursework for his PhD in linguistics at the University of Southern California, Ronnie moved back to Tulsa to teach courses in Chinese, Russian, and German at Booker T. Washington High School. That same year, Booker T. Washington, a historic Black high school in north Tulsa, was chosen to lead integration efforts in the city, twenty years after the *Brown v. Board* decision. The district started busing white students to the school.[54] Oral celebrated the move, expressing hope that it would "be more than an experiment" and that it would "be something living in the midst of all of us that demonstrates our real sincere feelings of brotherhood."[55] Despite being closer to home, Ronnie's relationship with his parents remained distant. He wore a beard and removed himself from the trust fund his father had established for his children. Oral and Evelyn, however, were hopeful. Evelyn told friends that it appeared Ronnie was coming around.[56]

If Ronnie was trying to distance himself from his father's ministry, Richard was increasingly being drawn in. In addition to his responsibilities for the prime-time specials, Richard was named president of the OREA in December 1973. This was a big responsibility. His new duties included "involvement in the production, distribution, talent coordination, and advertising of all programs in the national market." At the time, the *Contact* specials aired in 425 markets, 3 of which had audiences well over a million; the weekly half-hour program, *Oral Roberts Presents*, was on 300 stations; and the OREA distributed over 48 million pieces of mail each year.[57]

Richard was also going to be responsible for an ever-growing amount of money. The OREA's 1974 tax returns, according to an Associated Press (AP) story, reported $18.7 million ($98.1 million in 2021 dollars) in contributions, making up the bulk of its $20 million ($104.9 million) in total receipts. The organization's largest contribution, $6.2 million, was to ORU's operating funds, special events center, endowment fund, and scholarships. It spent another $5.6 million for radio and TV, $1.7 million for advertising, $1.2 million for postage, and $2.2 million for salaries. Richard's salary was $21,087. The OREA also paid $1,000 to the Billy Graham Evangelistic Association and $15 to the Optimist Club. Because the evangelistic association reported more exempt disbursements than receipts, it reported deficits for both 1973 and 1974: $677,743 in 1973 and $166,806 in 1974.[58] Not all the news that year was encouraging. The Better Business Bureau placed the OREA on its "Give, but Give Wisely" list for its refusal to provide the Washington-based group with financial information.[59]

The next year, 1975, the OREA showed gross receipts of $27.5 million ($132 million), of which $25.6 million ($123 million) came from contributions and gifts. The AP reported that the association listed its expenses at $24.37 million and a net worth of $7.69 million, up from $4.55 million at the beginning of the fiscal year. Again, ORU received the bulk of the OREA's contribution, a little over $7 million. Television and radio were the next biggest expenditure at $6.19 million. It also spent $2.8 million on religious literature, $1.1 million on *Abundant Life*, and $1.55 million on postage. Oral received a $29,000 salary ($140,000), plus perks, including a car, a house, and expenses. Richard was paid $25,000.[60]

Things were looking bright enough that ORU's student newspaper opened its April 11, 1975, issue with the headline, "ORU Becomes a True University." Just a few days prior, Oral announced that ORU was expanding to include graduate schools in business, theology, nursing, law, and medicine. The chairman of a visiting accreditation committee, a Dr. Carlson, praised ORU for being a "'distinctive educational institution' at a time when some are a 'pale copy of other colleges and universities.'"[61] The schools of law and medicine very quickly became controversial. Roberts had faced controversy before, but he quickly found himself in a fight with two of the most influential and secular professional organizations in the United States: the American Medical Association and the American Bar Association.

9

The Crown Jewel

ON APRIL 28, 1975, ORAL TOLD AN ORU CHAPEL AUDIENCE that that day would perhaps be "the second greatest moment in the history and the life of this university." To help them remember that April day, Oral asked them to get out a pencil and paper and draw a circle. He then asked them to put ORU at the center of the circle and to draw two lines inside the circle, one going left to right and the other top to bottom. They now had a circle with four spokes. The spokes, he said, represented the "four inescapable aspects of our human life": theology, business, law, and medicine. The announcement of these four new graduate schools marked the "beginning of the completion of the masterplan for Oral Roberts University," a master plan first revealed to Roberts thirteen years earlier when construction on the university started. Christian schools of theology, business, law, and medicine, said Lee Braxton, who had now been with the Roberts ministry for close to thirty years, was an "idea whose time has come."[1] The four graduate schools would be gradually phased in. The schools of theology and business were set to open in fall 1975, medicine in fall 1978, and law in fall 1979.

A year earlier, God had given Oral instructions for opening the medical school. This new command came while Oral was praying for the sick. He heard Jesus's words from the Gospel of Matthew: "They that are sick need a physician." Oral wasn't exactly sure what God was telling him, so he asked for clarification. God told him that he had already completed one part of the medical school by opening ORU, whose students would "go where My light is dim" and whose work would "exceed yours." Oral was still confused. God put it more plainly: "I want you to raise up Christian doctors who will accept My healing power in its fullness. *They will do all they can through prayer, and they will do all they can through medicine.*" These medical students would become "young *Lukes*" to Oral, and they would be accepted around the world as the representatives of Oral Roberts's healing ministry. Oral knew God's voice when he heard it, but he still had doubts. In 1975, at the time he announced his plans to expand ORU, Evelyn reassured her husband that he was following God's will, and, just in case there were any lingering doubts, a number of ORU students told the university president that they would gladly enroll in the medical school. The only thing that seemed like an impossibility at the time was welcoming the first class of medical students by fall 1978.[2]

Dr. James Winslow, the man Oral recruited to help him navigate the complications of opening a medical school, had first heard of the famous evangelist when he was completing his residency in orthopedic surgery in Memphis, Tennessee. A young patient's grandfather refused to allow the doctors to give his dying granddaughter cortisone, an experimental and potentially dangerous drug at the time. The reason? He said he had called Oral, and Oral had told him the little girl didn't need medicine but prayer. Though initially upset that Oral may have recommended withholding a lifesaving drug, the doctors concluded that it was unlikely the grandfather had given them an accurate account.[3]

Two years after Winslow moved to Tulsa in 1967, his wife, Sue, underwent a successful treatment of cancer and received the baptism of the Holy Spirit, an experience she encouraged her husband to pursue.[4] Dr. Winslow's and Oral's paths finally crossed in the early 1970s. At an ORU basketball game in 1970, the team's leading rebounder, Eddie Woods, fell on the floor and hit his head. Concerned, Winslow left his seat to check on the basketball star, who recovered and was able to return to the game. Coach Trickey asked Winslow if he would provide medical care for the team. Winslow said he would. Two years later, after injuring his knee playing golf, Oral visited Winslow's office, where Oral asked the surgeon if he ever prayed *with* his patients. Winslow apparently thought Oral had asked him if he ever prayed *for* his patients. After Winslow prayed for Oral's knee to heal, the two got into an argument over payment. Winslow's office apparently refused to charge ministers, so Oral offered a compromise; they would play golf together at the Southern Hills Country Club in lieu of pay. That summer, they played golf several times together and, according to Oral's account, learned a great deal from each other. Oral learned more about how medicine operated, and Winslow learned more about how prayer worked. Oral eventually grew comfortable enough to tell his newfound friend his plans for the medical school. After several moments of awkward silence, Winslow said he finally understood why they had been talking about the relationship between prayer and medicine and that he had come around to seeing that prayer and medicine worked best together. When Oral told Winslow he wanted to open the medical school in fall 1978, the surgeon told him that was impossible.[5]

Roberts broke ground for the graduate schools, whose total cost was projected at $60 million ($310 million in 2021 dollars), on his fifty-eighth birthday, January 24, 1976. Comedian Jerry Lewis, who was on campus directing the *Contact* spring special, and evangelist Corrie ten Boom participated in the groundbreaking. Lewis, speaking on behalf of "the crippled children of the world," celebrated the medical school "as one more tremendous cog in the wheel of victory" against disease, particularly muscular dystrophy. Oral was understandably excited. Posing for pictures with Dr. Winslow, who was holding a stethoscope, the beaming evangelist said, "I hope you don't hold that to my heart 'cause it's in my throat right now."[6]

Rather than going through the hassle of constructing several new buildings, Oral planned to add to the triangle-shaped Learning Resources Center (LRC). Like so many of his plans, this one came via an intimate talk with God. In their conversation, God instructed his servant to look at the LRC and to notice that it was only half finished. Oral responded that he had never noticed that before and that he didn't know he did things "half way." God wanted him to complete the LRC by making it a diamond. With the library and undergraduate and graduate programs under the same roof, Oral envisioned an educational plan he called "cross-fertilization." Theology students, for instance, would be required to take courses in management principles, business students would take courses in business ethics, and professors would teach both undergraduate and graduate students. Graduate students would also be required to sign the university's honor code, demonstrating, Roberts excitedly said, that "we are one family."[7]

The good news continued into early February. The ORU law school now had a name: the O. W. Coburn School of Law. On February 5, Oral announced that the law school's namesake, O. W. "Bill" Coburn, founder and president of Coburn Optical Industries, had donated a sizable amount—Roberts never revealed it, but he said it was the largest donation the school had ever received—to help finish the $10 million school. On why he earmarked his money for the law school, Coburn said, "We sense a great need for more 'honest' lawyers in our nation and we believe the atmosphere at Oral Roberts University will result in that type of law graduate."[8] Oral also announced Charles A. Kothe, a local attorney and close friend of Coburn, as dean of the school. Kothe, who had taught labor law at the University of Tulsa, echoed Coburn's sentiments for the need of a law school like ORU's: "This is not just another law school. The concept is so unique it may be called unique in the state of Oklahoma. Students here will follow the 'whole man' concept. The world today is so truly mechanized and produces so many brittle products, that this is important." He added that he wished he had had the type of cross-fertilization training that ORU would offer its law and other graduate students.[9]

The medical school was the first of the graduate schools to face opposition. In September 1976, the *Tulsa Tribune* published an article that had the potential to derail Oral's plans. Six years earlier, the California-based Carnegie Council on Policy Studies in Higher Education had suggested that new medical schools be built in nine American cities. Tulsa was on the list. Oklahomans responded by opening two new medical schools in the city. The Oklahoma College of Osteopathic Medicine and Surgery and a Tulsa branch of the University of Oklahoma College of Medicine were both opened in 1974.

Six years after its initial study, the Carnegie Council now said there were too many medical schools in the United States and suggested that state and federal authorities halt the construction of any new ones. Local administrators were worried that a third medical school in Tulsa would flood an already perilous market with too many physicians. The other Tulsa medical schools had already imposed voluntary enrollment limits for the upcoming school year. Robert Hansen, dean of the ORU dental school, said they hadn't read the first report and doubted that they would pay attention to the most recent one.[10]

Less than a week after announcing Coburn's donation, on Friday, February 11, 1977, Oral and Evelyn's oldest child, Rebecca, and her husband, Marshall Nash, were flying from Aspen, Colorado, to Tulsa when their twin-engine plane crashed in a wheat field in Anthony, Kansas. The Nashes and four others died in the crash. Rebecca Roberts Nash was thirty-seven, and Marshall Nash was thirty-eight. The Federal Aviation Administration (FAA) eventually concluded that a "two to three-second roller coaster" effect, during which the plane fell to pieces, preceded the crash. The federal authorities weren't able to determine if the crash was caused by the environment, the pilot, a malfunction, or some combination of all three. Right before the crash, the pilot, Louis Taylor, reported that they were flying through light snow but that there was no icing on the plane, which was equipped with deicing equipment. The FAA's investigation discovered that Taylor, who was using the plane for a sales demonstration, didn't have the multi-engine rating required to fly it. His employer, Catlin Aviation, accused Taylor of lying on his application. The plane, a Piper Navajo, also had a history of in-flight structural failures.[11] On the spring 1977 *Contact* special, Oral tearfully recounted the morning when the police told him his children were dead. He talked about the police officers telling him and Evelyn about the crash, and then, when he got to his grandkids' house, they were awake earlier than usual because they were excited to see their parents. Oral had to tell them they were dead.[12] A "home-going celebration" was held in Mabee Auditorium on February 14. Billy Graham sent his condolences. "Sometimes we have to look at heaven through tears. On these occasions, our tears become telescopes that bring heaven nearer," the evangelist wrote in a telegram.[13] Almost immediately, Oral and Evelyn appeared on television to talk about their grief. In the October issue of *Abundant Life*, Oral, still trying to find meaning in the deaths, said that their decision to go on television was a "seed" planted, and he was confident it would "bear fruit."[14]

On February 18, the ORU student newspaper reported that the ORU medical school encountered another problem. According to state and federal law, to be considered for accreditation, the school had to find a local hospital where its students could fulfill their residency requirements. One Tulsa hospital, St. Francis, declined affiliation; James Winslow had worked there, and Oral had probably hoped he would grease the skids for acceptance. This left the two other local hospitals, St. John's and Hillcrest, to enter into negotiations with. These types of talks, Winslow explained, were usually time-consuming, and he admitted ORU was "a little behind" where he wanted them to be. One major source of tension was the past behavior of ORU students, who apparently entered hospital rooms and prayed with patients without having proper consent. ORU students would have to start being more discreet, Winslow recommended. If the negotiations failed, Winslow said there was always the option that ORU could start its own hospital so its medical students would have a place to train.[15]

In March, Tulsa newspapers ran stories that ORU officials were considering opening a hospital. An inside source explained that the proposed hospital would also serve the needs of people throughout the country who had apparently voiced a desire to receive medical treatment at ORU. Such a hospital would have no effect on other Tulsa hospitals, the unnamed source added. Others obviously disagreed, believing that an ORU hospital would meet opposition from both north Tulsans, who had been trying to get a hospital of their own for years, and south Tulsans, who feared that another hospital on their side of town would lead to overbedding and closures.[16]

The ongoing negotiations between ORU and St. John's and Hillcrest hospitals picked up at the end of March. The two hospitals hoped, the *Tulsa Tribune* reported, "to forestall at least 'temporarily' the need for ORU to construct its own general hospital in order to provide necessary training facilities." Dr. John Alexander, president of St. John's medical staff, said that approval was likely considering a staff recommendation that would leave room for "other community hospitals" to participate in the future. ORU officials, however, still wouldn't rule out opening their own hospital; this meant, according to Provost Carl Hamilton, that "ORU will not have to make a decision about a facility of its own as soon as might otherwise have been necessary without such an agreement."[17]

On the spring 1977 *Contact*, which aired in April, Oral hinted at his idea to start a hospital. During his sermon, he spoke at length about the relationship between prayer and medicine and talked about the need for new medical-based centers that merged the two.[18] On September 7, 1977, Oral announced his plans to build the City of Faith Medical and Research Center. After the deaths of Rebecca and Marshall, Oral, Evelyn, and Richard traveled to their vacation home in California to grieve. While he was mourning, God said to Oral, "I will rain upon your desert." God further told the evangelist that he wanted him to complete the healing vision he had given him to take God's healing power to his generation. This vision could only be finished if Oral built a "new and different medical center" for the Lord, one where the powers of prayer and medicine could come together. The Lord gave further instructions: "In the new City of Faith on the ORU campus, I want my healing resources used. Prayer, but more than prayer. Medical science, but more than medical science I want an *atmosphere charged with faith and hope*; where My healing love fills the entire place." By demonstrating the power of merging prayer and medicine, the City of Faith would change the world.[19]

God did not stop there. He also showed Roberts how he wanted the buildings constructed. The three buildings were to be connected from a single base. At the center would be a 600-foot-high clinic flanked by a 300-foot-high hospital and a 200-foot-high medical research center. The complex would not be the "usual low-scattered buildings that are not always people-oriented. They are to be towering buildings, closely connected, built on a single base—a crown jewel rising in the sky, reaching up in praise to God, the Source of all healing."[20] Flowing directly in front of the City of Faith, Roberts envisioned a 100-foot-long pool, representing the "River of Life" described in the book of Revelation, lined with evergreen trees, symbolizing the "Tree of Life." Set directly at the base of the City of Faith was a pair of 60-foot-high bronze Healing Hands, with each hand representing a different approach to healing. The right hand represented the healing stream of God's power to heal through prayer. The left hand represented God's power to heal through medicine. "The symbolism of the Healing Hands standing tall where the stream meets THE CITY OF FAITH, visible both day and night, grabbed all that I know about God's healing power. I've seen those Hands in my spirit many times. I feel them touching my hands as I pray for people," Roberts wrote. "I understand how important hands are in God's healing process, both the laying on of hands through prayer AND the work of the hands of skilled and dedicated physicians."[21] Unused portions of the 80-acre property would be turned into playing fields for ORU's popular intramural sports program, giving patients the ability to "look out the hospital windows and see young people playing on the surrounding area," Oral added.[22]

His announcement preempted two possible objections: how he planned to finance such an expensive project, and how a 777-bed hospital would affect other Tulsa hospitals. The question about money was perhaps the easiest to address. By this time, Oral had shown a remarkable ability to raise money. He bragged that he had already spent $150 million for buildings and endowments and that the school's debt, about $15 million, would easily be paid back through dormitory fees. Besides, he had faith on his side. "We are going into this project without funds as usual," Oral said, "but I know God will see us through." Tulsa hospitals had no reason to worry, he explained, because most patients would be drawn from all over the world. With "2.5 million families as our partners in the U. S., many living in this region of the country," Oral anticipated that "many of them will use the center."[23]

Fund-raising started the same day. Initially priced at $100 million ($460 million in 2021 dollars), the City of Faith was Oral's most expensive project to date. Michael Cardone Jr., an ORU regent, donated $77,777. The number seven, considered to be the number of completeness and perfection, played a key role in Oral's announcement. When God spoke to Roberts, he said, "I told you there would be a Breakthrough from Heaven in '77. Therefore, you are to start in the fall of '77. This is the accepted time. People are ready for it." He also suggested that if supporters wanted to experience their own "Breakthrough from Heaven in '77," they needed to send a minimum of $77, which would pay for three-and-half yards of concrete, with the reinforced steel. If they wanted to send more than this amount, they needed to do it in multiples of $77.[24] If partners couldn't afford to give $77 at one time, they could make payments, he told a TV audience in December. After all, "seven dollars for 11 months is $77." He also distinguished between "valued partners," or people who simply wrote or did "anything for this ministry," and "chosen partners," people who gave at least $77 toward the construction of the City of Faith. These partners were going to be the "building stones in the City of Faith." At the time, in December, only 15 percent of the partners had sent money.[25]

Opinion in Tulsa was divided on the prospect of a new 777-bed hospital. The two dailies, the *Tulsa Tribune* and the *Tulsa World*, came out in support of the ambitious plan. The *Tribune* compared Oral's accomplishments to the NASA program, writing, the "accomplishments of Oral Roberts have only been slightly less amazing than our space program." Oral had an impressive track record of starting seemingly impossible projects and seeing them to completion. But none of these projects, including ORU, which was then valued at $150 million ($690 million in 2021 dollars), were as "mind-boggling" as the $100 million City of Faith. If the City of Faith could achieve its dream of drawing patients from around the nation and possibly the globe and could demonstrate the relationship between prayer and medicine, then it was worth the gamble. "As it is," the editorial concluded, "we can only wish him Godspeed."[26] The *Tulsa World* equally praised Oral's genius, adding that the possibility of opening such an expensive complex debt-free was a "feat that few organizations in the U. S. can accomplish."[27]

The medical community was less impressed. Despite assurances that the City of Faith would not add to an already weak health-care market by contributing to "overbedding" or a precarious labor supply, Tulsa hospital administrators were skeptical. They were also surprised. James Harvey, president of Hillcrest, said that Oral's sudden announcement was "highly unusual."[28] These administrators' concerns were legitimate. In October, the *Tulsa Tribune* reported that Oklahoma might have to cut 2,500 hospital beds. Tulsa County alone was at risk of having to cut 1,000 beds, a dire situation made worse if the City of Faith was built. The Department of Health, Education, and Welfare (HEW), in a September proposal, recommended a ratio of four hospital beds for every 1,000 persons in a hospital's service area. In 1975, there were an estimated 417,200 people in Tulsa, which meant, if the HEW's proposal was followed, the number of hospital beds would be approximately 1,669. In late 1977, there were 2,708 hospital beds, and, with new construction in two of the hospitals, St. Francis and St. John's, the number would climb to 3,028. If the City of Faith was approved, an additional 777 beds would be added.[29]

While ORU and local hospital officials were scrambling to suss out the implications of another hospital, news leaked that ORU banned fat and handicapped people from its campus. On September 22, 1977, the Oklahoma Coalition of Citizens with Disabilities (OCCD) and the American Civil Liberties Union (ACLU) charged the university with having "a de facto policy that discriminates against otherwise qualified handicapped individuals in its program and facilities." ORU, according to Mike Phillips, president of the OCCD, had several buildings on campus, including the LRC and the Prayer Tower, which were inaccessible to people in wheelchairs.[30] This was a violation of federal law. The Rehabilitation Act of 1973 prohibited discrimination on the basis of disability at institutions—public and private—that received federal grants and loans. In 1977, ORU received $586,425 in federal student aid and had used federal funds to construct several buildings in the past. The university agreed to comply with federal law. Within a few years, the university was made handicap accessible.[31]

The university was less willing to budge on its compulsory weight-loss program, the Pounds Off Program, called POPS in the student newspaper. Weight requirements were nothing new at a Roberts-run organization. Back in 1962, Oral required fat employees at the OREA to lose weight or risk disciplinary action. This type of oversight was expanded at ORU. In 1972, Oral became a devotee of Kenneth Cooper's revolutionary aerobics program, eventually building the $2 million Kenneth H. Cooper Aerobics Center on ORU's campus in 1974. POPS was created two years later. Incoming students had their body fat percentage, cardiovascular strength, resting and active heart rates, and blood pressure measured. The university also examined the students' past medical and diet history, gave them a dental exam, and tested their strength.

While all ORU students were required to take Aerobics I and II during their first two semesters and to participate in team and individual sports, fat students faced more scrutiny. Students who were deemed overweight—men exceeding 25 percent body fat and women exceeding 35 percent—were required to participate in a strict exercise and diet regime. These students were placed under medical supervision with the goal of losing one pound per week. If they failed to make satisfactory progress, students faced "physical probation" for a semester. If they continued to fail, they faced suspension from classes. Students in this situation were sent home to evaluate their dedication to ORU's strict lifestyle.

The national news media got wind of POPS in late 1977 when four expelled fat students joined the OCCD and the ACLU in the lawsuit. One suspended student, junior Debbie Padgett, received a letter in February 1977 notifying her that her course work was unsatisfactory and that she would have to drop 30 pounds, from 175 to 145 pounds, by the end of her senior year or she wouldn't be allowed to graduate. Padgett, who eventually transferred to Central State University (now University of Central Oklahoma), had mixed feelings about ORU. She still believed in its original mission but also felt sad: "It has so much potential, so many positive things about it, but you can't treat people this way. They just want lovely people. They treat you like you're not close enough to God or you'd lose weight."[32]

Another female student, Jerri Johnston, was denied readmittance for her junior year because, according to school officials, she failed to uphold her end of the contract she signed the previous year. They told her she could try again at the beginning of the spring semester if she lost 26 pounds. Her mother, who accompanied Jerri to enrollment to help her son enroll but also to learn more about why her honor-student daughter was denied readmission, described the scene in the weigh-in room as "going to the gallows." Johnston wasn't enrolled at ORU in fall 1977 but hoped to attend in spring 1978 to prove to the school that she was capable of losing the weight. To meet the weight requirements, she dedicated herself to a strict workout schedule and 750 calories a day. However, she had no interest in graduating from ORU. Her plan, instead, was to graduate from Oklahoma State University. Like Padgett, she had critical words for ORU. "I think I must have an outdated Bible," she said, "because mine doesn't say, 'Blessed are the thin for they shall inherit the earth.'"[33]

For fat activists, part of the growing "fat power" movement, ORU's weight-loss policy reeked of antifat bias, but for others, POPS was an appropriate response to a hedonistic culture. In January 1978, the popular health and fitness magazine *Prevention* polled its readers on their response to POPS. They responded 2-to-1 in favor of the university's policy.[34] Advice columnist Abigail Van Buren, popularly known as "Dear Abby," in response to a letter from a family member of one of the expelled ORU students, wrote, "It seems that your niece ate herself out of the university."[35]

By early 1978, the controversy surrounding handicap accessibility and POPS disappeared from the headlines as the fight over the City of Faith amped up. At the center of the struggle were attempts at the state and national level to control runaway health-care costs. In the years following World War II, American legislators noticed a severe shortage of hospitals in the United States, so they increased funding to build more. There were soon too many hospitals. In 1964, New York was the first state to try to lower costs by requiring hospitals to apply for a "certificate of need." Eight years later, twenty states required hospitals to demonstrate a "need" for their services. The basic assumption behind this requirement was that excess bed capacity, "overbedding," led to inflated health-care costs because hospitals had to pay staff to cover these empty beds, costs that the consumer was forced to eat.[36] In a city like Tulsa, therefore, with 1,000 unused beds and a combined indebtedness of $150 million, Oral had to demonstrate that a hospital the size of City of Faith was "needed."[37]

To get its certificate of need, ORU had to go through a multistep process. The first step was to submit its application to the Oklahoma Health Systems Agency (OHSA), a nonprofit but federally funded advisory board. The OHSA would then forward its recommendation for or against the City of Faith's certificate of need to the Oklahoma Health Planning Commission (OHPC), who would then have final say.

ORU submitted its application to the Oklahoma health review boards on December 2, 1977. In the 168-page application, ORU officials maintained that the City of Faith would be a national referral clinic, like the prestigious Mayo Clinic in Rochester, Minnesota, and that the hospital would focus on cancer and heart disease and would draw 90 percent of its patients from the more than 7.5 million people in the United States who supported the Roberts ministry. Oklahoma accounted for 144,000 constituents, neighboring states for 1,254,000, and the remaining states for 6,102,000. Out of these constituents, ORU officials estimated that the City of Faith would receive 609,730 referrals and 47,278 admissions among Roberts's followers. Notably, ORU didn't dispute that Oklahoma had too many hospital beds. Dr. Winslow said, "We're not trying to argue that point. What we're trying to say is that's not an issue with this particular institution." The initial fundraising had been impressive. The application noted that ORU had already raised $15 million for the project.[38]

Oral Roberts broke ground for the City of Faith on January 24, 1978. The day may have been foggy and overcast, reflecting, Oral said, the "condition that millions of people are in," but it was also a day of celebration. Lee Braxton called the City of Faith the "crown jewel of Oral's ministry," while Tulsa mayor Robert J. LaFortune praised Oral's contributions to Tulsa. It was time for Tulsans, the mayor remarked, to have a little faith in Oral

Roberts.[39] Starting in ORU's chapel, the ceremony ended with seventy-seven white doves being released into the cold air and twelve dignitaries, including state and local officials, wielding gold shovels.[40]

With battle lines clearly drawn by the end of January 1978, Drs. James Winslow and C. T. Thompson, an early critic of the hospital, appeared on a local TV news show six days after the groundbreaking. For several weeks, the local opposition had been coordinating their efforts in order to present a united front. In December, Hillcrest opted out of negotiations to train ORU medical students, which meant that St. John's followed suit because, as its chief executive officer said, they were only willing to work with ORU in conjunction with Hillcrest.[41] On January 17, the Tulsa Hospital Council held a closed-door meeting during which several hospital officials discussed the potential impact of the $100 million City of Faith. The council selected Hillcrest administrator James Harvey as its spokesperson. Harvey had already publicly voiced his opposition to ORU's proposed project.[42]

Thompson and Winslow's appearance revealed how deep the divide was between the two sides. It seems they couldn't even agree on the definition of the word "need." Thompson was the first to appear. He was clearly frustrated that he and Winslow weren't talking face-to-face. The hosts assured him that they would be happy to arrange a live debate between the two physicians. Thompson's case rested on a few arguments. First was ORU's claim that the City of Faith would be a long-distance referral hospital like Mayo, the Ochsner Clinic, Baylor Scott & White, or the Johns Hopkins Hospital. It was true that these hospitals drew from a larger radius than most hospitals, but even that was limited. Mayo, for example, received 89 percent of its patients from a 500-mile radius. These same illustrious hospitals also tended to not be attached to a medical school. On whether Oral's partners would come in the tens of thousands, how likely, Thompson wanted to know, would "a man from Iowa who sends $10 a year" travel to Tulsa for his physical? What operation would draw him to Tulsa? An appendectomy? For his daughter to deliver a baby? Quite simply, the City of Faith wasn't offering anything that the other Tulsa hospitals didn't already provide. He wanted to "believe that unless somebody could legally prove need and need being that we need a hospital here in Tulsa, Oklahoma, or the state needs a hospital, [he] would really like to believe that the certificate of need would not be given." He recognized, though, the political pressures the health-planning committees faced. Oral Roberts was a powerful man in Oklahoma.

As he had already done, Winslow didn't dispute that, according to the opposition's understanding of "need," the City of Faith failed to meet their criteria. The City of Faith, he repeated, wasn't going to draw from the local or even state health market but from a national one. There was already plenty of evidence that Oral's supporters wanted and needed a hospital like the City of Faith. Oral's partners had not just voiced their support in nearly 500,000 letters sent to ORU but had voted with their feet as well. Every year, Winslow explained, people came to Tulsa "for even less than full medical services." Twenty-five thousand people came for the annual seminars on ORU's campus; ORU would have an estimated 5,000 students by the time the City of Faith opened in 1981; and, in 1977, 250,000 people signed the register at the Prayer Tower. Besides a devotion to Oral Roberts's philosophy, these people brought something else with them: money. Rather than a discussion about how the City of Faith would adversely affect the other Tulsa hospitals, Winslow wanted to have one about how it would help them. He predicted that the City of Faith would attract so many patients that it wouldn't be able to keep up, therefore sending its patient overflow to the other hospitals.

Both sides also had different accounts of the collapsed negotiations between the ORU medical school and Tulsa's hospitals. Thompson said the hospitals had acted in good faith and that hospital administrators felt they were misled. They had been assured that ORU had no intent to build a hospital. This wasn't quite accurate, according to Winslow. Thompson, he said, would have no idea of the details because he wasn't present at any of the meetings. St. Francis, the hospital Thompson represented, refused to participate from the beginning. The other hospital administrators had known since April 6, 1977, that ORU would likely build a hospital teaching facility. At the time, they didn't know the type or size of this theoretical hospital, but ORU did not treat them in an "inconsistent way," Winslow remarked.[43]

With these arguments locked in, the two sides had their first public hearing on February 8, 1978. A three-member review committee of the OHSA heard six hours of testimony from seventy people. Sixty people were in favor of the City of Faith while ten opposed it. The opponents, most of whom represented the Tulsa Hospital Council, voiced concern that the City of Faith would lead to overbedding, higher medical costs, employee shortages, and duplication of services. Phil Goodwin, vice president of the council, was also bothered by Roberts's claim that no other hospital embraced the spiritual aspect of the healing process, because St. Francis and

St. John's were Catholic hospitals. In another testimony, the results of a Tulsa County Medical Society survey were revealed, indicating that 78 percent of Tulsa physicians opposed the City of Faith.[44] Earl Sneed, Oklahoma City attorney representing the Tulsa Hospital Council, wondered if the City of Faith would draw patients after Roberts's death.[45] William Paul, also a lawyer who represented the Tulsa Hospital Council, shared twenty-four letters from Oklahoma hospitals in opposition to ORU's proposal.[46]

ORU supporters again accused their opponents of acting in bad faith. One told the committee to "disregard any input" from the Tulsa Hospital Council and the Tulsa County Medical Society because, when the latter conducted their study, they didn't invite ORU "to discuss the issue, to try to determine which concerns of the hospitals were real and which were imagined." He added that the survey was untrustworthy because the people surveyed only received information mailed out by the Tulsa Hospital Council. The survey may have turned out differently if they had sent out ORU's material.

Winslow trotted out the oft-repeated argument that the City of Faith was seeking a national patient load and that it would contribute positively to the Tulsa labor market. They had already heard from 750 people who were interested in positions at the medical school and City of Faith. "The problem of numbers," he said, "is the wrong problem. The problem is one of selection." He mentioned some other impressive numbers. Each month, the Roberts ministry received on average 544,000 letters containing 402,000 prayer requests. They had been able to identify 99,255 medical problems and 72,761 mental and emotional problems. These partners had clearly expressed a want and a need for a place like the City of Faith.

Another supporter challenged the Tulsa Hospital Council's definition of "need." "Is a need," he asked, "merely the need for surgical steel, a room, a nurse, a doctor? Or does the need exist for a facility of the kind proposed by the City of Faith? In all of America you will not find a charismatic hospital. Is there a need on a national scope for this kind of facility?"[47] Seventy-one-year-old Lavenia James told the committee that she had had four surgeries for cancer before she was even forty. She was due for another when she heard about Oral Roberts. A recent examination showed that some scar tissue was the only remaining evidence of her cancer. She said she was grateful to God, and, she added, "I want that City of Faith."[48]

Roberts had the final word. The facility was needed not only for its unique vision of health care but also as a place where Roberts's constituents could freely carry out their faith. Roberts boiled the complicated matter of overbedding and health-care costs down to his supporters' First Amendment rights: "Have our people not the right to express their beliefs and have a place especially designed and constructed where they can put their beliefs into action in this country?"[49] He also introduced a letter from Billy Graham supporting the hospital. The three-member review committee recommended disapproval of the certificate of need.[50]

A few weeks later, on February 27, the OHSA Board of Trustees voted 19–6, also recommending disapproval. It did so on four grounds: the City of Faith would duplicate services already offered in Tulsa; it had failed to obtain affiliation and sharing agreements with other local hospitals; it would raise medical costs broadly across the region; and it had failed to adequately demonstrate a need for more hospital beds. Earl Sneed said the decision did not forbid Roberts from building a clinic, something he encouraged the evangelist to do, or a research center; it forbade just the hospital. City of Faith supporters had good reason to worry. The OHPC rarely overturned the OHSA's decisions. The OHPC was originally scheduled to hear the City of Faith's case on March 22, but it wouldn't meet until April 26.

The day wasn't all bad, though. The FAA concluded that the sixty-story clinic, measured to rise to 648 feet, posed no threat to air traffic. ORU agreed to place flashing lights on the top of the building and to keep the FAA informed of any construction. This approval was the final impediment to construction of the clinic.[51]

On March 8, Roberts asked his partners to write or call Oklahoma governor David Boren and to contact their state legislators expressing their support for the hospital.[52] Oklahoma political officials were soon flooded with letters from Roberts's followers. The *Tulsa Tribune* reported that Boren received an estimated 1,500 letters and as many as three hundred phone calls in one day. The letters offered a variety of reasons to support the City of Faith, including one that claimed Elvis Presley would still be alive if the hospital had been open. There were letters about the personal trauma of seeing a loved one get sick and die. One letter-writer had lost an uncle to cancer and a grandfather now had brain cancer. "I only wish we had a City of Faith." Some accused opponents of the hospital of being on the side of the devil and of deliberately trying to stifle the work of God. Some of these letters had an ominous tone, warning the governor and other government officials that, if they did not throw their political weight behind the City of Faith, God would kill them. Several writers reminded Governor Boren that they were Democrats and that they had voted for him for governor and planned to support his upcoming US Senate bid.[53]

On March 9, Oral traveled to Washington, DC, to meet with federal officials to request an investigation into the OHSA. Two of the board members who voted against the City of Faith apparently had conflicts of interest. One was an associate administrator at St. Francis Hospital, and the other had been associated with the Franklin Memorial Hospital and the First National Bank, both of Broken Arrow, Oklahoma. Shocked at the accusation, the latter board member told reporters that he was a member of the ORU Titan booster club. ORU also argued their application deserved special consideration in light of a federal law that granted extra attention to medical schools and special referral centers. The federal officials told Oral they could only start an investigation at the request of the state. The next day, Lloyd Rader, state welfare director and one of the three members of the OHPC, called federal offices and asked for an investigation into the OHSA. The Health Resources Administration, the federal agency running the investigation, said, though it wasn't committed to the hospital, some of the things its members had been told warranted a closer look. ORU later dropped its lawsuit.

In the meantime, Ken Caughman, OHSA board chairman, announced that the agency would reconsider the City of Faith application because ORU said the hospital was scaling down its cost from $93 million to $55 million. This was enough money to open with 294 beds in a facility that would eventually have 777. The OHSA was scheduled to rehear ORU's case on March 16.[54]

Oral's appearance on a local news show on March 14 was likely meant to clear up any lingering questions, but, at least on one issue, it only muddied the waters. Like so many debates over health care, the one over the City of Faith was focused on white people's needs. One of the panelists asked Roberts why he didn't open his hospital in north Tulsa, where the majority of Tulsa's Black residents lived. There were already five hospitals on the south side, so, clearly, another hospital wasn't needed there. It seems that about ten years prior, north Tulsa was cleared for a 125-bed hospital, a hospital that still hadn't been built. Maybe, Oral replied, the fault was with Black Tulsans. "Think," he said, "if they had united long ago they'd solved lots more of their problems and had much more equal rights and I for one would like to see that."[55]

Robert Goodwin, ORU graduate and editor of Tulsa's Black newspaper, the *Oklahoma Eagle*, penned an editorial two days after Oral's appearance. In it, Goodwin engaged a few of the arguments Roberts had made. First, he said north Tulsa needed a privately owned facility like the City of Faith because publicly owned clinics tended to be poorly run, offered inferior health care, and tended to be drop-off points for charity cases. Second, a north Tulsa hospital would improve relations between ORU and the rest of the city by encouraging graduates to stay in town. Third, a City of Faith-North branch could be an economic boon. People would only move to north Tulsa, Goodwin claimed, if it was in their economic interests to do so. Finally, he addressed Oral's characterization of north Tulsa. There were 150,000 people on the north side, the majority of whom were white. The problem wasn't division, but a lack of economic and political clout to demand and support a north-side hospital. He also wanted Oral to know that nobody from north Tulsa had opposed the City of Faith. That was south Tulsa.[56] Other Black Tulsans were less diplomatic. One letter to the *Oklahoma Eagle* accused Roberts of racism. Oral said he loved Tulsa, but it was clear that he only loved south Tulsa, the letter concluded. At the end of March, ORU aides and Black representatives met to discuss the City of Faith.[57]

At the state capital, politicians were looking for ways to help the City of Faith get approval. The debate over the hospital made its way into the state senate shortly after the OHSA rejected the City of Faith's application in the form of an amendment that sought to "grandfather" in its approval. The proposed law stated that any medical facility under construction would not have to go through the process of acquiring a certificate of need, effectively allowing ORU to finish its medical center. Predictably, both opponents and supporters of the bill traded barbs about whether it was aimed directly at the City of Faith. The bill's supporters argued that it was meant to help all facilities under construction, not just the City of Faith, and that Roberts would still have to go through the proper channels to get approval of the complex.[58] Opponents promised that if the bill ended up helping ORU, there would be a fight.[59]

By March and April, however, there was no doubt about which side state politicians endorsed. In a show of support, thirty-eight senators signed a letter addressed to the OHPC, who had yet to hear the case and had final say. The senate letter argued that the City of Faith would aid rural Oklahoma, improve the search for cures to deadly disease—most notably cancer—and bring a great deal of prestige and money to the state. John Young, the Democratic senator who circulated the letter, explained that the City of Faith would be a benefit to Oklahoma taxpayers, who were spending an average of $24,000 per medical student. The City of Faith, a private enterprise, would educate medical students at no cost to Oklahoma citizens.[60] A few weeks later, the senate passed a resolution endorsing the hospital. The author of the resolution, Democratic senator Gene Stipe, maintained that there was a conspiracy among the City of Faith's opponents to continue to corner the health-care market and blamed them for inflating the cost of hospital beds that made it impossible for the poor to pay for treatment.[61] David Floyd, a Democrat in the House, questioned the OHSA's constitutionality. He explained that Oklahoma's state constitution prohibited the state from giving exclusive right to any corporation; the OHSA was a nonprofit corporation that received federal funds. "I am appalled," he said, "that we have rules and regulations which prohibit or attempt to prohibit projects of this [City of Faith] caliber." He wanted to see the power transferred to a state-run planning committee, one that did not receive federal funds.[62] A few weeks later, the state House of Representatives also endorsed the City of Faith.[63]

The two sides in the battle over the City of Faith met again on April 26, 1978, to present their cases to the OHPC. In preparation for the meeting, Roberts told his supporters to write to the commission supporting the City of Faith. His plea worked. A month before the scheduled meeting, Dr. Hayden Donahue, the state's mental health director, and Lloyd Rader each received nearly 40,000 letters and hundreds of phone calls. Rader estimated that 250,000 letters flooded Oklahoma City, and that less than 1 percent were against ORU's facility.[64] By April 26, the three members of the commission had each received over 100,000 letters in support of the hospital and over 3,000 phone calls. Dr. Donahue reported that in one single day his office received 21,000 letters and 525 phone calls.[65]

There was little new either side offered the OHPC during the public hearing, which probably didn't bode well for ORU, considering that the commission's own study discovered not only few distant referral hospitals in the United States, but that the university also hadn't completed a market study to demonstrate its national draw.[66] Some powerful people, however, appeared on behalf of the City of Faith. Two state representatives, Democrats Guy Davis and Bernard McIntyre, and a state senator, Democrat John Young, were at the meeting to give their support. Young told the three-member review committee that his office had received 450 letters in support of the City of Faith and that the driving concern behind the City of Faith was freedom of religion. Davis was a little more accusatory in tone: "The City of Faith Hospital, let him [Oral] build it. If it be of man, your approval will mean nothing. It will never get off the ground. But I'll tell you, if it be of God, you can't stop it lest happily you be found guilty of fighting against God."[67]

After hearing comments from the standing-room-only audience, the OHPC voted to grant certification to the City of Faith. In their decision, the three-member commission ruled that hospital planners had demonstrated that there was a need for the hospital, that it would be adequately staffed, and that since it was being funded through contributions, it would not be a burden on taxpayers.[68] Construction began the same day.

There was still the problem of the medical school's accreditation. In spring 1978, it became increasingly clear that the medical school likely wouldn't open according to Oral's time line, which, God had told him, was that coming fall. The struggle for accreditation showed not just the external difficulties but the internal ones as well. In May 1977, Roberts achieved a major victory when he recruited Dr. Charles B. McCall to head the medical school. McCall, a graduate of Vanderbilt University and dean of the University of Tennessee College of Medicine, brought a sense of academic credibility with him, but he and Oral eventually butted heads over the opening of the medical school. As the fall 1978 semester loomed closer, Oral considered opening an unaccredited medical school, something McCall refused to do. At the end of July 1978, McCall resigned in protest, and Oral hired a more compliant dean. That same month, ORU announced that it was opening its medical school with twenty provisional students. In September, St. John's Hospital agreed to establish a "limited affiliation" with ORU, further paving the way for accreditation, which the hospital received in February 1979.[69]

The OHPC may have granted the City of Faith its certificate of need, but the Tulsa Hospital Council wasn't ready to give up. Their first step in opposition was the Tulsa District Court. When the district court finally heard arguments in November 1978, it entered the murky waters of the separation of church and state. In the court battle, both sides recognized the potential of the First Amendment. ORU's attorneys argued that the religious convictions of Roberts's followers naturally affected their health, and, therefore, "the religious orientation of the hospital was a health need and a proper concern for the commission." Earl Sneed challenged the university's stance, maintaining that granting the certification of need on the basis of religious philosophy was a direct violation of the separation of church and state.

In the final decision, which was handed down on December 1, 1978, the district court overruled the OHPC, determining that its approval of the certificate of need had violated the establishment clause of the First Amendment. Tulsa County judge Ronald Ricketts ruled that the City of

Faith's stated mission to provide holistic health care brought it within the bounds of the First Amendment's definition of religion because it promised to take care of patients' spiritual as well as physical needs. City of Faith planners, he further argued, had failed to adequately prove that the medical complex would attract enough of Roberts's constituents to justify its existence or that it was needed to train ORU's medical students. Ricketts, however, did not order a halt to the construction of the City of Faith.[70] A week later, the OHPC and ORU appealed to the Oklahoma Supreme Court to overturn the lower court's decision.[71]

The health commission and ORU were not alone in their frustration with the district court's decision. In February 1979, the state senate drafted a bill that would eliminate the legal obstacles that had stopped the City of Faith from being constructed. The bill proposed to repeal the requirement for a certificate of need. The House drafted its own resolution, which asked Governor George Nigh to disband the OHSA and replace it with a new agency, an agency more in tune with consumers' needs. The resolution stated that the health systems agency was controlled by people who were either related by blood or marriage to health-industry insiders, or had business dealings with them. Such relationships were unfair and violated the spirit of federal regulations.[72] With the bills in hand, Nigh sent a request to the secretary of the Department of Health, Education, and Welfare to consider a new agency that would perform health planning in the state.[73]

While state and federal officials were trading barbs over regulatory agencies, ORU was struggling to keep its head above water. The fund-raising demands of the City of Faith had put the ministry and university in dire straits. The budget needs for the ministry during the construction of the City of Faith rose to $10 million a month.[74] The initial fund-raising was impressive. Tax records for 1977–1978 show that Roberts's partners donated over $38 million, but by the summer of 1979 the well had run dry, prompting Roberts to ask for another $50 million during a July telecast. This development was troubling, since Oral had just raised $50 million in January 1979.[75] Roberts attributed the decline in donations to followers who had contributed early on in the project, and then word got out that the ministry "had all the money in the world." He explained that escalating costs and declining donations meant that construction costs were being paid from the university's operational funds. If sufficient funds were not raised, ORU would have to seriously consider eliminating its grants, effectively leading to fewer admitted students, and end construction on the City of Faith.[76]

Oral faced another potential crisis on March 9, 1979, when Tulsa newspapers reported that, after ten years of marriage, Patti and Richard were divorcing. Both parties later agreed that the marriage was unhappy from the beginning. Tellingly, Richard never mentioned Patti by name in his 1985 autobiography. In his account, the reasons for the divorce are vague and ill-defined, and, in the section dedicated to the marriage and divorce, he reminded the reader that he was the brains and talent behind the World Action Singers. He did, however, learn the valuable lesson that God allowed for second chances.[77]

Patti's account got more into the nitty-gritty of what it was like to be a Roberts. Talented and bright, Patti had always wanted to have a career free of Oral's name. In November 1976, she made the first move to distance herself from the Oral Roberts ministry by resigning from the television programs and starting Patti Roberts International Outreach. Her career soon took her overseas to England, Taiwan, and prerevolution Iran. In an April 1978 interview with the *Tulsa Tribune*, Patti dismissed rumors that her marriage was in trouble. The reason she stopped appearing on the Oral Roberts television specials was that she wanted a career of her own. "I can't be an extension of someone else all of my life," she told the newspaper, a statement that not only justified her decision but, perhaps unconsciously, also revealed her opinion of Richard.[78] In her 1983 autobiography, she explained that one of the major sources of tension in their marriage was that Richard wasn't doing enough to make a name for himself. "I wanted to be Patti, and I wanted Richard to be Richard," she wrote.[79] Oral, though hurt by the divorce, may have supported her independent ministry to get her out of the way, Patti later speculated. Like her father-in-law, she was strong-willed and opinionated, a deadly combination for any person in his employ, but especially hazardous for someone like Patti who opposed the City of Faith.[80] In her version, Oral was the first one to broach the subject of divorce. He likened it to cutting the tail off a dog: "I don't see any point in cutting the tail off the dog in small pieces. Why don't you lop it off and that will be that?" He told her to get it over with and to move on with her life.[81]

Shortly after agreeing with Richard to a divorce, Patti walked into Oral's study, only to see her soon-to-be ex-father-in-law and his two jet pilots hanging pictures. He called to her by her pet name, "Patrick, come here." He asked, "Do you think that picture's high enough? Does it look good on the wall?" "Yeah, Oral," she replied, "it looks wonderful." "Well, Patrick," Roberts said, "we'll see ya honey." Though certainly hurt, Patti expressed sympathy for Oral. "I think there comes a time when pain is so intense or the sense of futility so heavy, even for great spiritual leaders, and it is so close to you that you don't counsel, you don't do anything, you let it happen," she wrote. At this point in their lives, they "were all weakened by the years and years of pain." This encounter happened in 1979. Rebecca and Marshall had only been dead for two years, and the fight over the City of Faith was entering one of its hottest phases. Patti believed that Oral was simply too tired: "He had reached his limit."[82]

10

Called Home

A 900-FOOT JESUS APPEARED TO ORAL on May 25, 1980, at 7:00 p.m. as the evangelist stood praying in front of the half-finished City of Faith. For the next hour and a half, Jesus and Oral talked about the dire situation of the medical complex. The $50 million Oral raised the previous year was already gone, and with only a year to finish construction, he needed money. Oral was standing by himself when he suddenly felt that "someone was there besides myself," he told his partners in a September letter. When he opened his eyes, he saw Jesus looking at him. "His eyes . . . Oh! His eyes! He stood a full 300 feet taller than the 600-foot-tall City of Faith." This wasn't the first time Oral saw Jesus, but this time he was "face to face with the King of Kings." Jesus silently stared at the six foot three inch evangelist and lifted the sixty-story clinic off its base and said, "See how easy it is for Me to lift it?"[1]

Roberts knew immediately what Jesus was telling him; if he wanted to finish the City of Faith, he needed to put all his trust in God. The evangelist pleaded with Jesus that he and his loyal partners had already done all they could, but that things still seemed hopeless. Jesus reprimanded Oral, reminding him of the blessings that could be found through seed faith and that, though many of his partners had obeyed, many more had not: "I desire them to obey so I can *bless* them and *make* them a *blessing*."[2]

Oral moaned that he had already done everything he could. The burden was now on his partners, some of whom had obeyed God's command to donate but many had not. He was not asking for money simply for himself. He was doing it for them. He wrote, "You've got a need. You may have lost your job. Your creditors and the utility companies may have been threatening to turn off your lights or repossess your gas. Your house may be in danger. You may be with your back to the wall. You don't know what's going to happen."[3] These problems could be solved by sending money to help finish the City of Faith. "Do what I ask you to do, not for Oral Roberts but because I'm a man of God doing God's work, and because God says He'll multiply your seed."[4] Between 400,000 and 500,000 of Oral's followers responded to the September letter by mailing nearly $5 million over the next month.[5] The year 1980 ended up becoming the best fund-raising year of Oral's career; he raised nearly $88 million ($297 million in 2021 dollars).[6]

Smelling blood, Oral's critics pounced. Dr. C. T. Thompson wrote to Oklahoma newspapers with a recommendation that a meeting with a 900-foot Jesus merited news coverage. "If he was not here," the physician said, "then you must consider that Mr. Roberts has a healthy imagination at best or is a fraud at the very worst." Thompson, an early opponent of the City of Faith, had come to resent Oral. Claims like Oral's made Tulsa the "religious kook capital of the world," the physician complained. If any other person claimed to have talked with a 900-foot Jesus, that person would be locked up. People tolerated Roberts because he brought a lot of money to the city.[7] Tulsa photographer Stephen Reynolds poked fun at Oral's claim by designing a sign that read "Begin 900-foot Jesus Crossing." The poster, Reynolds explained, which one Tulsa Unitarian minister said helped fill his own church coffers, wasn't meant to be malicious. Any famous person who claimed to talk to a 900-foot Jesus could expect to be poked fun at.[8]

Several syndicated columnists were equally aghast. One hoped that this latest stunt would finally make Oral's impoverished supporters realize that he was a charlatan. Anybody who knew how much money Oral spent building a winning basketball team knew that he would never let a 900-foot prospect walk away.[9] Another told the story of Rose Emmett, supposedly one of Oral's millions of partners, who, though on a fixed income, sent money to Tulsa before her death. Her son-in-law said that the fund-raising letters, which were still being sent to the deceased woman, made him "boil." What kind of a person asked a poor woman "to go out and borrow the money if she didn't have it," he wanted to know. The columnist admitted that the "Lord works in mysterious ways," but that some of his "self-appointed 'crusaders'" wrote the book on chicanery.[10]

Oral also faced backlash from other Christians. Fundamentalist preacher Carl McIntire accused Roberts of going "berserk" and claimed that the Tulsa-based evangelist was "leading an awful lot of people astray from Christianity."[11] An Oklahoma City–based United Methodist Church official wrote a letter to the state bishop urging him to remind other Methodists that Oral's ministry wasn't affiliated with the denomination. He further accused Roberts of "empire building" and called his vision of a

900-foot Jesus a "fabrication." Nebraska bishop Monk Bryan said that though Oral had a "considerable enterprise there in Tulsa," the Methodist Church "should not give encouragement to anyone who bases his ministry on visions."[12]

The City of Faith wasn't the only ORU institution struggling in 1980. In January, the ORU basketball program was put on probation for a year. The alleged violations occurred during the tenures of coaches Jerry Hale (1975–1976) and Lake Kelly (1977–1978). One former player, Chuck Dahms, who transferred to Wake Forest after his sophomore season, said players were gifted cars, clothes, and cash. "There was plenty of other money given out," he remembered. When the NCAA launched its investigation in July 1978, ORU athletic director Bob Brooks dismissed the allegations as nothing more than the words of a few bitter ex-players, and Oral went on record saying that if the athletic department ever violated the university's code of conduct, he would immediately shut it down. In its investigation, the NCAA discovered that players were given cash to pay for airplane travel and for personal use, had their phone bills paid, were hired for jobs at inflated salaries, and lived in rent-free housing.[13]

Basketball sanctions aside, Oral scored a major victory in March 1981 when the Oklahoma Supreme Court reversed the Tulsa District Court's 1978 ruling. The OHPC had acted correctly, six of the nine justices argued, since the "'controlling' purpose of the hospital was not religious." In the majority opinion, Justice Ralph Hodges wrote that the hospital did not advance or prohibit the free exercise of religion. Just because "some religious group might receive some incidental benefit as the result of construction of the hospital is not controlling," the justice argued. The court also supported the City of Faith's holistic framework and agreed with Oral's contention that no other institution offered the type of spiritual and medical care the City of Faith promised.[14]

Rick Ford, attorney for the Tulsa Hospital Council, said the opposition had two choices. It could either get the court to rehear the case, which wasn't likely, or take the case to the US Supreme Court, where the most promising approach was to argue that the OHPC's decision violated the separation of church and state. Ford didn't think the matter was settled. The state court simply ruled that there had been no violation of church-state separation, not that the hospital was needed.[15] The Tulsa Hospital Council mulled appealing its case to the Supreme Court, but a month later, it decided to end its fight and welcomed the City of Faith into its ranks.[16]

Roberts and his supporters saw the court's order as evidence that God was on their side. Immediately upon hearing the court's decision, Roberts told James Winslow, "The ruling by the Oklahoma Supreme Court shows us once again God is God; when He speaks and His children obey, no power of man or devil can stop Him. I feel in my spirit a new wave of God's healing power is going to begin sweeping across the land."[17] Don Nickles, US senator from Oklahoma, similarly saw the court's order as a triumph of American freedom and Christian heritage. The nation had been through some rough times, but the City of Faith represented a spiritual rebirth. Nickles praised the state supreme court for resurrecting the Founding Fathers' vision of a country guided by Christian principles and reliance on God Almighty. Quoting one of his favorite Bible verses, Galatians 5:1, "Stand fast therefore in the liberty, wherewith Christ hath made us free, and be not entangled again with the yoke of bondage," Nickles argued that with the City of Faith—and Ronald Reagan's presidency—"we will have a rebirth of freedom, and that we will enjoy eternal life with God."[18]

More good news came in August. At its annual meeting in New Orleans, the House of Delegates of the American Bar Association (ABA) voted 147 to 127 to grant the O. W. Coburn School of Law provisional accreditation. Back in May, despite glowing reports for ORU's faculty, students, and facilities, an ABA committee recommended against accreditation on the grounds that the university violated the association's Standard 211, which prohibited discrimination on the basis of race, national origin, sex, and religion. The committee objected to ORU's requirement that all faculty and students sign the university's honor code, which not only placed limits on personal conduct but also professed a belief in Jesus Christ. The problem, according to a lawyer for the ABA, wasn't that ORU had a religious orientation—the ABA had accredited religious-oriented law schools in the past—but that it was blatantly discriminatory against people who didn't hold the same beliefs.[19] One major point of tension was how ORU would react to two homosexual professors who wanted to marry each other. They'd be fired, of course, Dean Charles Kothe said.[20]

In July, an Illinois federal district judge ruled that the ABA couldn't deny accreditation based on the school's religious policy, as long as the education met "'acceptable standards' of competency." For ORU to receive accreditation, the House of Delegates amended Standard 211 to allow for religious-based admission policies. These policies had to be stated up front and couldn't be used to avoid having a diverse student body.[21]

Standing before a crowd of thirteen thousand in ORU's Mabee Auditorium on November 1, 1981, Oral dedicated the City of Faith. Surrounded by fellow evangelists Pat Robertson, Rex Humbard, Kenneth Hagin, Kenneth Hagin Jr., and Demos Shakarian; former professional football player Rosie Grier; Oklahoma governor George Nigh; and Kenya's minister of higher education, J. Kamotha, Roberts proudly proclaimed that the City of Faith would be visited by an astonishing one million patients a year. Speaking on the theme "This Is a New Beginning for the Human Race," Oral said, with a bit of hubris, that the opening of the City of Faith was akin to the creation of the universe. "It's like the moment of creation, when time stood still. And every now and then in the history of the human race, time stands still when some great event is about to burst forth from over the horizon to touch human life in some significant way. Today once again time stands still, if only for a moment, for the power of prayer and medicine to be forever merged in the City of Faith."[22] And, as if the day could not get any better for the sixty-three-year-old evangelist, Congressman James Jones of Tulsa read a letter from President Ronald Regan, who congratulated the evangelist for opening the City of Faith free of debt and for showing the power of private initiative. After Jones read the letter, Roberts remarked, "I'm about to explode."[23] Tulsa mayor James Inhofe added to the excitement when he proclaimed that November 1 was going to be "City of Faith and We Love Oral Roberts Day" in the city.[24]

The thrill didn't last long. After it opened, the City of Faith immediately started losing money. In March 1982, Roberts apocalyptically told his TV viewers that the ministry was nearly broke and needed at least $10 million a month or the hospital and university would have to close. Pinning the blame on his partners, he said, "Some of our 'prayer partners' apparently think that building the City of Faith and opening it is the end of the picture. We're going to have to change that perception."[25]

The financial problems were a result of poor patient numbers. From November 1981 to January 1982, the hospital saw about thirty-four patients a day. This number increased to about fifty in June. The low numbers led to the first of several rounds of layoffs that would occur during the 1980s. In July 1982, the City of Faith announced that it was laying off 50 percent of its support personnel and demoting fifty registered nurses to a "cooperative arrangement" with a guaranteed salary at other institutions. Dr. James Winslow said the hospital had been overstaffed in comparison to demand, but he remained hopeful that someday, when things improved, the laid-off staff could be rehired. A hospital spokesperson stated that they had not considered the difficulty patients would have traveling to the hospital and that the hospital needed to diversify its services to attract more patients.[26] A few months later, in October, hospital administrators had reason to be a bit more optimistic. The City of Faith rehired some of the one hundred personnel that were laid off in July, and there was an increase in the number of patients. The hospital, though, was still operating at a loss, and Winslow predicted that it would not break even until 1984.[27]

It was at this time that the Roberts family faced another devastating tragedy. On June 9, 1982, Ronnie Roberts was found dead in his car of an apparent self-inflicted .25 caliber gunshot wound to the chest. There was no suicide note at the scene, but Richard Roberts and George Stovall, executive vice president of ORU, found several letters in Ronnie's apartment. In one of these letters, he reportedly wrote that he was excited to see Rebecca again and warned his children about the dangers of drugs. Ronnie was thirty-seven years old.[28]

It's not totally clear when Ronnie started using drugs, but, according to Oral in his 1995 autobiography, the signs were there almost immediately after his eldest son moved back to Tulsa in the mid-1970s. One afternoon, Oral and Evelyn visited Ronnie at his place, only to find him in bed. When they asked him if he was sick, he said there was nothing to worry about because he took a nap every afternoon. Oral had almost certainly encountered addicts during his career, but his strict Pentecostal upbringing and the lifestyle at ORU shielded him from personal exposure to drug use and drug addicts. By summer 1981, Oral finally confronted Ronnie about what was happening in his life. Ronnie broke down and admitted that he was a drug addict. In September 1981, Oral and Evelyn and the rest of the nation learned the depth of Ronnie's addiction when he was charged with forging prescriptions to secure five hundred tablets of the drug Tussionex, a cough suppressant. He pleaded guilty and was placed on probation in February 1982. As part of his guilty plea, he agreed to a six-month outpatient drug treatment program.[29]

Things deteriorated quickly. After his arrest, Ronnie and his wife, Carol, separated. He spent his last few months alone in a Tulsa apartment. The last few meetings with his parents were deeply tragic. To help his struggling son, Oral once again offered Ronnie a position at ORU if he met certain conditions; he would have to stop smoking and drinking and would have to cut his beard. Ronnie, as always, was flattered, but when his mom came to visit him on May 9, Mother's Day, he told her that he couldn't take a job just because of his last name. Evelyn believed that her son was hopelessly lost.[30] A few days before he took his life, Ronnie went to his father for money. In their last conversation, Oral told Ronnie that he was done giving him money to feed his addiction and said, "Settle it, Ronnie, my dear son, once and for all."[31]

In June 1982, *Christianity Today* published Oral's thoughts on the death of his son. In the statement, Oral touched on his son's great potential—not just academically but also spiritually—and his struggles. Ronnie told Evelyn before his death, "Mother, I can't cope anymore." Despite the grief, Oral said he felt at peace. "Two things remain: the Lord and heaven—the two that remain. From this day we shall enter a new dimension of God's grace, a renewed determination to bring God's healing love to this generation. Heaven is very real; God is so close. We still hurt, but we rejoice, too, because our God is still God."[32]

Ronnie's life hid another secret: he was gay.[33] His sexuality, even more than Richard and Patti's divorce and the financial problems facing the City of Faith, had the most potential to destroy Oral's ministry. Though Oral was never as vocal about his feelings toward homosexuality as many of his contemporaries, he, like most of them, was antigay. In 2007, an undated audio clip surfaced online of Oral talking about sex.

There's always a list of reasons that leads a person to commit suicide. In Ronnie's case, in the two years before his death, he had declared bankruptcy, been arrested, and divorced, a sequence of events that would wreak havoc on any person's mental well-being. But Ronnie wasn't like most people. His intellect, use of tobacco and alcohol, and beard made him the black sheep of his family. He was also the closeted son of one of the world's most famous evangelists, an evangelist who compared gay sex to a man trying to insert his penis into a woman's ear or nose or any other strange orifice, which Oral, in his Oklahoma drawl, pronounced "or-e-*fice*."[34]

Ronnie's death, much like Rebecca's in February 1977, was the impetus behind a major announcement at the City of Faith. In early January 1983, in a twelve-page letter and on his TV show, *Oral Roberts and You*, Oral told his partners about a seven-hour conversation with Jesus. This time they talked about the City of Faith's medical research center, which was still little more than an exterior shell after two years and had hired zero researchers. In their chat, Jesus told Oral that the City of Faith was going to discover the cure for cancer. The Lord reportedly told Roberts that he wouldn't have instructed him to build the twenty-story center unless he had a plan to attack "cancer in both a physical and spiritual way that is different than any cancer research programs in the world today."

He definitely didn't ask the evangelist to open the center only for it to stand empty.[35]

In the February 1983 issue of *Abundant Life*, Oral described cancer as a wild weed. You could chop it off at the surface, "but you'll never kill it out unless you get it at the roots." Satan, Oral believed, was responsible for cancer. On their own, prayer and medicine weren't enough to defeat cancer, Oral wrote. What was needed was the latest medical technology and treatment *and* prayer.[36] Dr. Winslow explained to reporters, "We're not substituting prayer for medicine, nor are we substituting medicine for prayer. We're trying to put them together."[37] Dr. Marc Rendell, a physician at the City of Faith who was previously a professor of internal medicine at Johns Hopkins University and chief of endocrinology at a US Public Health Service hospital, said that the medical establishment worshiped a false god—science—and needed to be reminded that all things, even medical advances, came from God.[38] *Lifeline*, the City of Faith's in-house publication, declared 1983 the "Year of Research."[39] A spokesman for the American Cancer Society didn't know how to respond to the claim that cancer had spiritual origins because, he said, "What we're dealing with [with Oral Roberts] is religious beliefs. We're dealing with science."[40]

Oral told his partners that a breakthrough could happen only if they sent enough money. In exchange for a $240 gift, Oral promised to send forty-eight cassette tapes on which he read and offered his commentary on the New Testament. He also told them to expect up to fourteen "spectacular things of miracle power," including financial success, better health, happier families, and increased mental ability.[41] Later in January, five thousand ORU students and staff circled the City of Faith in what officials called a "Jericho march against cancer." Just like at the battle of Jericho in the Old Testament book of Joshua, when the ancient Israelites marched around the city's walls until they were destroyed, Roberts explained, "our march today is a symbol of faith."[42]

Once again, Roberts's partners came through. One month after Oral announced the revelation, approximately 130,000 to 140,000 had responded, with about 80,000 requesting the tapes and pledging to support the research center.[43] By May, partners had donated $5 million to the research center.[44] Shortly after this fund-raising drive, Dr. Winslow announced that the City of Faith had purchased a $1.4 million nuclear magnetic resonance imaging unit that could be used for the treatment and research of cancer.[45] That same spring, 244 City of Faith employees lost their jobs, as operating losses climbed to $1 million a month.[46] They weren't broke, Oral said, but they were close. He was still under the obligation to God not to borrow money. At the time, he needed to raise about $10 million ($27 million in 2021 dollars) a month: $8 million for the City of Faith and $2 million for ORU.[47]

Widely publicized exposés documented that the medical complex was a "ghost town." In February 1983, the *Washington Post* reported that the hospital had opened only four floors and was using only 103 out of 294 beds. Most of the floors in the clinic were closed, and the research center was still a shell and had not opened for its stated purpose to research cancer.[48] In June 1983, the *Chicago Tribune* quoted local critics of Oral's medical complex. Marvin Cooke, a Methodist clergyman and director of the interfaith Tulsa Metropolitan Ministry Association, commented that the three-building medical complex looked "like a turkey, a gold-plated elephant." Ira Schlezinger, a vice president for Tulsa's Hillcrest Medical Center, said that the problems the City of Faith faced had been anticipated, calling them "fulfilled prophecies," and suggested that about half of the City of Faith's patients came from Oklahoma and a majority from Tulsa. He expressed concern that the City of Faith would further drain patients from the other Tulsa hospitals by placing a health maintenance organization (HMO) in the sixty-story clinic and that it had recently sent out a mass mailing to churches within a fifty-mile radius of Tulsa.[49]

Since the City of Faith opened in November 1981, administrators had tried several marketing techniques to attract patients, including advertisements in popular magazines like the *Saturday Evening Post* and local publications like *Tulsa Lifestyle*, TV spots, and a display at the Tulsa International Airport, which had the potential to be seen by 5 million travelers.[50] One of the most ambitious attempts was the City of Faith Gold Card Program, which promised members a free annual physical and discounts at the pharmacy, gift shop, and cafeteria. In its initial phase, launched in November 1982, the City of Faith distributed 1.2 million gold-colored patient cards and expected to distribute another 1.5 million.[51]

In August 1984, Oral said God spoke to him again. Things had been bleak for the entire Roberts organization since the beginning of the year. By June, 244 of the 907 employees at the City of Faith and 90 at the OREA had been laid off (40 had already lost their jobs in a previous round of cutbacks). ORU employees were placed on a four-day, thirty-two-hour workweek for June and July, direct mail correspondence was cut by 40 percent from one million pieces a month to 600,000, and ORU eliminated athletic scholarships for "minor sports" like men's and women's cross country, track and field, and tennis, and women's volleyball.[52]

On the August 19 episode of *Expect a Miracle with Oral and Richard Roberts*, Oral, recording from his hospital room at the City of Faith, where he recently had surgery to remove nasal polyps, recounted how Jesus had stood at the foot of his bed. Similar to their 1980 conversation, Jesus bemoaned that the devil was still trying to bring down the City of Faith and that Roberts's partners were not taking advantage of the hospital's excellent services. To save the City of Faith, Roberts had to plant a seed of his own. Jesus told Roberts to open the City of Faith to the poor and needy, even though most of them would be unable to pay their medical fees. If Oral obeyed, God would bless him as he had done early in Oral's ministry when he welcomed and prayed for the poor and "invalids" at his tent healing services. Jesus reminded Oral that he never charged any of these people for prayer and that now he needed to provide them with free medical treatment.

After a twenty-minute conversation, Jesus disappeared, and Oral's attention was drawn to another figure standing in the room. An angel, who Oral said "was so huge that his head touched the ceiling," picked up where Jesus left off. The angel said two words to Oral: "Dispatch me." Oral was admittedly confused by this instruction, but then he remembered Hebrews 1:14, where the ancient Christian writer said that God used angels to help the saved. Now that he understood, Oral dispatched the angel to bring the sick and needy to the City of Faith.[53] A minister in Del Rio, Texas, obeyed the message. After hearing Oral talk at a ministers seminar at ORU about his plan to open the City of Faith to the poor, the Reverend Michael Kyle set up a special fund at his home church to help poor people pay for travel to Tulsa. The church and local community jumped in to help. One church member offered free use of his personal airplane, and a Wendy's restaurant pledged 10 percent of whatever church members spent there on Sundays. Wendy's eventually sent a $500 check to the church.[54] In the fall of 1984, City of Faith officials shared that the hospital's daily patient load nearly doubled from 80 to 155, that most were paying patients, and that the hospital hired an additional 100 people.[55]

Despite Roberts's promises, charity was never a spending priority. In addition to his plan to help the needy, Roberts said he would spend $7 million over the next eighteen months on indigent care. The amount was later dropped to $2.4 million. In all, from 1982 to 1987, the City of Faith never spent more than $880,000 a year on charity care, and only a combined total of $1.2 million in 1984 and 1985. Dr. Pat Lester, one of the physicians at the City of Faith, expressed disappointment that helping the poor wasn't a higher priority, but as money grew tighter, he said, "that was the first thing to go."[56]

Facing mounting pressure, Oral returned to his roots. In October 1983, readers of *Abundant Life* learned that God had told him to hold major healing crusades once again after a twenty-year absence.[57] The crusades kicked off on February 26, 1984, but with a twist. With Oral in Tulsa and Richard, who started his own healing ministry four years earlier and would start his own daily TV show in September 1984, in Nigeria, the father and son duo were seen via satellite by more than 200,000 people in 211 US and Canadian cities. One attendee in Madison, Wisconsin, said it felt a "little less real, but it's still beautiful."[58] A month later, Oral and Richard traveled to Phoenix, where they filled the seven-thousand-seat Sundome.[59] Crusades were also scheduled for Roanoke, Virginia; Charlotte, North Carolina; Columbus, Ohio; Huntington, West Virginia; and Anaheim, California.[60]

The reason for this return to the revival circuit was obvious. Oral needed money. The cost to run ORU, the City of Faith, and his evangelistic association had climbed to $125 million ($335 million in 2021 dollars) a year. During the February 1984 satellite broadcast, he told the audience that he didn't want to give them the specifics on the financial crisis but wanted them to know that it was serious. "Give liberally to God," he then said, "and God will give liberally to you."[61] Richard, it seemed, picked up on his father's fund-raising tics. In Phoenix, he told the crowd that God instructed him to tell them "the number for today is $20. Everyone is to give a gift of $20." He went on, "God laid that on my heart."[62]

The problem with the revival circuit, Oral told *Charisma* magazine in June 1985, was his age. In his heart, he felt twenty-nine, but he knew that his sixty-seven-year-old body wouldn't "stand it." It pained him, he said, that his body as well as ORU and the City of Faith were keeping him from doing what God had originally called him to do: pray for the sick.

Oral wasn't the only person who yearned for personal connection. He believed that one of the reasons more than 150,000 people visited ORU each year was to have an encounter with one of the Robertses. Unfortunately, they had to leave disappointed because the family was too busy with their other jobs.[63] Jan Dargatz, spokesperson for ORU, agreed. She told newspapers that people wanted a "greater encounter with what Oral Roberts represents."[64] This was the reason Oral announced plans to build the $15 million, 300,000-square-foot Healing Center in Tulsa.

Announced in January 1985, the Healing Center represented how desperate the situation had become in Tulsa. On its surface, the center had the bells and whistles of a Christian theme park, much like Jim Bakker's Heritage USA in Charlotte, North Carolina. The seven-acre Healing Center would house the "Journey into Faith" center, where visitors could see depictions of Oral's life. During the "Walk through the Bible" portion, visitors would experience the parting of the Red Sea, the creation of the world, and Moses receiving the Ten Commandments on Mount Sinai. There would also be a gift shop, restaurant, marriage counseling center, and television studio. Exhibition designer Peter Wolf said he was loath to call it a theme park because even the best theme parks like Disneyland were two-dimensional. "Our challenge," he remarked, "is to give people an experience they haven't had before." The centerpiece was to be a glass-enclosed atrium where Roberts could preach and pray for the sick. He couldn't be there every day with set hours, according to Dargatz, because they needed to guarantee Oral's safety. Oral estimated that 2 million people would visit the Healing Center every year.[65] The Healing Center, he told *Charisma*, was the "most important thing" he'd ever done in his life.[66]

In reality, the Healing Center was a desperate attempt to raise money. In his talk with *Charisma*, he explained that one of the purposes of the center was to create a "living endowment"; in other words, a steady stream of money.[67] Dargatz opined that people who visited Tulsa would be more likely to give direct contributions.[68] Sociologist Jeffrey Hadden, one of the first scholars to take televangelism seriously, commented shortly after the Healing Center was announced that it was a "last-ditch effort to try to save Oral's shaky financial empire." He also believed that it was too late to help the evangelist: "I think he's pulled his last trick from the hat."[69] Two years later, a journalist for the *Miami Herald* reviewed the creation portion of the Healing Outreach Center. The reporter was impressed by most of it, though a little disappointed with the Way of Sin section, describing it as "uneventful." Admittance was free, but on the way out, visitors heard a short sermon where Oral talked about seed faith and were then handed pledge cards as they left.[70]

In June 1985, university officials told students they were closing the dental school. Richard blamed the dental students for the closure, claiming that only one graduate had fulfilled a promise made to become a "missionary dentist." Most graduates selfishly went into private practice instead, Richard complained. A second-year dental student quarreled with this account. Oral may not have been raising money for dental missions, but the students were. Four mission teams were already slated to start work that upcoming summer, and students were busy sending out support letters and receiving money. Dr. James Winslow was a little more sympathetic to the dental students' situation. He explained that the average student graduated with $35,000 of debt. Private practice was simply the best option to pay back this debt. A local dentist, who had worked as an adjunct instructor at the dental school, said the school was poorly prepared for the costs needed to keep a dental school running.[71]

In November, in another cost-cutting measure, ORU closed its law school and transferred its 200,000-volume law library, valued at $10 million, to Pat Robertson's upstart law school at CBN University (now Regent University). During a press conference, Oral said that Robertson, who went to Yale Law School, was better equipped to run a law school and that the transfer was a "testament that those working for Jesus Christ do this for one common good." He also referred to the transfer as an act of seed faith.[72]

On January 4, 1987, standing inside the still incomplete research center, Roberts told his television audience, which at the time was estimated to be about 1.4 million, about a recent confrontation with God. The initial conversation happened about a year earlier in March 1986; in that talk, Oral promised God he would raise $8 million for a medical missionary program; if he didn't do that, he said, God would "call him home." But eight months later he was still $4.5 million short, and Oral was getting nervous. With only a few months left, Oral asked his supporters to extend his life. "Let me live beyond March," he said.[73] On the same program, Evelyn looked at her husband and said, "Something's got to happen by March, honey. I certainly don't want God to take you after 48 years (of marriage)." On ABC's *Good Morning America*, Richard said he didn't want his father's upcoming birthday on January 24 to be his last.[74] Jan Dargatz said that Oral's comments shouldn't be taken as a negative thing, because the evangelist wasn't afraid to die: "He's looking forward to getting to heaven and finding out some answers to questions, such as why wasn't everybody healed?"[75] An ORU sophomore said, "If he says God spoke to him, God spoke to him. Oral Roberts is no flimflam man."[76] Frank Coyle, history professor at ORU, was a little more concerned about Oral's comments. He said that while he had never questioned Oral's sincerity, he felt there was something wrong with "putting a guilt trip like that on other people."[77] Oral's partners responded as they always did. They sent $1.6 million in cash and pledges in the ten days following his announcement.[78]

Others were less impressed with Roberts's exploitative tactics. At the end of the year, *Good Morning America* awarded Roberts—along with his counterpart Jim Bakker—a "Gimme a Break Award" for using the possibility of his death to bilk his supporters for their money, accusing him of turning God into a terrorist.[79] James Dobson, popular Christian psychologist and founder of Focus on the Family, said Roberts was "killing his ministry" with his radical claims and needed to seek psychiatric treatment. A former associate of Oral's confirmed Dobson's fear that the evangelist was suffering from mental illness, displaying signs of manic depression.[80]

Roberts's unfortunate remarks were a popular topic of conversation at a Christian fund-raising conference, cosponsored by the Billy Graham Center and Christian Stewardship Council, in Kansas City. The pastors, ministry executives, and fund-raisers in attendance accused Roberts of setting fund-raising back at least twenty years and of hurting their own efforts to raise money. Without discounting the importance of Oral's ministry, theologian Carl F. H. Henry remarked that Oral's plea "was hardly a gain for the evangelical Gospel." At the end of the conference, participants signed a pledge promising to "seek godly ways in raising and giving funds," because, "even with the best of intentions, mistakes have been made." A Gallup poll showed that Americans in general were growing tired of evangelists' fund-raising methods: 40 percent of Americans believed their fund-raising approaches were unethical, and over half believed there had been too many appeals for money over the past year and that money was misused or that the evangelists were dishonest.[81] In July and August 1987, the United Methodist Church separated itself from Oral by removing ORU from its list of approved seminaries and revoking Oral's elder status.[82]

Jeff MacNelly, cartoonist for the *Chicago Tribune*, drew Oral in a church belfry, the Church of Oral Roberts, holding two tablets resembling popular depictions of the Ten Commandments, "'Send more money or the preacher gits it.'—God." A police helicopter pilot nervously says, "We've got a weird situation here, Chief."[83] *Saturday Night Live* also poked fun at Roberts on its March 28 episode. Phil Hartman portrayed Oral, and Charlton Heston played God.

Chicago Tribune columnist Mike Royko wrote that Roberts had the chance to convert millions of atheists. Royko said that he had been an admirer of the Tulsa evangelist since he claimed to have seen a 900-foot Jesus lift the City of Faith off its foundation. He had seen quarterbacks shudder in fear at the mere sight of seven-foot linemen, while Roberts showed little to no fear when confronted with the 900-foot savior. Royko added that it would be a mistake to send Roberts money, since his death had the potential to be a great evangelistic tool. Just imagine, Royko wrote, if Roberts appeared on his television show, told his audience that they had fallen $2 million short of their goal, and immediately dropped dead. That might sound coldhearted, but if Roberts and his followers were sincere about converting the lost, they would heed his advice. Royko admitted that his plan would probably fail anyway, as Roberts would simply go on television and tell his audience that God had given him an extension.[84] This was a real possibility. At a February 18 chapel service, Oral told students and faculty that his homecoming wouldn't necessarily be immediate but could be "twenty years from now."[85]

Opinion in Tulsa also started to turn against Oral. Radio DJ John Erling said that a 600-foot Lassie the dog appeared to him in a vision and told him to build the Kennel of Care, a hospital for cats and dogs. The wonder dog also instructed him to ask his listeners to each send in $777 for the Kennel of Care, which would include golden fire hydrants. More seriously, Erling believed Oral was on his "last stand" and that with the failure of the City of Faith, "his back is up against the wall."[86] Even the usually friendly *Tulsa Tribune* issued a rebuke of Oral's death claim. A headline read, "Come off It, Oral," and the *Tribune*'s editor, Jenkin Lloyd Jones, accused his friend of "sacrilege" and suggested that only a "petty, vengeful or idiotic" God would hold Oral's life ransom for a few million dollars. The *Tribune* also found that Oral lived in a $500,000 house in Tulsa and used a $2.4 million mansion in Beverly Hills and a $553,000 house in Palm Springs, California, and that Richard's family had recently moved into a 7,000-square-foot house in Tulsa. Tax records revealed how much Oral's supporters had cut back on donations. From the $88 million peak in 1980, donations had dropped to $58 million in 1985.[87]

Tulsans, however, were in a tough position. While the city's oil-based economy had been in a slump, residents were grateful for the 2,500 jobs Oral provided. Mayor Dick Crawford, who had worked as a development officer at ORU for several years, said Oral could be "stubborn and arrogant," and when he felt like God had spoken to him, "it's damn the torpedoes." Kent Ingram, minister of evangelism at Boston Avenue United Methodist Church, said people in the city were hesitant to criticize Roberts because "in some ways he has put Tulsa on the map." Ingram, however, decried Oral for making God look "mechanistic and manipulative."[88] As people who worked intimately with Oral in the past, some Tulsans likely saw how much the stress of the City of Faith—and no doubt the trauma of losing two children—was having on him. The Reverend Warren Hultgren of Tulsa's First Baptist Church, longtime friend and golfing partner, said Oral didn't need criticism but help. "He's been zinged so bad," Hultgren said.[89]

March 22, 1987, marked the beginning of what Oral described as the most important prayer vigil of his life. He still needed to raise about $1.3 million before March 31, so he planned to temporarily move into the Prayer Tower for a nine-day vigil, leaving only for the essentials. Speaking from his private prayer room in the tower, Oral touched on the media blowup over his comments from January 4 and, predictably, spent much of the time talking about seed faith.[90] Richard called it the "most significant trip to the tower to date, since its construction in 1967. This vigil marks a momentous occasion for the entire body of Christ." His father, he said on his TV program, "will be in the prayer tower really travailing to rebirth what was created by the Apostle Paul and Doctor Luke 2,000 years ago— the combination of prayer and medicine." If Oral didn't start the medical missionary program, Richard added, it meant he was in "disobedience to God, and he will have no further purpose on this earth." In a letter to his supporters, Oral said he believed that the money was going to be raised, but if it wasn't, he would see them in heaven.[91]

Fortunately for Roberts, Jerry Collins, a former dog track owner and millionaire philanthropist from Florida, donated $1.3 million eight days before the evangelist was to be "called home." Never one to shy away from publicity, Collins stepped forward after he heard about Roberts's cries for money. He told reporters that he felt sorry for Roberts because the press had treated him so poorly in its portrayal of his fund-raising methods. By his own admission, Collins was an odd fit for Roberts. He was an infrequent church visitor, had once said Roberts needed psychiatric treatment, painted the evangelist's plea for money as "hari-kari," and added that if Roberts wanted to die, "he can go die."[92] Roberts, he explained, was simply a "medium to get [the money] to the students."[93] The money was raised, but the damage was done. Oral's reputation never recovered from his January 4 comments.

Oral wasn't the only TV preacher facing scandal. In 1986, a group of self-described skeptics smuggled a radio transmitter into Peter Popoff's healing service and discovered that, at the right frequency, 39.17 megahertz, they could pick up Popoff's wife, Elizabeth, giving details that she and other aides gathered from the audience before the service. Then, during the service, when Popoff called a specific name and ailments, it would appear as though he had received what charismatics call the "word of knowledge." A year later, the Peter Popoff Evangelistic Association filed for bankruptcy.[94]

On March 19, 1987, Jim Bakker, founder and president of the PTL Network, resigned from his position after admitting to a sexual encounter with twenty-one-year-old Jessica Hahn in a Clearwater Beach, Florida, hotel room in December 1980. Not long after his resignation, it was discovered that Bakker had paid Hahn $265,000 to remain quiet about their tryst. On the outside, Bakker's PTL empire was impressive. At its peak in 1986, it had 2,500 employees, annual revenues of $129 million, and a 2,300-acre theme park and ministry center, Heritage USA. That year, 6 million people visited Heritage USA, placing it third behind Disneyland and Disney World in attendance. Three years later, in October 1989, a federal jury convicted Bakker of several counts of mail and wire fraud for his fund-raising tactics while building Heritage USA. The judge sentenced him to forty-five years in prison, though he only served five.[95]

On October 17, 1987, Jimmy Swaggart was caught with a sex worker by one of his nemeses, Marvin Gorman, who blackmailed Swaggart into promising to publicly apologize to Gorman for lying about his own extramarital affairs. Gorman waited until February 1988 to take the evidence he had against Swaggart—photos of the Baton Rouge–based evangelist entering and exiting a hotel room known to be a place where sex workers took their clients—to the Assemblies of God. Confronted with the evidence, Swaggart, on February 21, 1988, put on a good show for the television audience and his church flock when he tearfully confessed to his transgressions. The Assemblies of God defrocked Swaggart in April when he refused to comply with a one-year suspension.[96]

The sins of the televangelists weren't necessarily isolated incidents. The titans of Wall Street in the 1980s, in some ways, were much like their counterparts in the evangelical world. They were outsiders and believed in taking risks. The renegades of Wall Street, Ivan Boesky, Carl Icahn, Dennis Levine, and Michael Milken, came from working-class, immigrant, and Jewish backgrounds; they were not the typical WASPs of the past. These new Wall Street leaders replaced traditional ideas of caution with ones of risk and debt. Their philosophy encouraged high-risk speculative investments, most clearly seen in the high-yield ("junk-bond") market and savings and loan (S&L) institutions, and it worked, at least temporarily. While there seemed to be an endless supply of money available, the junk-bond market quickly crashed. Starting with the arrest of Dennis Levine in May

1986 for insider trading and fraud, the image of Wall Street raiders as heroes began to collapse. The idea of finance as "a nonstop money machine" was over.[97]

Televangelism's and Wall Street's influence on American society were ubiquitous in the 1980s. In their rise and fall, they helped to shape the aesthetics and ethos of the Reagan years. They were symbols of the decade's glitz and glamour, embodying the decade's faith in growth and abundance. After the harsh years of the 1970s and Jimmy Carter's rebuke of American materialism and greed, Ronald Reagan offered a promising alternative. While Carter told Americans that they needed to learn to live with less and to stop measuring happiness with material goods, Reagan told them that they should never stop desiring more.[98] Instead, Americans should always be pursuing the next big thing. This optimism matched well Roberts's theology and his belief, despite all evidence to the contrary, that the City of Faith was going to be a success. The emphasis on the relationship between wealth and happiness and the idea that growth was limitless if one had enough faith fueled the evangelist's fevered expansion. The problem was that this faith in one's ability to create unlimited wealth and growth bred a sense of recklessness and invincibility. An economy based on so much speculation and debt could not last long.

The money Oral raised between January and March ran out quickly. By the end of October, journalists reported that the situation at the City of Faith continued to deteriorate. It was revealed that hospital administrators were in negotiations to seek outside control in the hopes of bringing financial stability to the project and that several top officials had resigned. There were also reports that Roberts's ministry was going to stop financing the clinic, and was telling physicians to open their own private practices since they would no longer be salaried employees of the City of Faith.[99] The following month, a group of seventy-six doctors took over the daily operations of the City of Faith's clinic.[100]

On March 28, 1989, Roberts once again went, hat in hand, to his supporters. During a taping of his weekly television show, *Expect a Miracle*, he said that he needed to raise $11 million by May 6 to pay for television airtime, ministry payroll, food at the university, and other supplies to appease creditors, who he said would "start dismantling" his ministry. The plea sounded a lot like previous ones. "People, this is serious. This is a life-and-death matter." He continued, "I believe you want me to continue coming on the air, saying 'Something good is going to happen to you,' because you need to hear a good word in an unhappy world." He also asked his supporters to give away personal valuables: "You can sell them or part of them and send the proceeds to the Oral Roberts Ministries." The ministry had been facing declining contributions since 1987. During that time, donations dropped from $5 million a month to $2.7 million. Roberts, of course, admitted no fault in this decline. Instead, he blamed Jim Bakker, Jimmy Swaggart, and a group of unidentified people "who have already said they're going to take over Oral Roberts University. They're going to take the Bible out and God out and the chapel out." He went on, "And I doubt that. I'm fighting. I won't give up. I won't quit. I'm believing in God."[101] Even if Roberts successfully raised the $11 million, he still faced an uphill battle. ORU had a total debt of $25 million.[102]

On Saturday, May 6, Oral told graduating seniors that the ministry was still $3.8 million short of the $11 million goal. "I want to remind you that things can be lost," he told them. Roberts and his son Richard expressed some hope that they would have the money by Monday. "Checks are coming in the mail, by Federal Express and from credit cards," Richard told a television audience. The father and son team also asked the students to pray that they could establish endowments of more than $100 million to fund various parts of the ministry. Mark Swadener, chief financial officer for the combined ministries, said that the ministry would probably be able to get a three-day extension if the money was not raised by Monday.[103]

On May 3, the *Tulsa World* reported that the NCAA was launching another investigation into the ORU men's basketball team. Just one day prior, the university had announced that it was dropping its affiliation with the NCAA and joining the National Association of Intercollegiate Athletics (NAIA), a lesser level of college sports. Though the move to the NAIA was certainly suspicious, Roberts said it was made for financial reasons.[104] Two weeks later, the *Tulsa World* reported that the $11 million goal was met, but the ministry's problems were far from over. The ministry still needed to find a way to raise $3.3 million a month in order to remain solvent.[105] Between faculty disgruntlement and turnover and low donation numbers—the ministry was only able to raise between $2.3 and $2.5 million a month—the next few months were disappointing.[106] On September 14, Roberts announced that he was being forced to close the medical school and hospital. With $25 million in debt, the ministry was also selling five ministry-owned houses, including the ones in which Oral and his son Richard lived, and a housing complex for married ORU students. The closings would affect nearly 600 hospital employees, 147 students, and 100 faculty members.

One medical student from San Jose, California, voiced disappointment. He was not surprised that the closures were happening, but for students the timing was bad. He explained that he and the other third-year medical students would not be able to transfer all their credits to another university and, therefore, would have to take some of the same classes again. "I've been here two and a half years and kind of watched things fall apart," he told the *Washington Post*. "I've watched doctors leave in droves. I've watched classmates leave in droves. . . . I frankly don't have a lot of confidence in the leadership here from what I've seen and experienced. You get told one thing and other things happen." Unless the ministry raised a $50 million endowment, Oral's dream project would close.[107] The day after the announcement, the *Tulsa World* praised Roberts for his poise in discussing the medical complex's closure.[108]

The miracle multimillion-dollar endowment never came. The City of Faith released its last patient on October 16, 1989. The clinic was the only part of the City of Faith that remained open.[109] After the closing of the City of Faith, ORU was stuck with 2.2 million square feet of hulking buildings. There were certainly ideas about what to do with the structures, some more feasible than others. Some suggested that Tulsa County buy the complex and turn it into a jail, a plan, according to the *Tulsa World*, that would be wildly impractical and expensive.[110] Others thought the Veterans Administration could move into the massive complex.[111] Just one month after the City of Faith released its final patient, ten potential tenants had toured the complex, four of whom remained interested at the end of November.[112] In January 1990, the *Tulsa World* reported that ORU had found at least one tenant, the Cancer Care Centers of America. The cancer treatment center signed a thirty-year lease for 250,000 square feet of space in the thirty-story hospital. The financial terms were confidential. Though the Care Center only took up 10 percent of the available 2.2 million square feet, ORU administrators hoped its presence would send a positive message to other potential tenants.[113]

Assessing the damage years later, Roberts pinned the blame on nearly everyone but himself. He predictably blamed the scandals surrounding Bakker and Swaggart for the decline in donations. Though the fall of these two television ministers had inflicted collateral damage on other Christian ministries, Roberts far overestimated their impact on his own. After all, his visions of a 900-foot Jesus and the 1984 hospital-bed encounter with Jesus happened before Bakker and Swaggart were exposed. Roberts ultimately concluded that televangelist scandals of the late 1980s were overblown and that the blowback on his ministry was unfair since, he said, "There had never been a stain morally, financially, or any other way on the Oral Roberts Ministries."[114]

Roberts also aimed his barbs at the medical establishment, whom he accused of working on the side of the devil to undermine the body of Christ. "Who was I, a healing evangelist, to tell medical people in all their greatness that many of them were missing the boat, that there was power in prayer, that they were falling short to practice medicine alone when people's spirits were crying out for medicine *and* prayer," he asked. He claimed that even the AMA's attitude toward the City of Faith grew more hostile throughout the 1980s. Every year, the governing body sent representatives to the hospital to make sure it was meeting its strict accreditation standards, but in one particular visit, he and the hospital administrators noticed a tension in the air that had never been there before. The medical site team was short with Roberts, ending the visit two days early and refusing to allow Roberts to respond to criticisms. When Roberts called the head of the AMA's liaison committee, a man who had generally been friendly toward Roberts and supported his vision to merge prayer and medicine, he refused the evangelist's request to send the site team back for a follow-up visit. Roberts was heartbroken: "But, [I called him by name], this kind of treatment has never happened before. We fully recognize the power of the AMA. All I'm asking is to be given the same kind of site team visits we've had each year."[115]

The *Tulsa World* was more measured in its conclusions. Two weeks before the City of Faith released its final patient, the newspaper suggested three reasons for the medical complex's failure. First, the type of long-distance referral hospital that Roberts envisioned did not exist because most medicine was routine and did not require travel. Second, the City of Faith had not had enough time to build a reputation. The type of reputation enjoyed by world-renowned hospitals like the Mayo Clinic was slowly earned. Finally, the City of Faith was too reliant on Roberts's supporters. As his television audience dipped during the 1980s, contributions naturally followed suit. The paper correctly pointed out that Roberts's visions likely helped to usher in the end, but observers could not deny the role Jim Bakker's and Jimmy Swaggart's misfortunes played in the failure.[116]

In a December 1989 interview, *Charisma* editor Stephen Strang asked Roberts how he would respond to his critics who say, "I told you so." Roberts said he did not know how to answer the question because he didn't "have any answers from a secular standpoint." He went on, "I operate from the spiritual realm." These critics, he continued, were the same ones who would have said that Jesus was a failure. After his death, they would have said, "See, I told you He was not the Messiah." It might not be obvious right now, Oral opined, but he was confident that, someday, millions of people would believe in God's healing power.[117]

Epilogue

Oral's problems continued into the early 1990s. Donations had been declining for several years. Between 1986 and 1989, annual giving to the Oral Roberts Evangelistic Association dropped from $48.6 million to $27.4 million. TV viewership dropped 50 percent, from roughly 1.1 million in 1986 to 521,000 in 1991, which, however, was an increase of 117,000 from 1990. The other way Oral communicated with his paying partners, the mail, also declined. In 1985, he distributed 27 million letters, magazines, and tracts. In 1989, he distributed 9 million. Giving to ORU dropped from $14 million in 1988 to $12.2 million in 1989. ORU was also facing several lawsuits for allegedly failing to pay debts ranging from $577 to $313,963. Some creditors expressed disappointment because ORU, though sometimes slow to make payments, had always been a reliable customer. The contractors complained that whenever they tried to collect their fees, ORU either ignored them or placed them on "terminal hold." At least one contractor said the university would have to start paying up front or provide cash on delivery. The single bright spot in this financial morass was the university's enrollment, which increased from 3,554 students in 1990 to 4,007 in fall 1991.[1]

There was no televised, tearful plea for money this time. Instead, referring to the crisis as a "private matter," the Robertses mailed letters to their prayer partners for help. In its initial reporting, the *Tulsa World* said Oral sent out one million letters, each of which asked for $500. Richard Roberts later refuted these numbers, claiming that they mailed 600,000 letters, individually tailored to what contributions had been made in the past. Ninety percent of the letters, the younger Roberts said, asked for $100 or less. It pained him to discuss the letter with the secular media, but since he lived in the "real world," he said, "if you're going to take a hit it's better to try and make sure that the hit is based on the facts." These facts, however, were murky. The November 1991 letter referred to a "satanic conspiracy," but because of "the enemies of this ministry," Oral and Richard refused to go into specifics. What mattered was that their supporters knew the situation was serious. If they didn't help, "all hell is going to break loose against this ministry," the letter read. The university's chief financial officer said they were tired of being the butt of jokes and that perhaps the only way to convince people that the crisis was real was to declare bankruptcy.[2]

There was some hope in March 1992 when reports surfaced that ORU had sold the City of Faith for an undisclosed amount to Mid-Continent Real Estate Corporation, who hoped to turn the two-million-square-foot complex into commercial real estate. However, Mid-Continent was unable to put the deal together.[3] There were other attempts to sell the City of Faith, including a $55.5 million sale that ended up with ORU and the potential buyer suing each other in court in 1995, but they all failed.[4] ORU continues to own and lease the three buildings, which are now named the CityPlex Towers.

Things again took a turn for the worse when, in early October 1992, Oral suffered a major heart attack. Just a year earlier, he had undergone two operations to widen his carotid arteries.[5] Complaining of chest pains after an appearance at the Trinity Broadcasting Network's studio in Tustin, California, the seventy-four-year-old Roberts was rushed by paramedics to Hoag Hospital, where he underwent an emergency angioplasty. A spokesperson for Hoag made it sound like there was nothing to worry about because the hospital performed about 200–300 angioplasties a year, but later reports revealed that Oral's heart attack was nearly fatal. In addition to the angioplasty, surgeons had to temporarily implant a pacemaker and a balloon pump through a leg artery. Oral's surgeon said it was cardiogenic shock, which had a fatality rate of 80–90 percent, that almost killed him.[6]

On January 27, 1993, three days after his seventy-fifth birthday, Oral announced that he was handing over the presidency of ORU to Richard. That this transition of power happened so soon after the heart attack was a coincidence. Two years earlier, Oral had stated his intent to step down when he turned seventy-five and that he would name Richard his successor. When Oral named Richard president, he told him to walk "in the footsteps of Jesus Christ," not Oral Roberts. Under his leadership, Richard promised to uphold the university's strict honor code and mandatory chapel attendance and that ORU would be "strong in athletics again." Chairman of the board of regents, Marilyn Hickey, downplayed any doubts about Richard's abilities by explaining that not only had the new president "gone through a lot of process" and had "been very open to training," but he also understood how the university operated because he had worked alongside his father for nearly thirty years.[7] At the May inauguration, Oral warned his forty-four-year-old son again, reminding him of something Billy Graham said during a 1987 visit, "If ORU ever departs from its original purpose as God's university, may a curse come upon it." He also joked, "I'm glad that the mantle is now on you, off of me."[8] After handing over control of ORU, Oral moved to Newport Beach, California, but he wasn't done working.

Nearly forty years before he left his post at ORU, Oral made clear his opinion on retirement. At a 1956 revival in Raleigh, North Carolina, he told the audience never to retire. "You ought to live all your life. Remember, age is not reckoned by years," he said. "It's reckoned by the way you believe and think. We all know people who are old at 20 and others who are young at 80. Keep busy doing good."[9] Keeping true to his word, he told interviewers in 1995 that he wasn't retired in "any sense of the word." The seventy-seven-year-old evangelist, just four years removed from the heart attack that nearly killed him, was still raising half of ORU's funds—hardly a long-term solution for the struggling university—was traveling across the country preaching thirty Sundays a year, playing nine holes of golf a day, and walking two miles every other day. His physicians also gave him a clean bill of health.[10] Oral's healing services may not have had the same energy as in the early years, but he continued to preach that "wherever the healing comes from, it's from God. Whatever is good, it's from God." The principles had remained the same, but the methods were not quite the same, he said, "because I'm not as young as I once was."[11]

Roberts, it seemed, had learned little from his downfall. Rather than using his experiences in the 1980s as an opportunity to reevaluate some of his teachings regarding wealth, he remained fully dedicated to the idea that the faithful can and should prosper. At a speaking engagement in Ventura, California, in May 1998, he told the six hundred people in attendance that if they gave to their church, God would give them "a thousand times more." He added that they shouldn't think about their offerings as money but as "seeds." "You're planting seeds that will bring you a harvest," he said. "The preacher needs to prosper before the people can prosper." He also prophesied that three people in the audience would become millionaires within the next six months. One audience member especially liked this part of the message, telling a journalist, "I might be one of them."[12] Oral also updated *The Miracle of Seed Faith*, originally published in 1970, for the new millennium in a book aptly titled *Seed-Faith 2000*. The book, perhaps other than some new anecdotes, provides little new insight.[13]

Oral's continued adherence to seed faith made him something of a relic in a prosperity gospel movement that still looked to him for inspiration but had moved on from the rigid laws of giving and receiving. The new generation of prosperity preachers both looked and acted different than the previous generation. For one, there were more women and people of color in positions of leadership. They also softened the harsh edges of what Kate Bowler has called *hard prosperity*, replacing it with *soft prosperity*. People like Creflo Dollar (who received an honorary doctorate from ORU in 1998 and served on its board of regents), T. D. Jakes, Eddie Long, Joyce Meyer, Paula White, and Joel Osteen still taught that wealth was a sign of faith, but for a cynical generation trained to be skeptical of tearful pleas for money, they have focused more on the returns than the giving or have couched their message of prosperity in more therapeutic, secular terms.[14]

On May 4, 2005, Evelyn Lutman Roberts, Oral's best friend for nearly seven decades, died after a fall in a parking lot. The fall caused massive internal bleeding in her brain, causing her to lapse into a coma from which she never regained consciousness. At her funeral five days later, Oral told an audience of three thousand in Tulsa about their last evening together. For the past seven years, they had a nightly routine consisting of seven kisses, plus "two more for the road," and a conversation about what they would want someone to say if one of them died. That last night, after Evelyn kissed him, Oral told her, "Evelyn, darling, I love you. Have a good night." After he received the phone call that Evelyn was in the emergency room, Oral heard from God: "I already have Evelyn in my arms." When he first saw her lying unconscious in the hospital bed, Oral recalled that his wife's face was "absolutely radiant." He went on, "I knew what I had heard from God was true." Alone in his condominium that night, Oral asked God if it was possible for Evelyn, who just a week before her fall made Oral promise not to keep her alive through artificial means, to live. God said no. The next day he and the rest of the family agreed to take Evelyn off life support. Three hours later, Richard called his father to tell him, "Dad, Mother's gone."[15] She was eighty-eight.[16]

It's not hyperbole to say that without Evelyn there would be no *Oral Roberts*. In their interactions on camera, they displayed a genuine affection for each other, but life as Oral's wife was far from easy. Her story is a fairly familiar one for women married to powerful—and selfish—men. By most accounts, Oral was a difficult person. His single-minded devotion to what he understood as God's call for his life meant he never let anything get in the way, even his family. He was also prone to devastating bouts of melancholy and wild, often unpredictable, mood swings. Patti Roberts believed that Evelyn's faith and courage made her the perfect mate for someone like Oral, whose frequent time away from home left her with the responsibility of raising four children on her own.[17] This unequal share of parental responsibilities also meant Evelyn had the thankless task of holding the family together through the stresses of a largely absent father.

Two years after Evelyn's funeral, in 2007, Oral found himself in Tulsa once again. Back in 1997, it looked like Richard had achieved some of his goals. ORU's enrollment had reached five thousand for the first time in its history, though the university included noncredit students in these numbers, a category not usually included in enrollment figures. Richard also claimed that ORU's debt had been cut in half and that the operating deficit had been eliminated.[18] Apart from the enrollment numbers, none of this was true. A 2007 *Tulsa World* report revealed that, despite Richard's claims, ORU continued to be mired in debt from 1993 to 2006, with expenses outpacing revenue by $73 million and its overall debt being $52.5 million.[19]

ORU's problems allegedly started at the top. Two lawsuits, the first filed on October 2, 2007, charged Richard, his wife, Lindsay, and the university's board of regents with a number of abuses, including wrongful termination and misuse of university money. For years, Richard and Lindsay had apparently been using university funds as their own personal piggy bank to pay for expensive home repairs, vacations for their daughters and their friends, clothing, cellphone bills, luxury cars, a horse stable for the exclusive use of the Roberts children, and Richard's 2006 campaign to be mayor of Tulsa, all of which violated the university's tax-exempt status. Lindsay also allegedly had inappropriate relationships with underage males and used her influence to reward nonacademic scholarships to friends and friends of her children, at least two of whom were academically ineligible to even be admitted to ORU. Richard also wasn't above abusing his power. Several university employees accused the president of coercive and intimidating behavior, which had the effect of creating a hostile work environment, and said he forced the university to hire a convicted sex offender to mentor ORU students. On October 17, the embattled fifty-eight-year-old university president took an indefinite leave of absence. Billy Joe Daugherty, ORU alum, former regent, and pastor of Victory Christian Church in Tulsa, was named interim president alongside Oral, who said that the university wouldn't survive without a Roberts at the helm.

Richard resigned on November 23. For the first time since its founding, there wasn't a Roberts in a position of leadership at ORU. In his resignation letter, he wrote, "I love ORU with all my heart. I love the students, faculty, staff and administration and I want to see God's best for all of them." He also explained that God told him that ORU would be blessed "supernaturally" if he resigned.[20]

Just days after Richard resigned, Mart Green, native Oklahoman and owner of the Mardel and Hobby Lobby chain stores, promised to donate $70 million to ORU. At a November 27 press conference, Green, who had no connection to ORU but called it "God's college," said he was going to immediately give $8 million but added that strings were attached to the remaining $62 million. Green hoped to address three major areas of concern: finances, leadership, and governance. For the first concern, $70 million would obviously go a long way toward helping the university's finances; second, Richard's resignation addressed the leadership problems; and third, the board of regents would have to agree to be more transparent and to do more to include the university faculty in its decision making. He also said that ORU and Oral Roberts Ministry would have to split, though one board member said the "spiritual connection between the two organizations will remain." Richard maintained his position as CEO of the ministry and, along with Oral, was named a "spiritual regent," a strictly honorific title that didn't allow them to vote on business matters.[21] Since then, ORU has added new buildings, stabilized its finances and enrollment, and even made a surprise run in the 2021 NCAA basketball tournament.[22] Oral would have been proud.

ORAL DELIVERED HIS LAST SERMON ON SUNDAY, SEPTEMBER 27, 2009. In Tulsa for the inauguration of ORU's third president, Mark Rutland, Roberts went off the beaten path to visit a small Native American church in rural Tulsa County. The church's senior pastor, Negiel Bigpond, said the visit was a surprise and that he initially hoped Roberts would stay for at least an hour; he stayed for three. After giving a sermon and praying for several people, Oral remarked, "I feel like I'm back in the tent."[23]

Granville Oral Roberts died on December 15, 2009, of complications with pneumonia at the age of ninety-one. He had been hospitalized a few days prior after a fall broke several bones. Richard described Oral's passing as "the most glorious, dignified, and wonderful homecoming" he'd ever witnessed. Oral spent his last day singing some of his favorite hymns, including songs like "God Is a Good God" that made his ministry famous. His singing was so loud, according to Richard, that he could be heard down the hall from his hospital room. Richard recounted that, between songs, knowing that his time was near, Oral proclaimed, "Praise God, I'm going home. I'm going home to my Evelyn." Richard, who had flown out to California with his sister Roberta to be by their father's side, said it was obviously a sad moment but that there was also rejoicing because they knew their father was now in heaven alongside his deceased wife and children, Rebecca and Ronnie, and a grandson, Richard Oral. "My father," Richard said, "is the greatest man of God I've ever known, and I've known some."[24]

Most obituaries agreed that Oral was one of the most influential figures in twentieth-century American religion, second only to Billy Graham. Others compared Oral's influence to that of Martin Luther King Jr. and Pope John Paul II. These same obituaries agreed that Oral, through television and ORU, brought faith healing and Pentecostalism to a mainstream audience. Jack Hayford, former president of the International Church of the Foursquare Gospel, said he didn't think the charismatic movement would have happened without Oral's influence. At the time of his death, 640 million people around the globe identified as Pentecostal-charismatic, many of them in the Global South, where Oral was still considered a hero. Visitors to African churches who mention they are from Tulsa are apparently asked if they knew Oral Roberts. Tulsa pastor Willie George praised Oral for showing Pentecostals that "we could have God's best," and for showing the world that God was a "good God." Roberts taught Pentecostals to "think big, to dare to dream." Presiding bishop Charles E. Blake, head of the Church of God in Christ, the nation's largest Black denomination, believed that Roberts should also be remembered for his work toward racial equality.[25]

There was less agreement about Oral's influence on the prosperity gospel. In its death notice, the *New York Times* described the evangelist as the "patriarch of the 'prosperity gospel'" for his message that "Christians who pray and donate with sufficient fervency will be rewarded with health, wealth, and happiness."[26] Journalist Matt Schudel noted that, unlike Jerry Falwell and Pat Robertson, Oral had little interest in shaping politics and social policy but rather focused on matters of faith and finance.[27] Ted Olsen of *Christianity Today* disagreed with the obituaries that made Roberts an architect of the prosperity gospel. The writers of those pieces had confused Oral with another Tulsa minister, Kenneth Hagin Jr. Instead of the prosperity gospel, Olsen thought Oral should be remembered for bridging the gap between Pentecostalism and mainstream evangelicalism by making practices like faith healing and speaking in tongues palatable to more sophisticated audiences.[28]

In his long life and career, Oral was controlled by two competing feelings. The first was a sense of divine calling. His mother was the first person to instill this sense into him. As a boy, she frequently reminded him of the fateful night when she vowed to dedicate him to God's service if he healed a neighbor's dying son. In a 1985 interview with *Charisma*, he said his most satisfying accomplishment was he had "obeyed Jesus." Oral believed that God had gone to other people to build ORU and the City of Faith, but he was different because he was the first person to listen.[29] In his 1995 autobiography *Expect a Miracle*, Oral said God had spoken to him twenty-three times. There were doubts along the way, but, he wrote, "I believed in God then; I believe in Him now that there is much more of the abundant life He is going to reveal. He will speak to many, many more to catch the vision and take it to suffering people everywhere. As one of the forerunners of God, I believe God cannot be God and do anything less."[30]

Oral had good reason to be so confident. Had he stayed a pastor with the Pentecostal Holiness Church, his life would have been fairly conventional. While his inherent skills as a preacher and communicator would have certainly guaranteed him a comfortable life in the denomination's hierarchy, the belief that God could heal the sick—alongside confidence in his own abilities—justified the risks that came with striking out on his own. Oral wasn't unique in his belief that God heals. When he entered the itinerant healing ministry in 1947, the competition was fierce. People like Jack Coe, A. A. Allen, W. V. Grant, Gordon Lindsay, and William Branham vied for a large, yet limited, audience. However, most of these healing evangelists of Roberts's generation, whether due to lack of finances or their own self-destructive behavior, faded. Oral was unique because he survived. Part of his genius was his ability to navigate the controversies that inevitably came with praying for the sick and to read cultural trends.

There was another side to Oral, though. He was deeply insecure. Wayne Robinson and Patti Roberts, both of whom were astute observers, noted how Oral's insecurities controlled him. Robinson believed it was Oral's desire to never be poor again that led him to spend a lifetime "constructing edifices which, once they [were] built, must be replaced by new structures—each time larger. Over and over again, these monuments declare,

'I ain't poor no more!' The *nouveau riche* tone of the ORU campus speaks of the poor boy who made it big." It's why he built University Village for his mother. Not only was she going to be living in an upscale, expensive retirement home, but it was also going to have a clear view of the university. Claudius would be able to spend her last few years alive in the luxury she could never afford for her son and look with pride at the glistening buildings and bright young Pentecostals walking to class.[31] Patti suggested that the "underlying insecurity that is often found in those who grew up in poverty" was behind her ex-father-in-law's prosperity message. A middle-class Presbyterian boy who received a brand-new bicycle at Christmas and knew he was going to be a wealthy adult wouldn't talk endlessly about seed faith the way Oral did.[32]

Nothing represented Oral's sense of divine calling and insecurities more than the City of Faith. The medical complex put Roberts into a nearly impossible situation. He was warned of the stakes in building the $100 million medical complex, but he ignored these risks because they were irrelevant in the face of God's command for him to build it. As the City of Faith's collapse looked more and more likely, the weaknesses at the center of Oral's prosperity theology became evident, pushing it to its limits as a fund-raising tool and worldview. Tailor-made for the United States' success- and celebrity-saturated culture, Oral's belief that there was a causal relationship between success and faith was inadequate to deal with the stresses of failure. His prosperity message was comforting when things were going well. All Oral had to do to know that faith unerringly led to riches and influence was to look around him. He may have grown up a poor, sickly, stuttering Pentecostal from Oklahoma's backwoods, but by the 1970s he was a prosperous, healthy, dapper Methodist with a hit TV series, a winning basketball team, and a growing university. His success showed that he had done everything right.

Oral's belief in his own righteousness—measured by the millions of people who supported him and the buildings on ORU's campus—made possible his outrageous behavior in the 1980s. The morbid nature of the fund-raising that reared its ugly head in January 1987 had been there for several years. Oral's ego and desperation were on full display starting in the early 1980s. He told readers of *Abundant Life* that they had to choose sides: his or the enemy's. In January 1980, he likened himself to the Old Testament prophet Elijah and suggested to readers that their very lives, health, and prosperity depended on supporting God's prophets like himself.[33] Two years later, in February 1982, he warned readers that if his ministry ended, his supporters would have nowhere to turn because there would be nobody to respond to their letters. Millions of hurting people wouldn't receive help if Oral's ministry stopped, one headline splashed across two pages read.[34] In February 1987, just one month shy of the deadline, Oral described his media critics as "gnats," bragged about his California residence ("Praise God, I'm no cheapskate," he said), implied that his onetime nemesis *Life* magazine went out of circulation because it published a negative article about him, and claimed that no person who had attacked ORU had prospered.[35] Several months later, after Jim Bakker's sexual affair and financial misdeeds were made public and while the City of Faith was still bleeding money, Oral asked readers if they would be like "the people who heard others laugh at Oral Roberts and then stopped giving" and subsequently lost out on healings and blessings—even the salvation of family members. Supporters could rest assured that he wouldn't make the same mistakes as Bakker because he operated his ministry with integrity.[36]

The mistake would be to see Roberts's rise and fall as an isolated incident—or simply a tale of the goddess Nemesis collecting her due—rather than as a microcosm of the state of evangelical Christianity at the end of the twentieth century. Though he tended to avoid the explicit white supremacist language and partisan bickering of some of his contemporaries, Roberts's prosperity theology is as much a part of the story. If white evangelicals' adherence to American nationalism reflects some of the most pernicious aspects of the nation's racism and sexism, Oral's devotion to things like seed faith and his belief in a causal relationship between faith and wealth—and its opposite—reflect the most damaging aspects of the nation's crass materialism, a problem inherent to capitalism. Roberts may have been right when he pointed out that he didn't accept the types of financial perks Jim and Tammy Faye Bakker did and that he had never been convicted of criminal conduct like Jim, but that didn't mean he wasn't operating from a similar mind-set, one that sought fulfillment and security (material and spiritual) through material things and viewed any checks on their power as illegitimate.

Roberts's theologies of prosperity and seed faith fostered a sense of invincibility and aversion to facts, or what Jim Bakker referred to as God's "special math." This prosperity theology required ever-increasing evidence of God's material blessings. For Roberts, the measure for God's grace and the quality of his relationship to God was physical buildings. This tendency was evidenced in his plans to start new construction projects even though he could not afford to pay for ongoing projects. It is hard to know if Roberts believed he would be able to build the multimillion-dollar healing center while the City of Faith was bleeding his ministry dry. He was in a bind, however. To admit that he had made a mistake or needed to cut back on building would have been unthinkable because it meant he had either misheard God's command or was lying about hearing from God in the first place. Even if it meant running his ministry into the ground or laying off workers, the image of physical growth was paramount. This demonstrable faith, best seen in the opulent lifestyles of rich pastors and endless construction projects (let's not forget that amid the ongoing financial crisis in the mid-1980s, Roberts proposed *more* construction), was ultimately self-defeating because it demanded "an endless cycle of bigger and better."[37]

The problem wasn't just with Oral Roberts, but with an evangelical culture that had become infatuated with money and influence. Every social order provides Christians with a unique set of challenges. Christians exist in an in-between place where they must navigate their lives amid the world in which they were born and the demands of their faith commitment, a commitment that is often at odds with the hegemonic culture. In the United States, the cultural concomitants of capitalism—its norms, beliefs, and values—are inescapable, as nearly all the nation's institutions (public and private) are geared toward protecting them. Christianity gives the lie to capitalism's core values of power and accumulation by directing our eyes toward "the love that moves the sun and the other stars." Roberts may have started his ministry with pure motives to give comfort to the sick and downtrodden, but he was eventually corrupted by power. In the end, Oral, along with the lieutenants who encouraged him, wasn't sufficiently rooted in the traditions of his own faith. If he had been, they would have stopped him from embracing the darker habits required to maintain his empire. In one of the last interviews before his death, he still couldn't give an honest reflection of what had happened. He told the interviewer, "I've never been sorry."[38]

Christians, however, shouldn't entirely flee the surrounding culture. Even if this were possible, Christians can and must engage with and speak in ways that make sense to contemporary ears. The struggle is how to do this without completely rejecting or accepting the dominant culture. In his own attempt to bridge this gap, Oral Roberts represented twentieth-century Christianity's greatest hopes and its worst failures.

A Note on the Sources

Oral Roberts was nothing if not prolific. He wrote several autobiographies, *Oral Roberts' Life Story* (1952), *My Twenty Years of a Miracle Ministry* (1967), *My Personal Diary of Our Worldwide Ministry* (1968), *My Story* (1961), *The Call* (1972), and *Expect a Miracle* (1995).

Over his long career, he published over 150 works on various topics, including salvation, healing, eschatology, pneumatology, evangelism, and seed faith. Some of these books include *Salvation by the Blood* (1938), *The Drama of the End-Time* (1941), *If You Need Healing—Do These Things* (1947), *The Fourth Man and Other Famous Sermons* (1951), *Deliverance from Fear and Sickness* (1954), *God's Formula for Success and Prosperity* (1956), *God Is a Good God* (1960), *Ten Greatest Miracles of Oral Roberts' Ministry* (1960), *Seven Divine Aids for Your Health* (1960), *This Is Your Abundant Life in Jesus Christ* (1960), *Expect a New Miracle Every Day* (1963), *The Baptism with the Holy Spirit and the Value of Speaking in Tongues Today* (1964), *Healing for the Whole Man* (1965), *How to Find Your Point of Contact with God* (1966), *God's Timetable for the End of Time* (1969), *The New Testament with Personal Commentary* (1969), *Miracle of Seed Faith* (1970), *How to Live Above Your Problems* (1974), *I Will Rain upon Your Desert* (1977), *Best-Loved Tent Sermons* (1982), *How I Learned Jesus Was Not Poor* (1989), *Seed-Faith 2000* (1999), and *The Ultimate Voice* (2008).

Members of Roberts's family also published useful books: E. M. Roberts and Claudius Roberts, *Our Ministry and Our Son* (1960), Evelyn Roberts, *His Daring Wife, Evelyn* (1976), Patti Roberts, *Ashes to Gold* (1983), and Roberta Roberts Potts, *My Dad, Oral Roberts* (2011). Former insiders have also had their say. The friendliest is Wayne Robinson, *Oral* (1976), while the most hostile is Jerry Sholes, *Give Me That Prime-Time Religion* (1979).

The Oral Roberts Evangelistic Association (OREA) published an enormous amount of literature. Some of the most valuable for tracing the evolution of Roberts's life and career are the ministry's monthly magazines, which went through a few name changes before settling in 1956 on *Abundant Life*: *Healing Waters* (1947–August 1953), *America's Healing Magazine* (September 1953–December 1955), *Healing* (January 1956–June 1956), and finally *Abundant Life* (July 1956–1991).

ORU also published its own material, including the *ORU Witness* (April–May 1964–Summer 1964), *Outreach* (Fall 1964–Winter 1968), and the student paper, *Oracle* (1966–). The short-lived law school had its own journal, *Journal of Christian Jurisprudence*. The City of Faith printed an in-house newsletter, *Lifeline* (1982–1985).

The Holy Spirit Research Center (HSRC) at Oral Roberts University houses the greatest collection of material on Oral Roberts. Its holdings include books, periodicals, audio recordings, crusade videos, chapel sermons, and OREA publications. The HSRC has also created the ORU Digital Showcase (https://digitalshowcase.oru.edu/hsrc/), which provides free global access to digitized materials. The online collection includes sermons, unpublished works, and digitized OREA and ORU publications. It has also digitized the periodicals of the Pentecostal Holiness Church, such as the *Pentecostal Holiness Advocate* and *East Oklahoma Conference of the Pentecostal Holiness Church*.

This biography relies heavily on contemporary newspaper accounts about Roberts. Despite his frequent claims that the press was overly hostile to him, most reporters seemed to have been either genuinely puzzled by him, which can sometimes read as hostility but was more often simple confusion about the beliefs and practices of Pentecostals, or in awe of his personality, drive, and success. Many of these newspapers, ranging from ones with national audiences like the *Los Angeles Times*, the *Chicago Tribune*, and the *Boston Globe* to small-town papers where Roberts held a crusade, can be found online at newspapers.com.

The digital age has also made it possible to see Roberts in action. Those interested can find footage of Roberts praying for the sick on YouTube. Oral's first and only fictional film, *Venture into Faith*, can be seen at the Internet Archive. A former OREA employee has uploaded *Contact* specials to the web (http://video.lemoin.com/VIDEO_playlist_ORU_SPECIALS .htm).

Oral Roberts, unlike his rival Billy Graham, has not captured the attention of scholars. There has only been one other serious attempt to study him: David Edwin Harrell Jr., *Oral Roberts: An American Life* (1985). In 2018, *Spiritus*, a journal published jointly by the ORU College of Theology and the HSRC, released an issue dedicated to Oral Roberts's life. The articles are a combination of historical and theological studies. When Roberts is mentioned in scholarly work, it is often in reference to his influence of faith healing (Joseph Williams, *Spirit Cure* [2013]) or the prosperity gospel (Kate Bowler, *Blessed* [2013]).

Oral Roberts and the Rise of the Prosperity Gospel shouldn't be the last word on Roberts. My hope is that other scholars much more capable than myself continue to study the life and times of Oral Roberts.

Notes

INTRODUCTION

1. Oral Roberts, "John Lennon's Letter," Chapel Transcript, January 26, 1973, 1–5.
2. Lindsey Neal, "The Gospel of John Lennon," *This Land*, March 7, 2011, https://thislandpress.com/2011/03/07/the-gospel-of-john-lennon/.
3. Patti Roberts, *Ashes to Gold* (Waco, TX: Word, 1983), 89–90.
4. *Rowan & Martin's Laugh-In*, season 6, episode 19, *Amazon Prime Video*, 52 minutes, February 5, 1973.
5. "Oral Roberts Visits the Barbershop," YouTube, accessed April 14, 2022, https://www.youtube.com/watch?v=YAyp6FSL8sE&t=10s.
6. *Rowan & Martin's Laugh-In*, season 6, episode 7, *Amazon Prime Video*, 52 minutes, October 23, 1972.
7. Oral Roberts, "Presentation of TV Equipment," Chapel Transcript, December 6, 1972, 15.
8. Oral Roberts, "Presentation of TV Equipment," 15.
9. "Roberts to Make TV Appearances," *Oracle*, February 2, 1973.
10. Oral Roberts, "Presentation of TV Equipment," 12.
11. David Edwin Harrell Jr., *Oral Roberts: An American Life* (Bloomington: Indiana University Press, 1985), 307. *Abundant Life* printed transcripts of some of these interviews. "Dick Cavett's Tough Questions," *Abundant Life*, June 1970, 10–12; "An Interview with Oral and Richard Roberts on the Mike Douglas Show," *Abundant Life*, December 1970, 10–12.
12. Oral Roberts, "About Television," Chapel Transcript, November 10, 1972, 7.
13. Edward B. Fiske, "The Oral Roberts Empire," *New York Times*, April 22, 1973.
14. For a concise history of the culture wars, see Andrew Hartman, *A War for the Soul of America: A History of the Culture Wars* (Chicago: University of Chicago Press, 2015).
15. For more on the Cold War liberal economic order, see Jonathan Levy, *Ages of American Capitalism: A History of the United States* (New York: Random House, 2021), 391–583.
16. Some of the best work on American consumption after World War II is Lizabeth Cohen, *A Consumers' Republic: The Politics of Mass Consumption in Postwar America*

(New York: Vintage Books, 2003). For more on the rise of the Sun Belt, refer to Bruce J. Schulman, *From Cotton Belt to Sunbelt: Federal Policy, Economic Development, and the Transformation of the South, 1938-1980* (New York: Oxford University Press, 1991).

17. Steven P. Miller, *The Age of Evangelicalism: America's Born-Again Years* (New York: Oxford University Press, 2014).

CHAPTER 1

1. Oral Roberts, *Expect a Miracle: My Life and My Ministry* (Nashville: Nelson, 1995), 18.

2. Oral Roberts, *Expect a Miracle*, 21-22; Oral Roberts, *My Story* (Tulsa: Summit Book Co., 1961), 3-5.

3. Oral Roberts, *Expect a Miracle*, 6-7; David Edwin Harrell Jr., *Oral Roberts: An American Life* (Bloomington: Indiana University Press, 1985), 9.

4. E. M. Roberts and Claudius Roberts, *Our Ministry and Our Son Oral* (Tulsa: Oral Roberts, 1960), 10-11.

5. E. M. Roberts and Claudius Roberts, *Our Ministry*, 13-26.

6. James R. Goff, *Fields White unto Harvest: Charles F. Parham and the Missionary Origins of Pentecostalism* (Fayetteville: University of Arkansas Press, 1988), 62-86; Randall Stephens, *The Fire Spreads: Holiness and Pentecostalism in the American South* (Cambridge, MA: Harvard University Press, 2008), 188-91; Gastón Espinosa, *William J. Seymour and the Origins of Global Pentecostalism: A Biography and Documentary History* (Durham, NC: Duke University Press, 2014), 41-47.

7. "Row at Bethel," *Topeka State Journal*, January 7, 1901; "Hindoo and Zulu," *Topeka State Journal*, January 9, 1901.

8. Espinosa, *William J. Seymour*, 53-95.

9. Frederick G. Henke, "The Gift of Tongues and Related Phenomena at the Present Day," *American Journal of Theology* 13, no. 2 (April 1909): 193-206; Robert Mapes Anderson, *Vision of the Disinherited: The Making of American Pentecostalism* (New York: Oxford University Press, 1979).

10. Oral Roberts, *Expect a Miracle*, 9.

11. Ellis Roberts, "God's Hand on My Life," *Healing Waters*, August 1951, 7.

12. E. M. Roberts and Claudius Roberts, *Our Ministry*, 27-29; Oral Roberts, "God's Hand on My Life," 6-7.

13. Oral Roberts, "God's Hand on My Life," 10; Oral Roberts, *My Story*, 9; Harrell, *Oral Roberts*, 15.

14. Oral Roberts, *Expect a Miracle*, 10-11; Oral Roberts, *Oral Roberts' Life Story* (Tulsa: Oral Roberts, 1952), 23.

15. E. M. Roberts and Claudius Roberts, *Our Ministry*, 31-32.

16. E. M. Roberts and Claudius Roberts, *Our Ministry*, 42-44.

17. E. M. Roberts and Claudius Roberts, *Our Ministry*, 33-35; Oral Roberts, *Expect a Miracle*, 3-4.

18. Oral Roberts, *Expect a Miracle*, 4. G. H. Montgomery, "She Named Him Oral," *America's Healing Magazine*, February 1954, 5.

19. Oral Roberts, "A Special Message to My Partners," *Abundant Life*, May 1967, 28.

20. U. S. Census Bureau, "County Table I—Farms and Farm Property, 1920," accessed February 17, 2022, https://www2.census.gov/prod2/decennial/documents /06229686v32-37ch5.pdf, 76.

21. Oral Roberts, "God's Hand on My Life," 7; Oral Roberts, *My Story*, 10.

22. W. David Baird and Danney Goble, *Oklahoma: A History* (Norman: University of Oklahoma Press, 2008), 75-90, 163-216.

23. E. M. Roberts and Claudius Roberts, *Our Ministry*, 36-37.

24. E. M. Roberts and Claudius Roberts, *Our Ministry*, 38.

25. Oral Roberts, *Expect a Miracle*, 14-16.

26. Oral Roberts, *Expect a Miracle*, 12-13.

27. Oral Roberts, *My Story*, 6-9.

28. Oral Roberts, *Life Story*, 35-37.

29. E. M. Roberts and Claudius Roberts, *Our Ministry*, 51.

30. E. M. Roberts and Claudius Roberts, *Our Ministry*, 51-53; Oral Roberts, *My Story*, 1-2.

31. Oral Roberts, *Expect a Miracle*, 20.

32. E. M. Roberts and Claudius Roberts, *Our Ministry*, 55; Oral Roberts, *Expect a Miracle*, 24; Oral Roberts, *My Story*, 15.

33. Oral Roberts, *Expect a Miracle*, 28.

34. Heather D. Curtis, *Faith in the Great Physician: Suffering and Divine Healing in American Culture, 1860-1900* (Baltimore: Johns Hopkins University Press, 2007).

35. Oral Roberts, *Expect a Miracle*, 10; Oral Roberts, *My Story*, 19.

36. Oral Roberts, *My Story*, 21; Oral Roberts, "Testimonies," *Pentecostal Holiness Advocate*, July 11, 1935, 14.

37. Oral Roberts, *Expect a Miracle*, 32.

38. Harrell, *Oral Roberts*, 5; "The Campaign Is Now Started," *Odessa (TX) American*, August 28, 1955.

39. Oral Roberts, *Expect a Miracle*, 33; Oral Roberts, *My Story*, 35-36.

40. Daniel Isgrigg and Vinson Synan, "An Early Account of Oral Roberts' Healing Testimony," *Spiritus* 3, no. 2 (2018): 170-72. This article reprinted the 1939 article in full.

CHAPTER 2

1. Oral Roberts, *Expect a Miracle: My Life and Ministry* (Nashville: Nelson, 1995), 42-43.

2. Evelyn Roberts, *His Darling Wife, Evelyn: The Autobiography of Mrs. Oral Roberts* (New York: Damascus House, 1976), 16-21.

3. James N. Gregory, *American Exodus: The Dust Bowl Migration and Okie Culture in Oklahoma* (New York: Oxford University Press, 1989), 3-19.

4. Evelyn Roberts, *His Darling Wife*, 16-17.

5. Evelyn Roberts, *His Darling Wife*, 35-37.

6. Josh McMullen, *Under the Big Top: Big Tent Revivalism and American Culture, 1885-1925* (New York: Oxford University Press, 2015), 11-13. Early nineteenth-century Methodists invented the camp meeting. John Wigger, *American Saint: Francis Asbury and the Methodists* (New York: Oxford University Press, 2009), 318-25.

7. Oral Roberts, *Expect a Miracle*, 40; Evelyn Roberts, *His Darling Wife*, 2-3.

8. Evelyn Roberts, "I Married Oral Roberts," *Healing Waters*, November 1952, 7.

9. Evelyn Roberts, *His Darling Wife*, 8.

10. *Discipline of the Pentecostal Holiness Church, 1933* (Franklin Springs, GA: Publishing House of the Pentecostal Holiness Church, 1933), 39-42.

11. W. O. Moore, "Fifty-Two Saved in Sand Springs Revival," *Pentecostal Holiness Advocate*, April 21, 1938, 13; "Wagoner Gains Fifty-Six Members," *Pentecostal Holiness Advocate*, July 14, 1938, 8; Oral Roberts, "From Evangelist Oral Roberts East Okla. Conference," *Pentecostal Holiness Advocate*, November 17, 1938.

12. Oral Roberts, "Is the World Overtaking You? Go Forward," *Pentecostal Holiness Advocate*, July 1, 1937, 12; Oral Roberts, "Lord, Teach Us to Pray," *Pentecostal Holiness Advocate*, March 10, 1938, 4.

13. "We Answer the Criticism," *Pentecostal Holiness Advocate*, May 11, 1938, 2. For more on the Pentecostal Holiness Church, see Joseph E. Campbell, *The Pentecostal Holiness Church, 1898-1948: Its Background and History* (Franklin Springs, GA: Publishing House of the Pentecostal Holiness Church, 1951), and David Edwin Harrell Jr., *Oral Roberts: An American Life* (Bloomington: Indiana University Press, 1985), 16-21.

14. Oral Roberts, "Relationship of Pastor and Evangelist," *Pentecostal Holiness Advocate*, April 21, 1938, 5.

15. "By Rev. Oral Roberts," *Pentecostal Holiness Advocate*, July 7, 1938, 15.

16. Evelyn Roberts, *His Darling Wife*, 4.

17. Oral Roberts, *My Story* (Tulsa: Summit Book Co., 1961), 44.

18. Evelyn Roberts, "I Married Oral Roberts," 7.

19. Evelyn Roberts, "I Married Oral Roberts," 7; Oral Roberts, *My Story*, 45.

20. Oral Roberts, *Expect a Miracle*, 45-48; Evelyn Roberts, *His Darling Wife*, 12.

21. Evelyn Roberts, "I Married Oral Roberts," 7 and 14.

22. Oral Roberts, *Expect a Miracle*, 48-49.

23. "Oral Roberts Reports," *Pentecostal Holiness Advocate*, February 20, 1941, 9 and 11; Harrell, *Oral Roberts*, 52.

24. Aimee Semple McPherson, *This Is That: Personal Experiences, Sermons, and Writings* (Los Angeles: Bridal Call, n.d.), 461-62.

25. "Anti-Christ: Where Is He Found?" *Household of God*, September 1906, 1. Also refer to Grant Wacker, *Heaven Below: Early Pentecostals and American Culture* (Cambridge, MA: Harvard University Press, 2001), 192-94.

26. Wacker, *Heaven Below*, 151-52; William H. Menzies, "Developing Educational Institutions," *Assemblies of God Heritage* 3, no. 2 (Summer 1983): 3.

27. Harrell, *Oral Roberts*, 17.

28. G. H. Montgomery, "Do We Need a Seminary?" *Pentecostal Holiness Advocate*, February 15, 1945, 2-3.

29. Oral Roberts, "God Is with Emmanuel College," *Pentecostal Holiness Advocate*, December 5, 1940, 3.

30. Roberts, "God Is with Emmanuel College," 3.

31. Evelyn Roberts, *His Darling Wife*, 45-46; Oral Roberts, *Expect a Miracle*, 53. Joe E. Campbell, "New Tabernacle at Fuquay Springs, N. C.," *Pentecostal Holiness Advocate*, January 1, 1942, 12.

32. Harrell, *Oral Roberts*, 55.

33. Evelyn Roberts, *His Darling Wife*, 46-47.

34. Oral Roberts, "Revival at Fuquay Springs," *Pentecostal Holiness Advocate*, August 20, 1942.

35. Harrell, *Oral Roberts*, 55-56.

36. Campbell, "New Tabernacle at Fuquay Springs, N. C."

37. Harrell, *Oral Roberts*, 56-57.

38. Oral Roberts, "We Need," *Pentecostal Holiness Advocate*, January 28, 1943, 3.

39. Oral Roberts, "Educational Activities," *Pentecostal Holiness Advocate*, February 24, 1944, 10.

40. Harrell, *Oral Roberts*, 59; Evelyn Roberts, "I Married Oral Roberts, Chapter II," *Healing Waters*, December 1952, 4.

41. Evelyn Roberts, *His Darling Wife*, 48.

42. Evelyn Roberts, *His Darling Wife*, 49.

43. Oral Roberts, *Life Story*, 57-58.

44. Oral Roberts, *Life Story*, 54-55 and 61-63.

45. Oral Roberts, *Expect a Miracle*, 56-61.

46. Harrell, *Oral Roberts*, 62-64; "Income of Nonfarm Families and Individuals: 1946," *Department of Commerce* (Washington, DC: 1948).

47. Evelyn Roberts, *His Darling Wife*, 52-55.

48. Oral Roberts, *Life Story*, 73.

49. Oral Roberts, *Life Story*, 83-87.

50. Oral Roberts, *Expect a Miracle*, 61-63.

51. Oral Roberts, *My Story*, 79-80.

52. Oral Roberts, *Life Story*, 68-69.

53. Oral Roberts, *Life Story*, 80-82.

54. Oral Roberts, *Life Story*, 88-90.

55. Oral Roberts, "The City-Wide Healing Revival," *Pentecostal Holiness Advocate*, May 22, 1947, 7.

56. Gilbert Bond, "I Made Oral Roberts Tough by Throwing Rocks in Front of Him," *Abundant Life*, May 1979, 20-21; Oral Roberts, *My Story*, 96; Oral Roberts, "1000 Attend Healing Service," *Pentecostal Holiness Advocate*, June 12, 1947, 2.

57. Evelyn Roberts, *His Darling Wife*, 61.

58. Oral Roberts, *My Story*, 51-55.

59. Harrell, *Oral Roberts*, 80.

CHAPTER 3

1. "Church Noise Curb Is Asked," *Tulsa World*, August 2, 1947; "Revival Feud Charge Filed," *Tulsa World*, August 6, 1947; "Church Shots Case Dropped," *Tulsa World*, August 9, 1947.

2. "A Personal Report from Bro. Roberts," *Healing Waters*, October 1948, 2.

3. Charlie Hazelton, "Summary of Oral Roberts Ministry during 1951," *Healing Waters*, February 1952, 3.

4. "Summary of the Oral Roberts' Ministry in 1952," *Healing Waters*, February 1953, 13.

5. G. H. Montgomery, "Anniversary," *Abundant Life*, June 1957, 2.

6. Oral Roberts, *Oral Roberts' Life Story* (Tulsa: Oral Roberts, 1952), 96-100.

7. Oral Roberts, "My Plans for the Future," *Healing Waters*, November 1950, 4.

8. Oral Roberts, "For Six Months of Each Year a . . . Tent Cathedral," *Healing Waters*, January/February 1948, 6.

9. "The Finest Gospel Equipment in America," *Healing Waters*, August 1948, 12.

10. "3,342 Come for Salvation during Roberts Campaign in Durham, N. C.," *Healing Waters*, August 1948, 1 and 9-10.

11. "Personal Word from Oral Roberts," *Healing Waters*, April 1949, 1 and 16; O. E. Sproul, "The Largest Tent Ever Constructed for the Gospel Ministry," *Healing Waters*, January 1950, 15; Vaden Roberts, "News about the Tent Cathedral," *Healing Waters*, January 1951, 14; G. H. Montgomery, "Looking Forward with Oral Roberts," *Healing Waters*, January 1952, 13.

12. "James H. Taylor Reports Jacksonville Ministers Banquet," *Healing Waters*, May 1949, 11 and 15.

13. "Oral Roberts Given Official Welcome," *Healing Waters*, May 1949, 2.

14. "Pastor Quits, Church Split by 'Healing Power' Dispute," *Newport News (VA) Daily Press*, April 9, 1952.

15. Reg. G. Hanson, "Information to Those Seeking Healing in the Roberts Healing Campaigns," *Healing Waters*, June 1948, 2; David Edwin Harrell Jr., *Oral Roberts: An American Life* (Bloomington: Indiana University Press, 1985), 95-96; John Kobler, "Oral Roberts: King of the Faith Healers," *American Magazine*, May 1956, 22.

16. "Oral Roberts Takes Crusade to New York," *Marysville (OH) Journal-Tribune*, March 26, 1958.

17. Harrell, *Oral Roberts*, 101.

18. Lee Wedman, "Thousands on Hand for Revival Meeting," *Vancouver (BC) Province*, August 29, 1953.

19. "Over 20,000 Pack Arena to Hear Tulsa Evangelist," *Raleigh (NC) News and Observer*, December 3, 1956; James Carty, "Get Back in Key, Roberts Pleads," *Nashville Tennessean*, December 1, 1958.

20. Harrell, *Oral Roberts*, 100.

21. Dan L. Thrapp, "Evangelist Oral Roberts Thrashing Devil in Tent," *Los Angeles Times*, October 7, 1951. For more on the day-to-day operations of Roberts's campaign, see Harrell, *Oral Roberts*, 88-106.

22. Rob Bell Jr., "Oral Roberts Winds Up Crusade at Fairgrounds Sunday Afternoon," *Nashville Banner*, November 29, 1958.

23. Oral Roberts, "Your Healing in the Roberts' Meetings," *Healing Waters*, September 1948, 2.

24. Oral Roberts, "God Delights in Supplying the . . . Wants of Men," *Healing Waters*, November 1948, 9.

25. Oral Roberts, "What God Has Shown Me," *America's Healing Magazine*, October 1954, 4.

26. Reg. G. Hanson, "The Blessed Hope and God's Gifts of Deliverance," *Healing Waters*, September 1948, 5; Reg. G. Hanson, "The Blessed Hope and God's Gifts of Deliverance," *Healing Waters*, October 1948, 11-12; Joe E. Campbell, "A Whole Gospel for the Whole Man," *Healing Waters*, December 1950, 10, 13, and 15.

27. Joel Carpenter, *Revive Us Again: The Reawakening of American Fundamentalism* (New York: Oxford University Press, 1997), 223-24.

28. Gil Rowland, "Christ's Coming Is Near Oral Roberts Tells 10,000," *Greenville (SC) News*, April 13, 1953.

29. Isa. 59:19.

30. Matthew Avery Sutton, *American Apocalypse: A History of Modern Evangelicalism* (Cambridge, MA: Belknap Press of Harvard University Press, 2014), 293-366.

31. Oral Roberts, *The Fourth Man*, rev. ed. (Tulsa: Oral Roberts, 1960), 70.

32. "The Sign-Gift Ministries," *Healing Waters*, August 1948, 12; Oral Roberts, "Your Healing in the Roberts' Meetings," 2 and 8.

33. "Looking Forward with Oral Roberts in 1953," *Healing Waters*, February 1953, 10.

34. Lee Braxton, "The Lee Braxton Story," *Healing Waters*, June 1951, 6.

35. Oral Roberts, *Life Story*, 103-8.

36. Gilbert Asher, "Pastor Realizes Dream, Far beyond Expectations," *Tulsa World*, September 8, 1949.

37. "A Miracle in Masonry," *America's Healing Magazine*, November 1954, 5.

38. "Lee Braxton Reports Amazing Progress and Problems of Healing Waters," *Healing Waters*, August 1950, 10.

39. Lee Braxton, "Healing Waters to Be Heard on 100 Stations," *Healing Waters*, March 1951, 13.

40. Lee Braxton, "Healing Waters Radio Meeting Success," *Healing Waters*, August 1951, 14.

41. Lee Braxton, "Oral Roberts Goes on ABC Network October 4," *America's Healing Magazine*, October 1953, 13; Lee Braxton, "Bible Deliverance Offers Us," *America's Healing Magazine*, November 1953, 12-13.

42. Harrell, *Oral Roberts*, 123.

43. G. H. Montgomery, "The March of Deliverance," *Healing Waters*, May 1953, 4; "Overseas Radio Stations," *Abundant Life*, November 1956, 13.

44. *Venture into Faith*, directed by Herb A. Lightman, 1952. The film can be viewed for free online: https://archive.org/details/OralRobertsVentureIntoFaith.

45. Lee Braxton, "Bible Deliverance Film Being Made," *Healing Waters*, August 1952, 10.

46. "Multitudes Attend Oral Roberts' Portland, Ore. Meeting," *Healing Waters*, November 1952, 2-3.

47. "Thousands Saved through 'Venture into Faith,'" *America's Healing Magazine*, November 1953, 11.

48. Lee Braxton, "'Venture into Faith,'" *America's Healing Magazine*, January 1954, 18; "Summary of Brother Roberts' Ministry for Year 1954," *America's Healing Maga-*

zine, February 1955, 10; "World Report on 'Venture into Faith,'" *America's Healing Magazine*, February 1955, 7 and 12.

49. "The Faith Healer," *Journal of American Medical Association*, January 28, 1956, 292.

50. "Questions Answered," *Apostolic Faith*, no. 11 (October–January 1908): 2.

51. Joseph Williams, *Spirit Cure: A History of Pentecostal Healing* (New York: Oxford University Press, 2013), 26–38.

52. Oral Roberts, "Your Healing in the Roberts' Meetings," 10.

53. "New Revivalist," *Life*, May 7, 1951, 73.

54. David Edwin Harrell Jr., *All Things Are Possible: The Healing and Charismatic Revivals in Modern America* (Bloomington: Indiana University Press, 1975), 106–12.

55. Harrell, *Oral Roberts*, 158–61.

56. G. H. Montgomery, "Ten Men and a Million Souls," *Healing Waters*, May 1953, 18; Oral Roberts, "My World Vision," *Healing Waters*, May 1953, 2–3 and 16.

CHAPTER 4

1. Amy Collier Artman, *The Miracle Lady: Kathryn Kuhlman and the Transformation of Charismatic Christianity* (Grand Rapids: Eerdmans, 2019), 64.

2. G. H. Montgomery, "Million Souls Crusade Draws Businessmen to Tulsa," *America's Healing Magazine*, October 1954, 14.

3. Oral Roberts, "My Plans for Television," *America's Healing Magazine*, January 1954, 12–14; G. H. Montgomery, "Previewing the Oral Roberts' TV Program," *America's Healing Magazine*, January 1954, 4; "'Your Faith Is Power' Catching Fire across America," *America's Healing Magazine*, March 1954, 8.

4. Oral Roberts, *The Call* (Old Tappan, NJ: Revell, 1971), 178. Evelyn Roberts, *His Darling Wife, Evelyn: The Autobiography of Mrs. Oral Roberts* (New York: Damascus House, 1976), 242.

5. Oral Roberts, *The Call*, 178; G. H. Montgomery, "The March of Deliverance," *America's Healing Magazine*, September 1954, 4.

6. Oral Roberts, *My Story* (Tulsa: Summit Book Co., 1961), 160–67.

7. Oral Roberts, "A Call to Action," *America's Healing Magazine*, June 1954, 12–13; Montgomery, "The March of Deliverance," 4.

8. Advertisement, *Healing Waters*, July 1950, 16.

9. David Edwin Harrell Jr., *Oral Roberts: An American Life* (Bloomington: Indiana University Press, 1985), 142.

10. Kimberly A. Neuendorf, "The Public Trust versus the Almighty Dollar," in *Religious Television: Controversies and Conclusions*, ed. Robert Abelman and Stewart M. Hoover (Norwood, NJ: Ablex, 1990), 71–84.

11. Montgomery, "Million Souls Crusade," 14; Lee Braxton, "Millions See the First Oral Roberts Telecast," *America's Healing Magazine*, March 1955, 22.

12. Braxton, "Millions See the First Oral Roberts Telecast."

13. Oral Roberts, *My Story*, 169–70.

14. Anita Snyder, "Turn Me Loose . . . I'm Going to Walk," *America's Healing Mag-*

azine, July 1955, 9–10 and 14; "Woman Leaves Wheel Chair, Walks First Time in Four Years," *Amarillo Globe-Times*, May 2, 1955.

15. Tommy Hicks, "I Saw Three Million People Bow before God," *America's Healing Magazine*, November 1954, 12–13 and 17.

16. Oral Roberts, "Diary of Our Trip to the Holy Land and South Africa," *America's Healing Magazine*, March 1955, 2–5.

17. Oral Roberts, "Expect Great Things from God," *America's Healing Magazine*, March 1955, 17.

18. Lee Braxton, "My Trip around the World by Clipper," *America's Healing Magazine*, May 1955, 10–11, 13, and 15.

19. "'I'm No Fraud,' Says Evangelist," *Sydney Morning Herald*, January 15, 1956.

20. "Papers Divided on Evangelist," *Tulsa World*, January 17, 1956; G. H. Montgomery, "Deliverance in Manila," *Healing*, March 1956, 13–15.

21. Oral Roberts, *My Story*, 173; G. H. Montgomery, "The Truth about the Melbourne Campaign," *Healing*, April 1956, 16.

22. "Oral Roberts Quits Hostile Australia," *Des Moines Tribune*, February 25, 1956.

23. Montgomery, "The Truth about the Melbourne Campaign."

24. Michael Reece, "Bibles, Ballyhoo in the Big Top," *Melbourne Argus*, February 9, 1956.

25. "Big Tent Filled to Hear Preacher," *Melbourne Age*, February 6, 1956.

26. Oral Roberts, *My Story*, 174.

27. Oral Roberts, *My Story*, 176.

28. "Crowd Chases, Abuses Faith Healer," *Melbourne Argus*, February 9, 1956.

29. "Council Checks on Oral," *Melbourne Argus*, February 8, 1956; "An Oral Examination," *Melbourne Argus*, February 7, 1956.

30. "Evangelist within Law," *Melbourne Age*, February 10, 1956.

31. Evelyn Roberts, *His Darling Wife*, 119.

32. "To the People of Melbourne and Australia," *Melbourne Age*, February 11, 1956.

33. "'Sinful, Faithless City' Too Much for Oral," *Melbourne Argus*, February 11, 1956.

34. Harry Robinson, "An Easy Choice," *Sydney Morning Herald*, April 14, 1967.

35. "The Back of Mr. Roberts . . . ," *Sydney Morning Herald*, February 12, 1956.

36. Oral Roberts, "My Fateful Journey Inside the Iron Curtain," *Abundant Life*, July 1960, 2–7.

37. Evelyn Roberts, *His Darling Wife*, 121.

38. Newton M. Minow, "Television and the Public Interest," American Rhetoric Online Speech Bank, May 9, 1961, https://www.americanrhetoric.com/speeches/newtonminow.htm.

39. Lee Braxton, "Man's Greatest Miracle—Our Greatest Opportunity," *Abundant Life*, November 1957, 20.

40. Jack Gould, "On Faith Healing," *New York Times*, February 19, 1956.

41. "The March of Deliverance," *America's Healing Magazine*, May 1955, 4.

42. "Roberts' Circular Letter," *New York Times*, March 4, 1956.

43. "To the Editor," *New York Times*, March 4, 1956.

44. "Oklahoma Faith-Healer Draws a Following," *Christian Century*, June 29, 1955, 749–50.

45. Harland G. Lewis, "Implications for the Churches," *Christian Century*, September 5, 1956, 1019-21.

46. "Mother, Ailing Child in Search of Miracle," *Tampa Bay Times*, September 4, 1958; "Cancer Boy Celebrates 1st Birthday at Home," *Tampa Tribune*, October 25, 1958; "Cancer Fight Ends for Terry Barker," *Tampa Bay Times*, May 21, 1959.

47. "Child Dies Awaiting 'Healing' Services," *Asheville (NC) Citizen-Times*, May 22, 1959.

48. Robert DeWolfe, "Diabetic Hears Evangelist, Discards Insulin, and Dies," *Detroit Free Press*, July 6, 1959.

49. "Oral Roberts Answers Your Questions," *Abundant Life*, December 1956, 11.

50. Oral Roberts, *Life Story*, 128.

51. "Oral Roberts Says 30,000 Converted on African Trip," *Tulsa World*, January 16, 1955.

52. "North Carolina Capital Visited by Great Revival," *Abundant Life*, February 1957, 11-12.

53. "Oral Roberts in Raleigh," *Raleigh (NC) Carolinian*, December 8, 1956.

54. Roberts, *The Call*, 93-104; Oral Roberts, *Expect a Miracle: My Life and Ministry* (Nashville: Nelson, 1995), 136-38.

55. "Negro Pastors Who Refused Segregated Seats at Oral Roberts Meet," *Pittsburgh Courier*, December 20, 1958.

56. Daniel Isgrigg, "Healing for All Races: Oral Roberts' Legacy of Racial Reconciliation in a Divided City," *Spiritus: ORU Journal of Theology* 4, no. 2 (2019): 234.

57. Oral Roberts, "Second Call to Arms," *America's Healing Magazine*, January 1955, 7.

58. "Indian Tribes Honor Oral Roberts," *Billings (MT) Gazette*, August 7, 1955; "Deliverance Is Brought to Crow Indian Reservation," *America's Healing Magazine*, November 1955, 6.

59. W. C. Armstrong, "A Contribution to His People," *Abundant Life*, October 1963, 21-23; "Roberts Named for Expo Honor," *Anadarko (OK) Daily News*, June 13, 1963. For more on Oral's relationship with his Cherokee ancestry, see Timothy Hatcher, "The Spirit of Immense Struggle: Oral Roberts' Native American Ancestry," *Spiritus* 3, no. 2 (2018): 177-98.

60. Margaret Oden, "World Outreach Conference Report," *America's Healing Magazine*, October 1955, 7; Napoleon Hill, "Whatever You Can Believe You Can Conceive and Achieve," *America's Healing Magazine*, September 1955, 7 and 10-14.

61. For a concise history of these various movements, see John S. Haller Jr., *The History of New Thought: From Mind Cure to Positive Thinking and the Prosperity Gospel* (West Chester, PA: Swedenborg Foundation Press, 2012).

62. Darren Grem, *The Blessings of Business: How Corporations Shaped Conservative Christianity* (New York: Oxford University Press, 2016), 196. For more on Peale, see Carol V. R. George, *God's Salesman: Norman Vincent Peale and the Power of Positive Thinking*, 2nd ed. (New York: Oxford University Press, 2019). For more on the relationship between businessmen and conservative politics, see Kevin M. Kruse, *One Nation under God: How Corporate America Invented Christian America* (New York: Basic Books, 2015).

63. Norman Vincent Peale, "Christ's Healing Power," *Healing Waters*, December 1949, 6-7.

64. Oral Roberts, "My Pledge to God . . . to Touch Neither the Gold Nor the Glory," *Healing Waters*, October 1951, 4.

65. John Kobler, "Oral Roberts: King of the Faith Healers," *American Magazine*, May 1956, 89–90.

66. "Revivalist Roberts Due Here in September," *Los Angeles Times*, July 21, 1951; "Roberts Starts Series Tonight," *Los Angeles Times*, September 28, 1951.

67. "Demos Shakarian Reports the Oral Roberts Campaign in Los Angeles," *Healing Waters*, December 1951, 11.

68. Demos Shakarian, as told to Elizabeth Sherrill and John Sherrill, *The Happiest People on Earth* (Lincoln, VA: Chosen Books, 1975), 118.

69. Oral Roberts, "Jesus' Law of Success," *America's Healing Magazine*, June 1955, 6.

70. For representative articles, see "What 10 Christian Businessmen Say about Giving," *America's Healing Magazine*, June 1955, 8–9 and 14; Carl H. Hamilton, "How Don Locke Found the Key to Success," *Abundant Life*, April 1962, 4–8. Oral Roberts and G. H. Montgomery, eds., *God's Formula for Success and Prosperity* (Tulsa: Oral Roberts, 1955).

71. Lizabeth Cohen, *A Consumers' Republic: The Politics of Mass Consumption in Postwar America* (New York: Vintage Books, 2003).

72. For the best history of the prosperity gospel, refer to Kate Bowler, *Blessed: A History of the American Prosperity Gospel* (New York: Oxford University Press, 2013).

73. Oral Roberts, *This Is Your Abundant Life in Jesus Christ* (Tulsa: Abundant Life Publications, 1962), 51–59.

74. Mann, "Supersalesman of Faith Healing," *Christian Century*, September 5, 1956, 1019.

75. "Holy Hijacking," *Flash*, April 7, 1956; "Australia Boots Out Religion Racketeer," *Flash*, April 14, 1956; "How Scripture Shark Makes Holy Hysteria a Lucrative Gimmick," *Flash*, April 21, 1956.

76. George W. Cornell, "Oral Roberts a Powerhouse of Modern Evangelism," *Oneonta (NY) Star*, March 31, 1958.

77. Harrell, *Oral Roberts*, 176–77.

78. "From the Pen of Oral Roberts," *Abundant Life*, October 1958, 14.

79. "Over 500 Newspapers Carry 'Abundant Life' Column," *Abundant Life*, November 1957, 2; "Does Your Paper Carry This Column?" *Abundant Life*, November 1959, 6.

80. Max Roser and Esteban Ortiz-Ospina, "Literacy," Our World in Data, last revision September 20, 2018, https://ourworldindata.org/literacy.

81. Hilliard Griffin, "More Than a Million," *Abundant Life*, October 1956, 9–10.

82. Hilliard Griffin, "We Must Fulfill the Great Commission," *Abundant Life*, October 1957, 20.

83. "Keeping Posted . . . ," *Abundant Life*, February 1962, 13.

84. "Evangelist Shops Here for Marble," *Rutland (VT) Daily Herald*, May 3, 1957.

85. Raymond Gary, "God's Answer to the Impossible," *Abundant Life*, August 1957, 22; "Gary Praises Oral Roberts at Ceremony," *Tulsa World*, May 23, 1957.

86. "The Abundant Life Building Takes Shape," *Abundant Life*, March 1958, 27.

87. Oral Roberts, "This Is the House the Lord Told Me to Build," *Abundant Life*,

April 1959, 4-6; "World Evangelist Oral Roberts to Dedicate Tulsa Headquarters," *Lawton (OK) Constitution*, May 1, 1959; "Dedicated to the Glory of God," *Abundant Life*, July 1959, 14-15.

88. Lee Braxton, "ORU Today," *Abundant Life*, February 1970, 21; Oral Roberts, *Expect a Miracle: My Life and Ministry* (Nashville: Nelson, 1995), 158.

89. "School Planned by Oral Roberts," *Tulsa World*, December 26, 1961.

CHAPTER 5

1. Charley Zaimes, "Oral Roberts—Crusader for Christ—Family Man, Lover of Sports," *Allentown (PA) Morning Call*, July 5, 1958.

2. "Evangelist's Wife Tells of Life as Helpmeet, Mother," *Bradenton (FL) Herald*, May 11, 1958.

3. Evelyn Roberts, *His Darling Wife, Evelyn: The Autobiography of Mrs. Oral Roberts* (New York: Damascus House, 1976), 104-6.

4. "Evangelist's Wife Tells of Life as Helpmeet, Mother."

5. Evelyn Roberts, *His Darling Wife*, 188-89, 195, and 197-98.

6. "Evangelist's Wife Tells of Life as Helpmeet, Mother."

7. Evelyn Roberts, *His Darling Wife*, 129.

8. Oral Roberts, *Expect a Miracle: My Life and My Ministry* (Nashville: Nelson, 1995), 203.

9. Evelyn Roberts, *His Darling Wife*, 129-30.

10. Yvonne Nance, "Evelyn Roberts," *Abundant Life*, May 1965, 24.

11. Oral Roberts, *Expect a Miracle*, 201-5.

12. Oral Roberts, *Expect a Miracle*, 163.

13. Oral Roberts, *Expect a Miracle*, 158-62.

14. Oral Roberts, *Expect a Miracle*, 169-71; David Edwin Harrell Jr., *Oral Roberts: An American Life* (Bloomington: Indiana University Press, 1985), 209.

15. Harrell, *Oral Roberts*, 209.

16. Oral Roberts, "A Spiritual Revolution throughout the Earth," *Abundant Life*, May 1962, 8-10; "Roberts to Train Natives," *Tulsa Tribune*, April 19, 1962.

17. Oral Roberts, *Expect a Miracle*, 164-66.

18. "O. R. U. Construction Progress," *Abundant Life*, October 1962, 24.

19. US Department of Education, *120 Years of American Education: A Statistical Portrait*, ed. Thomas D. Snyder ([Washington, DC]: National Center for Education Studies, 1993).

20. George Marsden, *The Soul of the American University: From Protestant Establishment to Established Nonbelief* (New York: Oxford University Press, 1994), 10-16.

21. "Ronald Reagan's 'Morality Gap' Speech (1966)," DIVA, Bay Area Television Archive, accessed April 21, 2022, https://diva.sfsu.edu/collections/sfbatv/bundles/229317.

22. Darren Dochuk, *From Bible Belt to Sun Belt: Plain-Folk Religion, Grassroots Politics, and the Rise of Evangelical Christianity* (New York: Norton, 2011), 52-74.

23. "Frenzy of Faith in a Man's Touch," *Life*, August 3, 1962, 12-21.

24. Wayne Robinson, *Oral: The Warm, Intimate, Unauthorized Portrait of a Man of God* (Los Angeles: Acton House, 1976), 68-69. For the press release, see R. F. De-Weese, "A Statement," *Abundant Life*, October 1962, 22.

25. Oral Roberts, "The R. O. Corvin Story," *Abundant Life*, January 1963, 7-9.

26. Harrell, *Oral Roberts*, 211.

27. William C. Armstrong, "Divine Moment," *Abundant Life*, February 1963, 2-3.

28. Bob Foreman, "Regents Tour Site, Hear Evangelist," *Tulsa Tribune*, November 26, 1962.

29. Armstrong, "Divine Moment," 4.

30. Armstrong, "Divine Moment," 6-7.

31. Doyle Helbling, "34 Regents Accept Challenge," *Abundant Life*, March 1964, 18-21.

32. Oral Roberts, "The Growth of a Miracle," *Abundant Life*, February 1964, 5; Robinson, *Oral*, 127.

33. Oral Roberts, "Silver Anniversary of Oral Roberts University," *Oral Roberts University 25th Silver Anniversary* (1990), ORU Archival Collection, 5-6.

34. "Ministers' Seminar," *Abundant Life*, April 1963, 2-11.

35. William C. Armstrong, "Released for Service," *Abundant Life*, July 1963, 14-17; Yvonne Nance, "Youth Set on Fire," *Abundant Life*, September 1963, 2-7; Doyle Helbling, "International Seminar," *Abundant Life*, February 1964, 10-11; William C. Armstrong, "Disciples: 1964," *Abundant Life*, April 1964, 6-11.

36. Oral Roberts, "We Are Releasing a New Force," *ORU Witness*, April-May 1964, 2.

37. Oral Roberts, "The President's Report," *Abundant Life*, February 1970, 5.

38. Harrell, *Oral Roberts*, 217-18.

39. Foreman, "Regents Tour Site, Hear Evangelist."

40. Harrell, *Oral Roberts*, 214-15.

41. Harrell, *Oral Roberts*, 222.

42. Oral Roberts, "How You Can Light an Eternal Flame at Oral Roberts University," *Witness*, April-May 1964, 21-24; William C. Armstrong, "A Time for Titans," *Abundant Life*, March 1966, 2-15.

43. "Big Development for ORU Outlined," *Tulsa Tribune*, December 4, 1964.

44. Lee Braxton and Clinton Davidson, "How You Can Become a Partner in Soul Winning through a Christian Will," *Abundant Life*, October 1960, 18; "'I Was So Excited to Learn ...,'" *Abundant Life*, March 1966, 21.

45. Oral Roberts, "Expecting a Miracle," Partner's Seminar Transcript, January 25, 1969, 2.

46. "Make Your Life Count Twice for God," *Abundant Life*, June 1962, 20.

47. "Big Development for ORU Outlined."

48. John D. Messick, "Learning Resources Center," *Witness*, April-May 1964, 6-9; Oral Roberts, "How You Can Light," 22; "Learning Resources Center," *Outreach*, Fall 1964, 26; William Steif, "College Founded by Evangelist Gets $3.5 Million U. S. Money," *Memphis Press-Scimitar*, July 15, 1965.

49. "About the Cover," *ORU Witness*, July 1964, 5; "Our New University," *Tulsa Tribune*, March 16, 1965.

50. William Steif, "$3.5 Million for Oral Roberts University," *Washington Daily*

News, July 14, 1965; "ORU Campus Busy as Staff Prepares for Opening Day," *Tulsa Tribune*, August 10, 1965; "Aid to Religion," *Uniontown (PA) Herald*, August 31, 1965; "Aid to Religion," *Marion (IN) Chronicle*, August 31, 1965.

51. Oral Roberts, *Expect a Miracle*, 145.

52. "ORU Buys 'Dial-a-Lesson' RCA Unit for $500,000," *Tulsa Daily World*, June 5, 1965; Peggy Dunsmoor, "Computerized Lessons for Oral Roberts U," *Tulsa Daily World*, June 20, 1965; "Data Retriever at ORU Is Examined by Experts," *Tulsa Daily World*, October 1, 1966; Frank Leslie, "ORU Information Dial Topic of Symposium," *Tulsa Daily World*, September 17, 1966; Joyce Louis, "New Oral Roberts University Is 'Educator's Dream,'" *Oklahoma Journal*, April 30, 1966, 1; Kyle Goddard, "Intellectual Mount Everest Growing in ORU's Grading," *Tulsa Tribune*, August 25, 1967. Messick's description can be found in Bob Foreman, "Electronic Teaching at Roberts U," *Tulsa Tribune*, March 16, 1964.

53. "Language Cassette Lab Aids Learning Process," *Oracle*, October 1, 1971, 1; Mike Henry, "New Curriculum Lab Offers Wide Scope of New Media," *Oracle*, December 10, 1971, 2.

54. Goddard, "Intellectual Mount Everest Growing in ORU's Grading."

55. Richard White, "Lose Fat or Job, Staff Told," *Tulsa Tribune*, March 26, 1962; "Weight Control Program Fair?" *Tulsa Tribune*, April 3, 1962.

56. "Unusual Health Center for ORU," *Tulsa Tribune*, August 25, 1964; "ORU Buying 'Glass Man,'" *Tulsa Daily World*, November 26, 1964; James C. Spalding, "A New Concept of Health at O. R. U.," *Outreach*, Fall 1964, 16-18.

57. Lee Braxton, "The Prayer Tower Goes Up at ORU," *Abundant Life*, May 1966, 18-19.

58. Oral Roberts, "Why Build a Prayer Tower?" *Outreach*, Winter 1966, 9.

59. Oral Roberts, *Expect a Miracle*, 164.

60. "Student Opinions—Why a Prayer Tower?" *Oracle*, November 21, 1966, 3.

61. Harrell, *Oral Roberts*, 227.

62. Robinson, *Oral*, 76.

63. Oral Roberts, *Expect a Miracle*, 179-80; Harrell, *Oral Roberts*, 243-44.

64. Philip Lee, "The Curious Life of *In Loco Parentis* at American Universities," *Higher Education in Review* 8 (2011): 65-90.

65. Lee Braxton, "Interview with Lee Braxton," *ORU Witness*, July 1964, 21.

66. Harrell, *Oral Roberts*, 239-44.

67. "What We Have to Say Is Vitally Important . . . ," *Oracle*, May 22, 1971, 2.

68. "Code of Honor," *Oracle*, February 21, 1966, 2.

69. Jerry L. Martin, "Honor Code Sees Upgrade," *Oracle*, April 14, 1967, 2.

70. Mel Goard and Eric Fiscus, "Do You Belong?" *Oracle*, March 17, 1967, 1.

71. "School for Squares," *Tulsa Tribune*, April 4, 1967.

72. "Our New University," *Tulsa Tribune*, March 16, 1965.

73. 91 Cong. Rec. S115 (November 18, 1969) (statement of Sen. Randolph).

74. "Off to a Good Start," *Tulsa Daily World*, June 18, 1969.

75. Oral Roberts, "Quest for the Whole Man," *Abundant Life*, November 1965, 25.

CHAPTER 6

1. Bob Foreman, "Record Construction Year Seen for Tulsa," *Tulsa Tribune*, December 28, 1964; Bob Foreman, "Economic Value of ORU Is Told," *Tulsa Tribune*, December 8, 1966; "ORU's Value to Community Stressed," *Tulsa Tribune*, August 2, 1967; "Tulsa: Mecca for Conservative Folks," *Wichita Beacon*, October 1, 1971; "In Just a Few Years, Tulsa Has Become a University City," *Tulsa Daily World*, February 25, 1976.

2. Wayne Robinson, *Oral: The Warm, Intimate, Unauthorized Portrait of a Man of God* (Los Angeles: Acton House, 1976), 110-11; Patti Roberts, *Ashes to Gold* (Waco, TX: Word, 1983), 91; David Edwin Harrell Jr., *Oral Roberts: An American Life* (Bloomington: Indiana University Press, 1985), 472.

3. Bob Frazier, "Billy Graham Brings Message (and Good News)," *Eugene (OR) Guard*, August 3, 1950; Oral Roberts, *The Call* (Old Tappan, NJ: Revell, 1971), 115.

4. William Martin, *A Prophet with Honor: The Billy Graham Story*, 2nd ed. (Grand Rapids: Zondervan, 2018), 258-62; "Billy Graham Is Handsome, Laughing, and Sincere," *Melbourne Age*, February 13, 1959.

5. Oral Roberts, *The Call*, 116-18.

6. "The Future of Evangelism: Is the Concept Still Valid?" *Christianity Today*, January 7, 1966, 44-47.

7. Hugh McCullum, "100 Lands in Evangelical Drive," *Toronto Telegram*, October 22, 1966; Hugh McCullum, "Killers-Turned-Christian Hear Dr. Billy Graham's Revival Pledge," *Toronto Telegram*, October 26, 1966; Hugh McCullum, "Lion Calls for Tolerance," *Toronto Telegram*, October 27, 1966; Hugh McCullum, "Evangelists Want Social Action," *Toronto Telegram*, November 3, 1966.

8. Martin, *A Prophet with Honor*, 331-40.

9. Hugh McCullum, "Battle over the New Morality," *Toronto Telegram*, October 29, 1966.

10. R. O. Corvin, "Oral Roberts and R. O. Corvin Attend World Congress on Evangelism in Berlin," *Abundant Life*, January 1967, 24-26.

11. "Overflow Crowd of Delegates Bombards Panel with Questions on Healing," *Abundant Life*, February 1967, 20-22.

12. "Overflow Crowd of Delegates," 23.

13. "Evangelist Roberts Unveils New Image of Balanced Ministry at Congress," *Albuquerque Journal*, November 3, 1966.

14. Beth Macklin, "Dr. Billy Graham Coming to Tulsa," *Tulsa Daily World*, November 10, 1966.

15. Frank Leslie, "Oral Roberts U., in First Year, Solving Problems," *Tulsa World*, April 9, 1966; Bill Sampson, "ORU Glances Back at First Year, Likes It," *Tulsa Tribune*, June 17, 1966.

16. Bill Sampson, "ORU Works Steadily toward Its Next Goal—Accreditation," *Tulsa Tribune*, June 18, 1966; Joyce Louis, "New Oral Roberts University Is 'Educators' Dream,'" *Oklahoma Journal*, April 30, 1966; "ORU Launches Its Second Year of Studies Today," *Tulsa Daily World*, September 9, 1966.

17. "ORU Okayed for Oklahoma Accreditation," *Oracle*, February 17, 1967, 1.

18. Bob Foreman, "ORU Opens Big Fund Campaign," *Tulsa Tribune*, December 6,

1966; "Oral Roberts University," *Tulsa World*, December 8, 1966; Frank Leslie, "ORU Begins First Local Fund Drive," *Tulsa World*, December 7, 1966.

19. "Development Council for ORU Plans $2.5 Million Fund Drive," *Tulsa Tribune*, July 29, 1967; "ORU Fund Hits $750,000; $50,000 Given by Trust," *Tulsa Daily World*, August 25, 1967; "ORU Fund-Raisers Seek More Individual Donors," *Tulsa Tribune*, January 15, 1968.

20. Oral Roberts, "God Is Not Yet Done with Man," *Abundant Life*, June 1967, 10-13.

21. Billy Graham, "Why I Believe in Christian Education," *Abundant Life*, June 1967, 15-17.

22. 90 Cong. Rec. H113 (April 3, 1967) (statement of Rep. Edmondson).

23. "ORU Students to Attend Brazilian Crusade," *Oracle*, May 23, 1966, 1.

24. Patti Roberts, *Ashes to Gold*, 44-45.

25. Patti Roberts, *Ashes to Gold*, 48-49. Here are the *Abundant Life* pieces: Oral Roberts, "The Brazil Story," November 1966, 2-20; Oral Roberts, "The Brazil Story Part Two," December 1966, 12-28; "Our Partners Write about the Brazil Crusade," January 1967, 31.

26. "Viet Nam: Where Do We Go from Here?" *Christianity Today*, January 7, 1966, 30-31.

27. Irving Spiegel, "Vietnam Protests Assailed by Rabbi," *New York Times*, May 7, 1967; John Leo, "Episcopal Diocese Calls for Voice for the Vietcong," *New York Times*, May 10, 1967. Also see Max Hastings, *Vietnam: An Epic Tragedy, 1945-1975* (New York: Harper Perennial, 2018), 379-92.

28. Martin, *A Prophet with Honor*, 349-51.

29. Oral Roberts, "With Our Men in Vietnam (1967)," *Oral Roberts Collection*, Holy Spirit Research Center, 3.

30. Oral Roberts, "God Doesn't Look at Skin Color," Chapel Transcript, September 26, 1989, 11.

31. Oral Roberts, "With Our Men," 5 and 15.

32. Oral Roberts, "With Our Men," 12 and 14.

33. Oral Roberts," With Our Men," 16.

34. "Oral Roberts Finds Journey to South Vietnam 'Sobering,'" *Tulsa Tribune*, July 22, 1967; Oral Roberts, "Mission to Vietnam," *Abundant Life*, October 1967, 5-20; Oral Roberts, "With Our Men," 19.

35. Oral Roberts, "God's Time for Indonesia," *Abundant Life*, November 1967, 5; "Friendship Tour to Indonesia," *Outreach*, Summer 1967, 6-9; Beth Macklin, "ORU Students Learn 'Laying On of Hands,'" *Tulsa Daily World*, August 3, 1967.

36. Hilliard Griffin, "Abundant Life Youth Teams," *Abundant Life*, March 1959, 10-11.

37. "Chilean Talks with Oral Roberts about University," *Enid (OK) Eagle*, May 1, 1967.

38. Philip Jenkins, *The Next Christendom: The Coming of Global Christianity* (New York: Oxford University Press, 2011).

39. Beth Macklin, "ORU Eyes Role in Chile College," *Tulsa Daily World*, December 3, 1967; Darline Ulseth, "Nichols Organizes Crusade," *Oracle*, December 11, 1967, 1.

40. "Chile 1964: CIA Covert Support in Frei Election Detailed," The National Security Archive, updated September 27, 2004, https://nsarchive2.gwu.edu//news/20040925/index.htm.

41. Macklin, "ORU Eyes Role in Chile College."

42. Macklin, "ORU Eyes Role in Chile College."

43. Robinson, *Oral*, 49–54.

44. Bob Foreman, "ORU's Dr. Messick Retiring," *Tulsa Tribune*, January 19, 1968.

45. Nell Jean Boggs, "ORU Dean: I Was Fired," *Tulsa Tribune*, March 22, 1968.

46. Robinson, *Oral*, 121–22.

47. Kyle Goddard, "Faculty Endorsement Key to Naming of ORU's Dean," *Tulsa Tribune*, January 26, 1968.

48. Roberts, *The Call*, 130–31.

49. Randy Krehbiel, "Turning Point," *Tulsa World*, August 28, 1994.

50. Robinson, *Oral*, 92–93.

51. Nell Jane Boggs, "Dean of Theology out in Policy Dispute," *Tulsa Tribune*, March 19, 1968; Boggs, "ORU Dean."

52. Nell Jane Boggs, "Roberts May Set Methodists 'On Fire,' Cleric Says," *Tulsa Tribune*, April 6, 1968.

53. Robinson, *Oral*, 60.

54. Robinson, *Oral*, 75.

55. Robinson, *Oral*, 66–67.

56. Amy Collier Artman, *The Miracle Lady: Kathryn Kuhlman and the Transformation of Charismatic Christianity* (Grand Rapids: Eerdmans, 2019), 4–8.

57. Oral Roberts, "Let's Go Back to the Bible," Laymen's Seminar, November 7, 1969, 16.

58. Emily Yoffe, "The Double Life of Finis Crutchfield," *Texas Monthly*, October 1987, 102–6 and 189–98.

59. Robinson, *Oral*, 82–83; Yoffe, "The Double Life," 190.

60. Robinson, *Oral*, 76.

61. Robert Allen, "The Will of God, Says Oral Roberts," *Oklahoma's Orbit*, May 5, 1968, 4; Robinson, *Oral*, 76.

62. Evelyn Roberts, *His Darling Wife, Evelyn: The Autobiography of Mrs. Oral Roberts* (New York: Damascus House, 1976), 177–84.

63. "God Is in the Now," *Texas Methodist*, March 24, 1972, 4; Harrell, *Oral Roberts*, 297; Ron Smith, "'Justify Cost,' Meeting with OREA Managers," Meeting with OREA Managers, December 18, 1973, 3.

64. Nancy Gregorik, "Oral Roberts' Crowds Shrink," *Detroit News*, July 12, 1967.

65. Robinson, *Oral*, 75.

66. John Wigger, *PTL: The Rise and Fall of Jim and Tammy Faye Bakker's Evangelical Empire* (New York: Oxford University Press, 2017), 27–29.

67. Roberts, *The Call*, 185–87.

CHAPTER 7

1. Oral Roberts, "Getting Your Needs Met," Chapel Transcript, March 14, 1969, 16–17.

2. Oral Roberts, "Getting Your Needs Met," World Action Conference, June 14, 1969, 16–19.

3. David Edwin Harrell, *Oral Roberts: An American Life* (Bloomington: Indiana University Press, 1985), 269–70; Jim E. Hunter Jr., "'Where My Voice Is Heard Small': The Development of Oral Roberts' Television Ministry," *Spiritus: ORU Journal of Theology* 3, no. 2 (2018): 246–47; "How to Reach Youth: Get Their Attention," *Shreveport (LA) Times*, May 31, 1970; "Special Wins T. V. Academy Nominations," *Oracle*, April 30, 1971, 3; Oral Roberts, "Ministering to People's Needs," Regents Banquet, May 5, 1973, 3–4; "Oral Roberts Special Features Special Guests," *Lafayette (LA) Daily Advertiser*, December 14, 1974.

4. Oral Roberts, "Carrying Out the Honor Code," Faculty Orientation Transcript, August 24, 1971, 7.

5. Evelyn Roberts, *His Darling Wife, Evelyn: The Autobiography of Mrs. Oral Roberts* (New York: Damascus House, 1976), 133–37.

6. Patti Roberts, *Ashes to Gold* (Waco, TX: Word, 1983), 56.

7. Patti Roberts, *Ashes to Gold*, 60–61.

8. Evelyn Roberts, *His Darling Wife*, 138–40.

9. "Richard Roberts Ministers in Song at Dayton Crusade," *Abundant Life*, December 1968, 6–8.

10. Patti Roberts, *Ashes to Gold*, 69–71 and 76.

11. Robert J. Thompson and Steve Allen, "Television in the United States," *Encyclopedia Britannica*, accessed April 25, 2022, https://www.britannica.com/art/television-in-the-United-States; "Variety Shows," PBS, Pioneers of Television, accessed April 25, 2022, https://www.pbs.org/wnet/pioneers-of-television/pioneering-programs/variety-shows/.

12. "Music with a Message," *Boston Globe*, May 31, 1970; "Evangelist's Special TV Show Has Something for All," *Ontario (CA) Daily Report*, November 14, 1970; "Hollywood Stars Join Tennis Professionals," *Deseret News*, May 14, 1976; Edward Fiske, "The Oral Roberts Empire," *New York Times*, April 22, 1973.

13. Darlene Ulseth, "KORU Interviews Ralph Carmichael," *Oracle*, October 20, 1967, 1.

14. Harrell, *Oral Roberts*, 267.

15. "Oral Roberts University Called 'Expensive TV Set,'" *Calgary Herald*, October 24, 1969.

16. Amy Collier Artman, *The Miracle Lady: Kathryn Kuhlman and the Transformation of Charismatic Christianity* (Grand Rapids: Eerdmans, 2019), 114–56.

17. Oral Roberts, *The Call* (New York: Doubleday, 1972), 193.

18. Oral Roberts, "Let's Go Back to the Bible," Laymen's Seminar, November 7, 1969, 2.

19. "OR-106H Summer Special," accessed April 25, 2022, http://video.lemoin.com/VIDEO_playlist_ORU_SPECIALS.htm; "OR-114H Summer Special," accessed April 25, 2022, http://video.lemoin.com/VIDEO_playlist_ORU_SPECIALS.htm.

20. "How to Reach Youth." For more on Christian rock and roll, refer to Gregory Alan Thornbury, *Why Should the Devil Have All the Good Music? Larry Norman and the Perils of Christian Rock* (New York: Convergent, 2018); Randall Stephens, *The Devil's Music: How Christians Inspired, Condemned, and Embraced Rock 'n' Roll* (Cambridge, MA: Harvard University Press, 2018).

21. "OR-101H A Venture into Faith," accessed April 25, 2022, http://video.lemoin .com/VIDEO_playlist_ORU_SPECIALS.htm.

22. Oral Roberts, "Let's Go Back to the Bible," 14.

23. Oral Roberts, "Presentation of TV Equipment," Chapel Transcript, December 6, 1972, 6-7.

24. Greg Broadd, "New Housing Project Here Unusual," *Tulsa Daily World*, December 21, 1969; Oral Roberts, "Fund Raising Dinner," ORU Archives, November 20, 1970, 4; "In Just One Month," *Abundant Life*, July 1970, 23; Bob Foreman, "'Village' Plans Expansion Wing," *Tulsa Tribune*, April 5, 1972.

25. Oral Roberts, "Presentation of TV Equipment," 7-8.

26. Oral Roberts, "Presentation of TV Equipment," 7; Renee Colwill, "Television Special Uses Mabee Center Setting," *Oracle*, October 13, 1972, 1.

27. Bob Foreman, "New ORU Center for Whole Community," *Tulsa Tribune*, July 16, 1970; Ronald E. Butler, "ORU's Center to Seat 10,252," *Tulsa Daily World*, October 16, 1970; "Smoking to Be Allowed in New Center at ORU," *Tulsa Daily World*, December 27, 1970; Tony Solow, "City, County Increase Share of ORU Paving Project," *Tulsa Tribune*, June 5, 1972; Don Bachelder, "Tulsa Area Building Bustin' Out All Over," *Tulsa Daily World*, July 16, 1972.

28. "Plans for ORU," Chapel Transcript, March 17, 1971, 1-6; "Roberts Unveils Projects," *Oracle*, March 26, 1971, 1.

29. "Roberts Unveils Projects," 1.

30. "Plans for ORU," 9; "ORU Starts Site Work on $2.5 Million Chapel," *Tulsa Sunday World*, February 20, 1972.

31. Wayne Robinson, *Oral: The Warm, Intimate, Unauthorized Portrait of a Man of God* (Los Angeles: Acton House, 1976), 28.

32. Oral Roberts, "Fund Raising Dinner," 1.

33. Robinson, *Oral*, 99-109.

34. Harrell, *Oral Roberts*, 279-80.

35. Oral Roberts, "I've Been Up in the Prayer Tower Alone with God," *Abundant Life*, June 1969, 2.

36. Kate Bowler has brilliantly called this *hard prosperity*. Kate Bowler, *Blessed: A History of the American Prosperity Gospel* (New York: Oxford University Press, 2013), 97.

37. Oral Roberts, *Miracle of Seed Faith* (Tulsa, OK: Oral Roberts), 21.

38. Harrell, *Oral Roberts*, 461-62.

39. Bowler, *Blessed*, 77.

40. James T. Patterson, *Restless Giant: The United States from Watergate to Bush v. Gore* (New York: Oxford University Press, 2005), 62-66.

41. Oral Roberts, "How You Can Live above Your Shortages," *Abundant Life*, March 1974, 3

42. Evelyn Roberts, "God Has No Shortages," *Abundant Life*, March 1974, 10.

43. Oral Roberts, "Getting Your Needs Met," World Action Conference, June 14, 1969, 17-19.

44. Robinson, *Oral*, 144-45.

45. Jerry LeBlanc, "Oral (Whirr, Beep) Roberts," *Chicago Tribune*, April 9, 1972.

46. Harrell, *Oral Roberts*, 313–15 and 354–55. For the country club dues, see Jerry Sholes, *Give Me That Prime-Time Religion* (New York: Hawthorn Books, 1979), 132.

CHAPTER 8

1. Patti Roberts, *Ashes to Gold* (Waco, TX: Word, 1983), 89–90.

2. "OR-106H Summer Special," *Contact*, accessed April 25, 2002, http://video .lemoin.com/VIDEO_playlist_ORU_SPECIALS.htm.

3. Robert H. Boyle, "Oral Roberts: Small but Oh, My," *Sports Illustrated*, November 30, 1970, 64; Jeff Prugh, "Oral Roberts U.—High Scorers for the Gospel," *Los Angeles Times*, March 6, 1972; Edward B. Fiske, "The Oral Roberts Empire," *New York Times*, April 22, 1973; David Kucharsky, "It's Time to Think Seriously about Sports," *Christianity Today*, November 7, 1975, 18–20.

4. Prugh, "Oral Roberts U." For more on the violence at sporting events in the early 1970s, see Dwight Chapin, "Violence, Vulgarity, and Basketball," *Los Angeles Times*, March 19, 1972.

5. Boyle, "Oral Roberts"; Edward B. Fiske, "Oral Roberts College Has Grown in 7 Years," *New York Times*, June 13, 1972. For the study on Tulsa's segregation, see Reynolds Farley and Alma F. Taeuber, "Racial Segregation in the Public Schools," *American Journal of Sociology* 79, no. 4 (January 1974): 888–905.

6. Prugh, "Oral Roberts U."

7. Paul Attner, "Fuqua's Bombing Gives Life to Oral Roberts' Run and Gun," *Washington Post*, March 21, 1972.

8. Jeff Prugh, "Oral Roberts Trying for a Miracle," *Los Angeles Times*, December 12, 1975; Boyle, "Oral Roberts."

9. Prugh, "Oral Roberts U."; Dave Kindred, "Praise the Lord, Pass the Shots, and Oral's Rebounders Get It Done," *Louisville Courier-Journal*, March 15, 1974.

10. Prugh, "Oral Roberts U."

11. John Peterson, "Faith, Not Fame, Lures Hoop Giant," *Dayton (OH) Daily News*, April 16, 1967.

12. Peterson, "Faith, Not Fame, Lures Hoop Giant."

13. Kenneth Denlinger, "Gospel Isn't Always True," *Washington Post*, February 18, 1972; Ken Hayes, "Hayes Recounts Time at ORU," *Inside Tulsa Sports*, March 20, 2013, https://tulsa.rivals.com/news/hayes-recounts-time-at-tu.

14. Dennis Eckert, "Roberts' Evangelistic Fervor Propelling ORU Cagers," *Tulsa Tribune*, October 27, 1971.

15. "Trickey Goes to Oral Roberts U.," *Murfreesboro (TN) Daily News Journal*, April 3, 1969.

16. Ken Bunch, "Trickey Looks Forward to 'Big Things' at ORU," *Tulsa Daily World*, November 6, 1969; Boyle, "Oral Roberts."

17. Ronald E. Butler, "ORU Eyes New Era with Accreditation," *Tulsa Daily World*, April 1, 1971; Jesse Owens, "ORU Acquires NCAA Membership," *Tulsa Daily World*, July 21, 1971.

18. David Edwin Harrell, *Oral Roberts: An American Life* (Bloomington: Indiana

University Press, 1985), 244; Dan Presley, "Titan Talk . . . ," *Oracle*, March 10, 1972, 5; Jeff Prugh, "Oral Roberts Trying for a Miracle," *Los Angeles Times*, December 12, 1975.

19. "Trickey to Resign as Cage Coach at Oral Roberts," *Bloomington (IL) Pantagraph*, February 5, 1974; Frank Boggs, "The Season Is Over for Trickey," *Oklahoma City Daily Oklahoman*, March 16, 1974; Jack Patterson, "The Sad Story of Ken Trickey," *Akron (OH) Beacon Journal*, March 17, 1974.

20. Jim Benagh, *Making It to #1: How College Football and Basketball Teams Get There* (New York: Dodd, Mead, 1976), 10 and 15.

21. Tony Kornheiser, "Moses Malone of Rockets," *New York Times*, November 7, 1976.

22. "ORU Investigation No Laughing Matter," *Shreveport (LA) Journal*, February 22, 1977.

23. Jerry Sholes, *Give Me That Prime-Time Religion: An Insider's Report on the Oral Roberts Evangelistic Association* (New York: Hawthorn Books, 1979), 109-17; Harrell, *Oral Roberts*, 363-64.

24. John Underwood, "The Desperate Coach," *Sports Illustrated*, August 25, 1969, 70-71.

25. John Matthew Smith, *The Sons of Westwood: John Wooden, UCLA, and the Dynasty That Changed College Basketball* (Urbana: University of Illinois Press, 2013), 195-99. For the Wooden quote, see, "Tall Stories," *Sports Illustrated*, May 22, 1972, 11.

26. John Husar, "Word Spread thru Hoops," *Chicago Tribune*, February 5, 1973.

27. Sam Goldaper, "Oral Roberts Brings Out Faithful," *New York Times*, December 5, 1971.

28. "Miracle U," *Newsweek*, February 7, 1972.

29. Goldaper, "Oral Roberts Brings Out Faithful."

30. Tom Sears, "Oral Roberts—Cagey Conman or Fan," *Daily Chronicle (IL)*, January 30, 1973.

31. Gene Dennison, "National Image of ORU Is Pointed Up by Recruiting," *Tulsa Tribune*, February 10, 1971.

32. Husar, "Word Spread thru Hoops."

33. Prugh, "Oral Roberts U."

34. "Athletics Dormitory Fundraising Brochure" (1974), ORU Library, Holy Spirit Research Center, 2.

35. Oral Roberts, "Carrying Out the Honor Code," Faculty Orientation Transcript, August 24, 1971, 11.

36. Rick Perlstein, *Reaganland: America's Right Turn, 1976-1980* (New York: Simon & Schuster, 2020), 346-49; Randall J. Stephens, "'It Has Come from the Hearts of the People': Evangelicals, Fundamentalists, Race, and the 1964 Civil Rights Act," *Journal of American Studies* 50 (2016): 559-85; Miles S. Mullin, "Neoevangelicalism and the Problem of Race in Postwar America," in *Christians and the Color Line: Race and Religion after Divided by Faith*, ed. J. Russell Hawkins and Philip Luke Sinitiere (New York: Oxford University Press, 2013), 15-44; Joseph Crespino, "Civil Rights and the Religious Right," in *Rightward Bound: Making America Conservative in the 1970s*, ed. Bruce J. Schulman and Julian E. Zelizer (Cambridge, MA: Harvard University Press, 2008), 90-105.

37. Jesse Curtis, *The Myth of Colorblind Christians: Evangelicals and White Supremacy in the Civil Rights Era* (New York: New York University Press, 2021), 1-6.

38. "OR-101H A Venture into Faith," accessed April 25, 2022, http://video.lemoin.com/VIDEO_playlist_ORU_SPECIALS.htm. For more on Oral's colorblind theology, see Daniel Isgrigg, "Healing for All Races: Oral Roberts' Legacy of Racial Reconciliation in a Divided City," *Spiritus: ORU Journal of Theology* 4, no. 2 (2019): 227-56.

39. "Seed-Faith Living Broke Our Poverty Cycle," *Abundant Life*, October 1974, 8-11.

40. Oral Roberts, "Observance of Black Heritage Week," Chapel Transcript, February 17, 1971, 7.

41. "Prayer for Governor George Wallace," Chapel Transcript, September 13, 1972.

42. "Roberts Says Church Future Grows Exciting," *Tulsa Daily World*, December 4, 1968; Oral Roberts, "A Message to Pastors," audio recording, December 3, 1968, Oral Roberts University, Holy Spirit Research Center, https://digitalshowcase.oru.edu/or_sermons/5/.

43. Prugh, "Oral Roberts U."

44. Oral Roberts, "Hate, Love and the Christian," *Abundant Life*, March 1968, 12.

45. Oral Roberts, "Observance of Black Heritage Week," 7.

46. "'Nixon's the One' at ORU," *Oracle*, October 25, 1968; "Oracle Political Poll Shows Nixon Leading," *Oracle*, October 27, 1972.

47. Henry Smith, "Black Students 'Cut Off,'" *Oracle*, December 4, 1970, 2.

48. "Black Awareness Chapel," Chapel Transcript, February 18, 1972, 4-7.

49. Isgrigg, "Healing for All Races," 240; "ORU Honors First Black Mayor of Mississippi Town," *Oracle*, September 22, 1972, 1; "Evers Voices Opinions," *Oracle*, October 6, 1972, 1.

50. "Will Focus on Attitudes," *Oracle*, December 15, 1972, 1.

51. Jesse Jackson, "1978 ORU Commencement Address," April 30, 1978, ORU Library, Holy Spirit Research Center, https://digitalshowcase.oru.edu/oruarchives/1/.

52. "Oral Roberts Prophetic Word at Azusa 1996 with Carlton Pearson," accessed April 25, 2022, https://www.youtube.com/watch?v=vdXRuVaLkFU.

53. Isgrigg, "Healing for All Races," 245.

54. "History," Booker T. Washington High School, accessed April 25, 2022, https://btw.tulsaschools.org/about-us/history.

55. Oral Roberts, "Booker T. Washington High School Desegregation Announcement," April 10, 1973, Oral Roberts University, Holy Spirit Research Center, https://digitalshowcase.oru.edu/or_speeches/6/.

56. Harrell, *Oral Roberts*, 324.

57. Rhonda Schell, "OREA Appoints New President," *Oracle*, January 25, 1974, 1.

58. "Oral Roberts Group Gets Some $19 Million," *Lawton (OK) Constitution*, October 1, 1977.

59. Carol Langston, "Oral Roberts Agency Silent on Donors," *Oklahoma City Daily Oklahoman*, September 30, 1977.

60. Bill Johnson, "Oral's Ministry Measured in Followers and in Dollars," *Oklahoma City Daily Oklahoman*, December 10, 1977.

61. "ORU Becomes a True University," *Oracle*, April 11, 1975, 1.

CHAPTER 9

1. Oral Roberts, "Announcement of Medical School," Chapel Transcript, April 28, 1975.

2. Oral Roberts, "Here's How It All Began," *Abundant Life*, February 1976, 3-11.

3. Oral Roberts, *Expect a Miracle: My Life and My Ministry* (Nashville: Nelson, 1995), 254.

4. David Edwin Harrell Jr., *Oral Roberts: An American Life* (Bloomington: Indiana University Press, 1985), 374.

5. Oral Roberts, *Expect a Miracle*, 254-62.

6. Lynne Somers, "ORU Breaks Ground for Med School," *Tulsa Daily World*, January 25, 1976.

7. Oral Roberts, "Announcement of Medical School," 5-8. Also see "Graduate Schools Open Doors," *Oracle*, September 29, 1975, 1.

8. "Coburn School of Law to Open at ORU in '79," *Oracle*, February 6, 1976, 1.

9. David MacKenzie, "Gift Boosts ORU Law School Plans," *Tulsa Daily World*, February 6, 1976.

10. Linda Daxon, "Med College Freeze Urged," *Tulsa Tribune*, September 2, 1976.

11. Vern Stefanic, "Oral Roberts' Daughter, 5 Others Die," *Tulsa Daily World*, February 13, 1977; Larry Levy, "'Roller Coaster' Action Preceded Crash of Plane," *Tulsa Tribune*, February 23, 1977; "Pilot in Fatal Roberts' Kin Crash Misrepresented Himself, Employer Says," *Oklahoma City Daily Oklahoman*, February 20, 1977.

12. "OR-135H Oral Roberts in San Francisco," *Contact*, accessed April 26, 2022, http://video.lemoin.com/VIDEO_playlist_ORU_SPECIALS.htm.

13. "3,000 at Plane Victims' Rites," *Tulsa Daily World*, February 15, 1977.

14. Oral Roberts, "I Will Rain upon Your Desert," *Abundant Life*, October 1977, 3.

15. Kathlyn Auten and Rick Barney, "Med School Hangs on Hospital," *Oracle*, February 18, 1977, 2.

16. Janet Pearson, "Plans Being Drawn for Hospital at ORU," *Tulsa Tribune*, March 12, 1977.

17. Linda Daxon, "Hospitals May Join ORU Medical Plan," *Tulsa Tribune*, March 28, 1977.

18. "OR-135H Oral Roberts in San Francisco," *Contact*, accessed April 26, 2022, http://video.lemoin.com/VIDEO_playlist_ORU_SPECIALS.htm.

19. Oral Roberts, "I Will Rain," 5.

20. Oral Roberts, "I Will Rain," 7.

21. Oral Roberts, "I Will Rain," 8.

22. Bob Foreman, "ORU to Build $100 Million Med Center," *Tulsa Tribune*, September 7, 1977.

23. Foreman, "ORU to Build $100 Million Med Center."

24. Oral Roberts, "I Will Rain," 9 and 12-13.

25. "Oral Roberts and You," Transcript, December 3, 1977.

26. "Oral's Moon-Shot," *Tulsa Tribune*, September 8, 1977.

27. "A Healing Ministry," *Tulsa World*, September 9, 1977.

28. Jim Killackey, "Tulsa Health Officials Fear Impact of Giant ORU Hospital," *Oklahoma City Daily Oklahoman*, September 9, 1977.

29. Laurie Mower, "State Faces 2,500-Bed Cut in Hospitals," *Tulsa Tribune*, October 6, 1977.

30. "ORU Official Says No Discrimination," *Clinton (OK) News*, September 23, 1977.

31. Yvonne Rehg, "Schools Work to Satisfy 'Handicap' Law," *Tulsa Tribune*, September 26, 1977; Debbie Quantock, "Renovation for Handicapped to Be Complete by 1980," *Oracle*, April 21, 1978, 1; "Disabilities Coalition and ORU Work Well," *Oracle*, November 10, 1978, 1.

32. Brenda Stockton-Hiss, "Student Feels Victimized by Mandatory Weight Program," *Oklahoma City Daily Oklahoman*, March 24, 1978.

33. Doug Hicks, "Weight Fought for ORU Readmission," *Tulsa World*, December 18, 1977.

34. Mark Bricklin, "Whole People, Fat People and God at Oral Roberts U.," *Prevention*, April 1978, 78–83.

35. Abigail Van Buren, "Obese Bounced from College," *Sarasota (FL) Journal*, May 22, 1978. For more on POPS, see Jonathan Root, "Pounds Off for Jesus: Oral Roberts University and the Fat Body, 1976–1978," *Fat Studies* 4, no. 2 (2015): 159–77.

36. Paul Starr, *Social Transformation of American Medicine* (New York: Basic Books, 1982), 398–99; "Certificate of Need (CON) State Laws," National Conference on State Legislatures, accessed April 26, 2022, http://www.ncsl.org/research/health/con-certificate-of-need-state-laws.aspx.

37. "Tulsa Hospitals Opposing City of Faith Complex," *Oklahoma City Daily Oklahoman*, January 26, 1978; Jim Killackey, "Experts Clash on ORU Hospital Impact," *Oklahoma City Daily Oklahoman*, February 7, 1978.

38. Janet Pearson, "ORU Application Due for Medical Complex," *Tulsa World*, December 2, 1977; Jim Killackey, "Oral Roberts Hospital Plan Filed," *Oklahoma City Daily Oklahoman*, December 3, 1977.

39. "City of Faith Groundbreaking," Chapel Transcript, January 24, 1978, 3; Cathy Carothers, "Ground Broken for City of Faith," *Communique*, Spring 1978, 1.

40. Will Sentell and George Prothro Jr., "Health Board Moves Up ORU Hearing Date," *Tulsa Tribune*, January 25, 1978.

41. Janet Pearson, "Hillcrest Panel Says No to ORU," *Tulsa World*, December 22, 1977.

42. "Opponents Unite on City of Faith," *Tulsa Tribune*, January 18, 1978.

43. "Channel 8 Interview about the City of Faith with Dr. C. T. Thompson and Dr. James Winslow," ORU, Holy Spirit Research Center, January 30, 1978, https://digitalshowcase.oru.edu/cof/1/.

44. "City of Faith Still on Hold," *Oracle*, February 17, 1978, 1.

45. Janet Pearson, "ORU Hospital Bed Disapproved," *Tulsa World*, February 17, 1978.

46. Janet Pearson, "Need for ORU Hospital Argued before Agency," *Tulsa World*, February 10, 1978.

47. "City of Faith Still on Hold."

48. Pearson, "Need for ORU Hospital Argued before Agency."

49. Larry Levy and George Prothro Jr., "Roberts Wins One, Loses One," *Tulsa Tribune*, February 28, 1978.

50. Will Sentell, "Faith City Plan Ruling Set Feb. 16," *Tulsa Tribune*, February 10, 1978.

51. Levy and Prothro, "Roberts Wins One, Loses One"; Janet Pearson, "Health Systems Trustees Reject ORU Hospital Plan," *Tulsa World*, February 28, 1978.

52. Will Sentell, "38 Senators Sign Letter Backing City of Faith," *Tulsa Tribune*, March 10, 1978.

53. Will Sentell, "Oral's Campaign," *Tulsa Tribune*, March 15, 1978.

54. Janet Pearson, "ORU Maintains Foes' Interests Are in Conflict," *Tulsa World*, March 8, 1978; George Prothro Jr., "ORU Hospital Charges Traded," *Tulsa Tribune*, March 8, 1978; George Prothro Jr., "Fate of Hospital Is Still Uncertain," *Tulsa Tribune*, March 10, 1978; Janet Pearson, "U. S. to Investigate Legality of ORU Hospital's Hearings," *Tulsa World*, March 16, 1978; George Prothro Jr., "ORU Withdraws Bid for OHSA Probe," *Tulsa Tribune*, March 30, 1978.

55. "Oral Roberts Answers Questions on City of Faith—Channel 8," Transcript, March 14, 1978, 16.

56. Robert K. Goodwin, "Roberts Challenged N. Tulsa Hospital Urged," *Oklahoma Eagle*, March 16, 1978.

57. "Roberts Misinformed," *Oklahoma Eagle*, March 16, 1978; George Prothro Jr., "ORU Aides, Blacks Hold Hospital Talk," *Tulsa Tribune*, March 29, 1978.

58. Richard Tapscott and George Prothro Jr., "'Faith' Dispute Snares Senators," *Tulsa Tribune*, March 2, 1978.

59. Will Sentell, "If Bill Aids ORU, Fight Vowed," *Tulsa Tribune*, March 6, 1978.

60. Sentell, "38 Senators Sign Letter Backing City of Faith."

61. "'City of Faith' Endorsed," *Oklahoma City Daily Oklahoman*, March 29, 1978.

62. "Channels of Review for ORU 'City of Faith' Attacked by Supporter in House," *Oklahoma City Sunday Oklahoman*, March 26, 1978.

63. "House Endorses City of Faith Hospital," *Oklahoma City Daily Oklahoman*, April 6, 1978.

64. Michael Lee, "Letter Deluge Backs City of Faith," *Oklahoma City Daily Oklahoman*, March 30, 1978; Prothro, "ORU Withdraws Bid for OHSA Probe."

65. Judy Fossett, "ORU Vote to Ease Postal Load," *Oklahoma City Daily Oklahoman*, April 26, 1978.

66. Oklahoma Health Planning Commission, *Proposed City of Faith Hospital* (Oklahoma City: OHPC, 1978), 62-74.

67. "Oklahoma Health Planning Commission," ORU, April 26, 1978, 7-8.

68. Jim Killackey, "Oral Roberts Gets Go-Ahead for City of Faith," *Oklahoma City Daily Oklahoman*, April 27, 1978.

69. Harrell, *Oral Roberts*, 376-78.

70. Jim Killackey, "ORU Hospital Plan Approval Overruled," *Oklahoma City Saturday Oklahoman & Times*, December 2, 1978.

71. John Greiner, "Supreme Court to Hear Fight for City of Faith," *Oklahoma City Saturday Oklahoman & Times*, December 9, 1978.

72. Mike Hammer, "City of Faith Bill Jeopardizes Funds, Official Warns," *Oklahoma City Daily Oklahoman*, February 9, 1979.

73. "Health Planning War Heats Up," *Oklahoma City Sunday Oklahoman*, February 25, 1979.

74. Harrell, *Oral Roberts*, 389.

75. "Million Send $50 Million," *Oklahoma City Sunday Oklahoman*, January 7, 1979.

76. "Roberts Sets City of Faith Funds Plea," *Oklahoma City Daily Oklahoman*, July 13, 1979.

77. Richard Roberts, *He's the God of a Second Chance* (n.p.: Richard Roberts, 1985), 29-36.

78. "Exploring Her Potential Is a New Goal for Patti Roberts," *Tulsa Tribune*, April 13, 1978.

79. Patti Roberts, *Ashes to Gold* (Waco, TX: Word, 1983), 88.

80. Patti Roberts, *Ashes to Gold*, 127.

81. Patti Roberts, *Ashes to Gold*, 129.

82. Patti Roberts, *Ashes to Gold*, 140.

CHAPTER 10

1. "Oral Roberts Talks of Talking to 900-Foot Jesus," *Tulsa World*, October 16, 1980.

2. Oral Roberts, "I Must Tell Somebody . . . and I Must Tell You, Dear Partner . . . ," *Abundant Life*, September 1980, 10 and 12.

3. Roberts, "I Must Tell Somebody," 11.

4. Roberts, "I Must Tell Somebody," 9.

5. Gail Mitchell, "Roberts Raises $5 Million after Talk with Jesus," *Oklahoma City Daily Oklahoman*, October 31, 1980.

6. Bruce Buursma, "Oral Roberts and His Skeptics," *Chicago Tribune*, January 3, 1982.

7. Covey Bean, "Roberts' Appeal Details Face-to-Face Talk with Jesus," *Oklahoma City Daily Oklahoman*, October 16, 1980.

8. "Roberts' Claim Satirized in Photographer's Poster," *Sapulpa (OK) Daily Herald*, December 18, 1981.

9. David Rossie, "Oral in Wonderland Meets the 900-Foot-Tall Jesus," *Binghamton (NY) Press and Sun-Bulletin*, November 2, 1980.

10. Lewis Grizzard, "Sorry, Oral, This Giver's Dead," *Edmond (OK) Sun*, November 2, 1980.

11. "N. J. Preacher Calls 'Vision' a Hoax," *Hackensack (NJ) Record*, November 30, 1980.

12. "Methodist Official: Roberts' Vision Fake," *Tampa Tribune*, December 13, 1980.

13. Tom Flynn, "NCAA Conducts Basketball Inquiry," *Oracle*, September 8, 1978, 1; "ORU Hit with One-Year Probation," *Oklahoma City Daily Oklahoman*, January 30, 1980.

14. Ed Montgomery and Jim Killackey, "Court Clears City of Faith Legal Blocks," *Oklahoma City Daily Oklahoman*, March 25, 1981.

15. Chuck Ervin, "Court Ruling Clears Way for City of Faith Opening," *Tulsa World*, March 26, 1981.

16. Jim Killackey, "Tulsa County Hospital Council Buries Hatchet with Oral Roberts," *Oklahoma City Daily Oklahoman*, April 16, 1981.

17. James Winslow, "Oklahoma State Supreme Court Rules in Favor of the City of Faith," *Abundant Life*, May 1981, 2. Also see Kay Atkins, "Roberts Says City of Faith Go-Ahead a Landmark Decision," *Oklahoma City Daily Oklahoman*, March 27, 1981.

18. Don Nickles, "The Spiritual Rebirth of Our Nation," *Abundant Life*, May 1981, 5.

19. Lee Strobel, "ABA Ponders Oral Roberts Issue," *Chicago Tribune*, August 10, 1981.

20. Oral Roberts, *Expect a Miracle: My Life and My Ministry* (Nashville: Nelson, 1995), 305.

21. "Judge: No Basis," *Streator (IL) Times*, July 18, 1981; Strobel, "ABA Ponders Oral Roberts Issue"; Lee Strobel, "ABA to Accredit Roberts Law School," *Chicago Tribune*, August 13, 1981.

22. "This Is a New Beginning for the Human Race," *Abundant Life*, December 1981.

23. Sue Smith, "10,000 Gather to Honor Evangelist Oral Roberts," *Oklahoma City Daily Oklahoman*, November 1, 1981. For the text of the president's letter, see "Congratulations from President Reagan," *Abundant Life*, December 1981.

24. "What God Has Done," *Abundant Life*, December 1981.

25. Don Hayden, "Finances a Crisis, Oral Roberts Says," *Oklahoma City Daily Oklahoman*, February 26, 1982. Also refer to "School Needs 'Miracle,' Oral Roberts Letter Says," *Oklahoma City Saturday Oklahoman & Times*, March 6, 1982; Jim Etter, "Roberts' Letter Called Immoral," *Oklahoma City Daily Oklahoman*, April 1, 1982.

26. "City of Faith Trims Payroll," *Oklahoma City Daily Oklahoman*, July 8, 1982.

27. R. Claire Shannonhouse, "City of Faith Hospital Short of Plan to Have 777 Beds and Be Debt-Free," *Oklahoma City Sunday Oklahoman*, October 31, 1982.

28. Mike Kimbrell, "Oral Roberts' Son Found Dead in Car," *Tulsa World*, June 10, 1982; Bob Bonebrake, "Reasons behind Suicide of Evangelist's Troubled Son Are Still a Mystery," *Oklahoma City Daily Oklahoman*, June 20, 1982.

29. "Oral Roberts' Son Given Probation on Drug Charges," *Kansas City Times*, February 20, 1982.

30. David Edwin Harrell Jr., *Oral Roberts: An American Life* (Bloomington: Indiana University Press, 1985), 338–39.

31. Roberts, *Expect a Miracle*, 208.

32. "A Minister's Son Ends His Life," *Christianity Today*, July 16, 1982, 40.

33. Randy R. Potts, "Gay, Closeted and Buried in History: My Uncle's Life Was Erased. Mine Won't Be," *Guardian*, June 13, 2016, https://www.theguardian.com/world/2016/jun/13/oral-roberts-oklahoma-gay-culture-closeted.

34. "Oral Roberts R.I.P (w/Classic Sex Sermon)," The Young Turks, accessed April 27, 2022, https://www.youtube.com/watch?v=_-BxqfAM1Ag.

35. "Evangelist Claims Cancer Revelation," *Oklahoma City Daily Oklahoman*, January 3, 1983; Bruce Buursma, "Another Fund-Raising 'Message from Jesus,'" *Chicago Tribune*, January 29, 1983.

36. Oral Roberts, "A Breakthrough for Cancer Is Coming," *Abundant Life*, February 1983, 3–8.

37. Dan Balz, "Oral Roberts Quotes Plea from God," *Washington Post*, February 2, 1983.

38. Anne Reifenberg, "Officials of Ailing Hospital Still Trust Oral Roberts' Vision," *Jackson (MS) Clarion Ledger*, April 22, 1984.

39. "1983 Declared Year of Research," *Lifeline*, January 1983, 1.

40. Bart Ziegler, "Oral Roberts' Promise from God Draws Dollars to Find Cancer Cure," *Tampa Tribune*, May 28, 1983.

41. Buursma, "Another Fund-Raising 'Message from Jesus'"; Russell Chandler, "Talked with Jesus, Evangelist Says," *Los Angeles Times*, January 18, 1983.

42. "ORU Stages Cancer March," *Oklahoma City Daily Oklahoman*, January 25, 1983.

43. Balz, "Oral Roberts Quotes Plea from God."

44. "$5 Million Sent to Fight Cancer," *Oklahoma City Daily Oklahoman*, May 28, 1983.

45. "City of Faith Prepares for NMR Unit," *Lifeline*, May/June 1983, 1 and 7.

46. Paul Taylor, "Evangelist's Hospital Finds Debt in Empty Beds," *Washington Post*, July 5, 1984.

47. Balz, "Oral Roberts Quotes Plea from God."

48. Balz, "Oral Roberts Quotes Plea from God."

49. Bruce Buursma, "Oral Roberts' Clinic May Need Cash Cure," *Chicago Tribune*, June 5, 1983.

50. "Major COF Marketing Thrust Begins," *Lifeline*, October 1982, 1 and 10.

51. William B. Luttrell, "Gearing Up for the Partners," *Lifeline*, December 1982, 2.

52. Robby Trammell, "ORU Programs Caught in Fund Squeeze," *Oklahoma City Daily Oklahoman*, June 19, 1984.

53. *Expect a Miracle with Oral and Richard Roberts*, August 19, 1984, https://digital showcase.oru.edu/cof/25/; Oral Roberts, "Oral Roberts, Open My City of Faith to the Poor and Needy," *Abundant Life*, August/September 1984, 2–6. Also see "'Poor of the World' Enlisted by Roberts to Save Hospital," *Oklahoma City Daily Oklahoman*, July 16, 1984.

54. "Churches Begin Programs to Send the Poor and Needy in Their Communities to the City of Faith," *Abundant Life*, October 1984, 12.

55. "Free Treatment to Poor Raises Hospital's Spirits," *Saskatoon (SK) Star-Phoenix*, October 22, 1984.

56. Chris Adams, "City of Faith: A Promise Unfulfilled," *Tulsa World*, September 30, 1989.

57. Oral Roberts, "Back on the Evangelistic Field," *Abundant Life*, October 1983, 3.

58. Linda Thomson, "An Old Fashioned Revival—via Satellite," *Madison (WI) Capital Times*, February 27, 1984; Richard Lessner, "Healer Packs Sundome," *Phoenix Arizona Republic*, March 11, 1984.

59. Lessner, "Healer Packs Sundome."

60. "Oral Roberts and Richard Roberts Healing Crusades," *Abundant Life*, July 1984, 20.

61. Thomson, "An Old Fashioned Revival."

62. Lessner, "Healer Packs Sundome."

63. "Oral Roberts Shares His Heart," *Charisma*, June 1985, 57.

64. Peter Larson, "Biblical Miracles Will Be Re-created at Evangelist's Theme Park," *Minneapolis Star Tribune*, July 13, 1985.

65. Larson, "Biblical Miracles Will Be Re-created at Evangelist's Theme Park"; "Evangelist Plans Groundbreaking for City of Faith Healing Center," *Oklahoma City Sunday Oklahoman*, May 5, 1985; "The Miracle Healing Center," *Abundant Life*, February/March 1985, 6-7.

66. "Oral Roberts Shares His Heart," 58.

67. "Oral Roberts Shares His Heart," 58.

68. Larson, "Biblical Miracles Will Be Re-created at Evangelist's Theme Park."

69. Larson, "Biblical Miracles Will Be Re-created at Evangelist's Theme Park."

70. Martin Merzer, "Bible Trip Is in Disney World Image," *Miami Herald*, March 8, 1987.

71. "ORU Phasing Out School of Dentistry," *Tulsa World*, June 22, 1985.

72. Gary Percefull, "ORU Transfers Law School to Virginia," *Tulsa World*, November 2, 1985.

73. "Oral Roberts Pleads for Money to Help Him Live Past March," *Oklahoma City Daily Oklahoman*, January 6, 1987.

74. John Omicinski, "Desperate Offerings?" *Jackson (TN) Sun*, February 1, 1987.

75. Jim Jones, "Tulsans Wince at Roberts' Plea," *Fort Worth Star-Telegram*, January 18, 1987.

76. Martin Merzer, "Roberts Appeal Reaps Harvest of Criticism," *Miami Herald*, March 8, 1987.

77. Jones, "Tulsans Wince at Roberts' Plea."

78. Griff Palmer, "Supporters Send Cash, Pledges to Oral Roberts," *Oklahoma City Daily Oklahoman*, January 16, 1987.

79. "Good Morning America 'Gimme a Break Awards' 1987," accessed March 24, 2021, https://www.youtube.com/watch?v=Ermcnzxjoko.

80. Bruce Buursma, "Oral Knows Exactly What He's Doing, Biographer Says," *Jacksonville Florida Times Union*, July 18, 1987.

81. "Roberts' Fund Plea Criticized," *Oklahoma City Daily Oklahoman*, March 13, 1987; Bruce Buursma, "Raising Money or Raising Cain?" *Chicago Tribune*, March 20, 1987.

82. "University Loses Methodist Certification," *Port Huron (MI) Times Herald*, July 11, 1987; Billie Cheney Speed, "Methodist Ruling on Elders May Affect Oral Roberts," *Atlanta Journal*, August 15, 1987.

83. Jeff MacNelly, cartoon, *Chicago Tribune*, January 9, 1987.

84. Mike Royko, "Roberts Has Chance to Convert Millions," *Burlington County (NJ) Times*, January 29, 1987.

85. Oral Roberts, "Update on the City of Faith," February 18, 1987, ORU Library, Holy Spirit Research Center, https://digitalshowcase.oru.edu/cof/23/.

86. "Public Doesn't Quite Know How to Take Oral Roberts Anymore," *Columbus (OH) Republic*, January 25, 1987.

87. Omicinski, "Desperate Offerings?"; Merzer, "Roberts Appeal Reaps Harvest of Criticism."

88. Bill Walker, "Oral Roberts: Putting God's Way to Test," *Fresno Bee*, March 12, 1987; Jones, "Tulsans Wince at Roberts' Plea."

89. Jones, "Tulsans Wince at Roberts' Plea."

90. "Fundraising for City of Faith from the Prayer Tower," March 22, 1987, ORU Library, Holy Spirit Research Center, https://digitalshowcase.oru.edu/cof/24/.

91. Cathy Milam, "Roberts Will Begin Vigil Sunday," *Tulsa World*, March 21, 1987.

92. Jay Hamburg, "Millionaire a Mix of Flash, Bounty," *Orlando Sentinel*, March 30, 1987.

93. Jennie Hess, "Roberts' Rescuer Has a Giving Nature," *Atlanta Constitution*, March 30, 1987.

94. John Dart, "Skeptics' Revelations," *Los Angeles Times*, May 11, 1986; Mark Oppenheimer, "Peter Popoff, the Born-Again Scoundrel," *Esquire*, February 27, 2017, https://www.gq.com/story/peter-popoff-born-again-scoundrel.

95. John Wigger, *PTL: The Rise and Fall of Jim and Tammy Faye Bakker's Evangelical Empire* (New York: Oxford University Press, 2017).

96. Ann Rowe Seaman, *Swaggart: The Unauthorized Biography of an American Evangelist* (New York: Continuum, 1999), 326-63.

97. Doug Rossinow, *The Reagan Era: A History of the 1980s* (New York: Columbia University Press, 2015), 208-9; Steve Fraser, *Every Man a Speculator: A History of Wall Street in American Life* (New York: HarperCollins, 2005), 525-72; Robert M. Collins, *Transforming America: Politics and Culture in the Reagan Years* (New York: Columbia University Press, 2007), 94-100. For some of the best work on Wall Street during the 1980s, refer to James B. Stewart, *Den of Thieves*, rev. ed. (New York: Simon & Schuster, 2010); Connie Bruck, *Predator's Ball: The Junk-Bond Raiders and the Man Who Staked Them* (New York: Simon & Schuster, 1988).

98. Jimmy Carter, "Address to the Nation on Energy and National Goals," July 15, 1979, The American Presidency Project, accessed February 14, 2018, https://www.presidency.ucsb.edu/documents/address-the-nation-energy-and-national-goals-the-malaise-speech; Ronald Reagan, "Ronald Reagan's Announcement for Presidential Candidacy," November 13, 1979, The American Presidency Project, accessed March 18, 2014, https://www.presidency.ucsb.edu/documents/remarks-announcing-candidacy-for-the-republican-presidential-nomination-2.

99. "Money Woes Shake Oral Roberts' City of Faith Hospital," *Oklahoma City Saturday Oklahoman & Times*, October 31, 1987.

100. "76 Doctors Plan to Run Oral Roberts' Hospital," *Oklahoma City Daily Oklahoman*, November 4, 1987.

101. Gil Broyles, "Roberts Ministry Needs $11 Million, Roberts Says," *Tulsa World*, March 28, 1989.

102. Chris Adams, "ORU Took Mortgages in '88 to Pay Bills?" *Tulsa World*, March 29, 1989.

103. Cathy Milam and Kay Johnson, "Donations Fall Short of Oral Roberts' Goal," *Tulsa World*, May 7, 1989.

104. Ted Bakamjian, "NCAA Probed ORU Program," *Tulsa World*, May 3, 1989.

105. Janet Pearson, "Roberts Says Goal Met," *Tulsa World*, May 17, 1989.

106. Chris Adams, "ORU: Departures in Med School," *Tulsa World*, July 17, 1989; Cathy Milam, "Doctors Say ORU School in Trouble," *Tulsa World*, July 23, 1989.

107. Arnold Hamilton, "Oral Roberts to Shut Down Hospital and Medical School at Tulsa," *Washington Post*, September 16, 1989. Also refer to "Closings, Sales Latest Roberts Ministry Woes," *Tulsa World*, September 14, 1989; Chris Adams, "Debt Defeats Roberts' Dream," *Tulsa World*, September 14, 1989.

108. Jenk Jones Jr., "Roberts Gives Class Performance in Announcing Hospital Closing," *Tulsa World*, September 15, 1989.

109. "Roberts' City of Faith Keeps Clinic; Hospital's Final Patient Checks Out," *Oklahoma City Daily Oklahoman*, October 18, 1989.

110. Cathy Milam, "Callers Have Schemes to Help Oral and Save the City of Faith," *Tulsa World*, September 20, 1989; "No Place for Jail," *Tulsa World*, October 12, 1989.

111. "VA Urged to Study City of Faith Move," *Tulsa World*, October 23, 1989.

112. David Blum, "City of Faith Courts Prospects," *Tulsa World*, November 21, 1989.

113. Cathy Milam, "Illinois Cancer Center Signs Lease on City of Faith," *Tulsa World*, January 25, 1990.

114. Roberts, *Expect a Miracle*, 295.

115. Roberts, *Expect a Miracle*, 298.

116. "Fiasco on 81st Street," *Tulsa World*, October 2, 1989.

117. "Oral Roberts: Victory out of Defeat," *Charisma*, December 1989, 90.

EPILOGUE

1. Cece Todd, "Support Erodes," *Tulsa World*, November 13, 1991; Cathy Spaulding, "ORU Dragging Feet, Contractors Say," *Tulsa World*, December 16, 1991.

2. Cathy Milam, "Robertses Ask Contributors for $500 Each," *Tulsa World*, November 12, 1991; Todd, "Support Erodes"; "Roberts Steamed at Money Jokes," *Oceanside (CA) North County Times*, November 20, 1991.

3. Cynthia Dees, "City of Faith Complex Sold," *Tulsa World*, March 20, 1992; Karen M. Thomas, "City of Faith Puts Faith in Auction," *Chicago Tribune*, September 29, 1992.

4. Jean Pagel, "Oral Roberts University Involved in Suit over Skyscrapers," *Fort Worth Star-Telegram*, September 1, 1996.

5. "Roberts Recovering from Heart Surgery," *Oklahoma City Daily Oklahoman*, March 16, 1991.

6. Marla Cone, "Oral Roberts Stable after Heart Problem," *Los Angeles Times*, October 8, 1992; "Oral Roberts Makes Strong Recovery," *Oklahoma City Daily Oklahoman*, October 10, 1992.

7. Kelly Kurt, "Richard Succeeds Oral," *Tulsa World*, January 28, 1993.

8. Wesley Brown, "Oral Passes Torch to Son during Commencement," *Tulsa World*, May 2, 1993.

9. "Over 20,000 Pack Arena to Hear Tulsa Evangelist," *Raleigh (NC) News and Observer*, December 3, 1956.

10. Bill Swindell, "Oral Keeps Busy Pace," *Tulsa World*, August 18, 1995.

11. Scott L. Miley, "Oral Roberts Shares Candid Moments," *Indianapolis Star*, August 19, 1995.

12. Pamela J. Johnson, "Oral Roberts Preaches on Faith and Finances to 600 in Ventura," *Los Angeles Times*, May 18, 1998.

13. Oral Roberts, *Seed-Faith 2000* (Tulsa: Oral Roberts, 1999).

14. Kate Bowler, *Blessed: A History of the American Prosperity Gospel* (New York: Oxford University Press, 2013), 107-27.

15. Bill Sherman, "Roberts Comes Home," *Tulsa World*, May 10, 2005.

16. "Evelyn Roberts, Wife of Oral Roberts, Dies," *Tulsa World*, May 4, 2005.

17. Patti Roberts, *Ashes to Gold* (Waco, TX: Word, 1983), 92.

18. "ORU Marks Record Student Enrollment," *Tulsa World*, September 19, 1997.

19. Ziva Branstetter, "Debt Weighs Down ORU," *Tulsa World*, November 4, 2007; Ziva Branstetter, "ORU Was Warned by the IRS," *Tulsa World*, October 16, 2007; April Marciszewski, "ORU in Debt $52.5 Million," *Tulsa World*, October 25, 2007.

20. "Former ORU Professors Suing University," *Tulsa World*, October 2, 2007; Justin Juozapavicius, "College's President, Wife Accused of Improprieties," *Fort Worth Star-Telegram*, October 6, 2007; Andrea Eger, "Robertses Deny Lawsuit's Allegations on ORU," *Tulsa World*, October 9, 2007; "Revised Lawsuit against ORU Makes New Allegations," *Tulsa World*, October 12, 2007; "Roberts Taking Leave of Absence," *Tulsa World*, October 17, 2007; Ziva Branstetter, "Richard Roberts Resigns as Oral Roberts University President," *Tulsa World*, November 24, 2007; "Richard Roberts: God Told Me to Resign," *Tulsa World*, November 28, 2007.

21. "$70 Million to ORU," *Tulsa World*, November 28, 2007; Ziva Branstetter, "An Angel for ORU," *Tulsa World*, November 28, 2007; John Estus, "How Fortune Came to Shine on ORU," *Oklahoma City Daily Oklahoman*, November 29, 2007.

22. Paul Putz and Jonathan Root, "ORU Basketball Fans Know to 'Expect a Miracle,'" *Christianity Today*, March 26, 2021, https://www.christianitytoday.com/ct/2021/march-web-only/oral-roberts-oru-ncca-basketball-history-christian.html.

23. Bill Sherman, "Oral Roberts Visits Native American Fold," *Tulsa World*, October 3, 2009; Jeffrey Smith, "Oral Roberts' Last Sermon Delivered to Local Native American Church," KOTV, Tulsa, December 16, 2009, https://www.newson6.com/story/5e366fe02f69d76f6207fb9f/oral-roberts-last-sermon-delivered-to-local-native-american-church.

24. Bill Sherman, "Son Describes His Father's Passing as 'Glorious, Dignified,'" *Oklahoma City Daily Oklahoman*, December 16, 2009.

25. Bill Sherman, "A Lasting Influence," *Tulsa World*, December 20, 2009.

26. Keith Schneider, "Oral Roberts, Fiery Preacher with Vast Empire, Dies at 91," *New York Times*, December 16, 2009.

27. Matt Schudel, "Oral Roberts, Key Figure in Growth of Pentecostalism, TV Ministry," *Boston Globe*, December 16, 2009.

28. Ted Olsen, "Why the Oral Roberts Obituaries Are Wrong," *Christianity Today*, December 16, 2009, https://www.christianitytoday.com/news/2009/december/151-34.0.html.

29. "Oral Roberts Shares His Heart," *Charisma*, June 1985, 56-57.

30. Oral Roberts, *Expect a Miracle: My Life and My Ministry* (Nashville: Nelson, 1995), 384.

31. Wayne Robinson, *Oral: The Warm, Intimate, Unauthorized Biography of a Man of God* (Los Angeles: Acton House, 1976), 76.

32. Patti Roberts, *Ashes to Gold*, 91.

33. Oral Roberts, "A Hard-Hitting Message to Help You Get Your Needs Met When Times Are Hard," *Abundant Life*, January 1980, 1-7.

34. "If This Ministry Stops, Your Letters to Me Will Not Be Answered," *Abundant Life*, February 1982, 7.

35. Oral Roberts, "Update on the City of Faith," ORU Chapel, February 18, 1987, ORU Library, Holy Spirit Research Center, https://digitalshowcase.oru.edu/cof/23/.

36. Oral Roberts, "Now the Truth . . . ," *Abundant Life*, September/October 1987, 11.

37. Bowler, *Blessed*, 109.

38. Bill Sherman, "In His Own Words," *Tulsa World*, December 20, 2009.

INDEX

Titles published in the

LIBRARY OF RELIGIOUS BIOGRAPHY SERIES

Orestes A. Brownson: American Religious Weathervane
by Patrick W. Carey

The Puritan as Yankee: A Life of Horace Bushnell
by Robert Bruce Mullin

A Life of Alexander Campbell
by Douglas A. Foster

Duty and Destiny: The Life and Faith of Winston Churchill
by Gary Scott Smith

Emblem of Faith Untouched: A Short Life of Thomas Cranmer
by Leslie Williams

Her Heart Can See: The Life and Hymns of Fanny J. Crosby
by Edith L. Blumhofer

Emily Dickinson and the Art of Belief
by Roger Lundin

God's Cold Warrior: The Life and Faith of John Foster Dulles
by John D. Wilsey

A Short Life of Jonathan Edwards
by George M. Marsden

The Religious Journey of Dwight D. Eisenhower: Duty, God, and Country
by Jack M. Holl

Charles G. Finney and the Spirit of American Evangelicalism
by Charles E. Hambrick-Stowe

William Ewart Gladstone: Faith and Politics in Victorian Britain
by David Bebbington

One Soul at a Time: The Story of Billy Graham
by Grant Wacker

An Odd Cross to Bear: A Biography of Ruth Bell Graham
by Anne Blue Wills

*A Heart Lost in Wonder: The Life and Faith of **Gerard Manley Hopkins***
by Catharine Randall

*Sworn on the Altar of God: A Religious Biography of **Thomas Jefferson***
by Edwin S. Gaustad

*The Miracle Lady: **Katherine Kuhlman**
and the Transformation of Charismatic Christianity*
by Amy Collier Artman

***Abraham Kuyper**: Modern Calvinist, Christian Democrat*
by James D. Bratt

*The Religious Life of **Robert E. Lee***
by R. David Cox

***Abraham Lincoln**: Redeemer President*
by Allen C. Guelzo

***Charles Lindbergh**: A Religious Biography
of America's Most Infamous Pilot*
by Christopher Gehrz

*The First American Evangelical: A Short Life of **Cotton Mather***
by Rick Kennedy

***Aimee Semple McPherson**: Everybody's Sister*
by Edith L. Blumhofer

*Mother of Modern Evangelicalism:
The Life and Legacy of **Henrietta Mears***
by Arlin Migliazzo

*Damning Words: The Life and Religious Times of **H. L. Mencken***
by D. G. Hart

***Thomas Merton** and the Monastic Vision*
by Lawrence S. Cunningham

*God's Strange Work: **William Miller** and the End of the World*
by David L. Rowe

***Blaise Pascal**: Reasons of the Heart*
by Marvin R. O'Connell

Occupy Until I Come: **A. T. Pierson** *and the Evangelization of the World*
by Dana L. Robert

The Kingdom Is Always but Coming: A Life of **Walter Rauschenbusch**
by Christopher H. Evans

Oral Roberts *and the Rise of the Prosperity Gospel*
by Jonathan Root

Strength for the Fight: The Life and Faith of **Jackie Robinson**
by Gary Scott Smith

A Christian and a Democrat: A Religious Life of **Franklin D. Roosevelt**
by John F. Woolverton with James D. Bratt

Francis Schaeffer *and the Shaping of Evangelical America*
by Barry Hankins

Harriet Beecher Stowe: *A Spiritual Life*
by Nancy Koester

Billy Sunday *and the Redemption of Urban America*
by Lyle W. Dorsett

Howard Thurman *and the Disinherited: A Religious Biography*
by Paul Harvey

We Will Be Free: The Life and Faith of **Sojourner Truth**
by Nancy Koester

Assist Me to Proclaim: The Life and Hymns of **Charles Wesley**
by John R. Tyson

Prophetess of Health: A Study of **Ellen G. White**
by Ronald L. Numbers

George Whitefield: *Evangelist for God and Empire*
by Peter Y. Choi

The Divine Dramatist: **George Whitefield**
and the Rise of Modern Evangelicalism
by Harry S. Stout

Liberty of Conscience: **Roger Williams** *in America*
by Edwin S. Gaustad